TRAVELS INTO BOKHARA

TRAVELS

INTO

BOKHARA

CONTAINING

THE NARRATIVE OF A VOYAGE
ON THE INDUS

FROM THE SEA TO LAHORE AND
AN ACCOUNT OF A
JOURNEY FROM INDIA TO

CABOOL, TARTARY AND PERSIA

IN THE YEARS 1831, 1832 AND 1833

BY LIEUT. ALEXANDER BURNES, F.R.S.

OF THE INDIA COMPANY'S SERVICE

Edited by
KATHLEEN HOPKIRK
Introduced by
WILLIAM DALRYMPLE

ELAND
LONDON

The three-volume edition of Burnes's *Travels into Bokhara*
was first published by John Murray in 1835
This edited edition first published by Eland Publishing Limited
61 Exmouth Market, London EC1R 4QL in 2012

ISBN 978 1 906011 71 0

Cover Image:
Sir Alexander Burnes in the costume of Bokhara
by kind permission of John Murray

Typeset by Antony Gray
Printed in the United Kingdom by MPG Biddles

CONTENTS

PART ONE
THE NARRATIVE OF A VOYAGE ON THE INDUS

PART TWO
AN ACCOUNT OF A JOURNEY FROM INDIA TO CABOOL, TARTARY AND PERSIA

EDITOR'S NOTE

Burnes's book was originally published in three volumes and I have, inevitably, had to condense some passages and omit others altogether, but this single-volume version is still very much Burnes's work. I have only intruded my own comments where something – perhaps obvious at the time – may need to be explained to a modern reader, and I believe his good spirits, and irrepressible interest in everything he encountered, still come across today, in spite of the more ponderous style of writing of the 1830s. Spellings of proper names may at first seem bizarre, for there was no standard transliteration in Burnes's day, and he evidently tried to render them as phonetically as possible. (For instance, 'Daoodpootra' would usually now be spelt 'Daudputra'.) But I have kept the original spellings, because in some cases there is no easily found modern equivalent. Where there is, I have put it in square brackets the first time the word is encountered.

For anyone wanting to read more on the subjects covered in this book, I would suggest John Keay's *India* for the historical background to the Indus voyage and India's highly complicated history in general, and Peter Hopkirk's *The Great Game* for the Central Asian journey and the political contest between Russia and British India. I found them both invaluable.

INTRODUCTION

In the Spring of 1831, Sindhi villagers taking a morning walk along the banks of the Indus might have stumbled across a rather unusual sight: five huge dapple-grey Suffolk dray horses being punted peacefully upriver, in the company of a gilt velvet-lined state carriage. Floating past the crumbling remains of the former riverside camps of Alexander the Great, Hindu temples, Sufi shrines and Mughal fortresses, the five Suffolk drays munched their way up the Indus until they reached Lahore, the capital of the Sikh leader Ranjit Singh to whom the horses and carriage were being sent as diplomatic gifts. On the way, 'the little English elephants' caused a sensation among the horse-obsessed Punjabis who had never seen their like before: 'For the first time,' wrote their minder Alexander Burnes, a young Scottish officer in the service of the East India Company, 'a dray horse was expected to gallop, canter and perform all the evolutions of the most agile animal.'

In the days that followed, the Suffolk drays and their minder were given a state reception. A guard of cavalry and a regiment of infantry were sent to meet them. 'The coach, which was a handsome vehicle, headed the procession,' wrote Burnes, 'and in the rear of the dray horses we ourselves followed on elephants, with the officers of the maharajah. We passed close under the city walls and entered Lahore by the palace gate. The streets were lined with cavalry, artillery and infantry, all of which saluted as we passed. The concourse of people was immense; they had principally seated themselves on the balconies of houses, and preserved a most respectful silence.'

The British party was led across the courtyard of the old Mughal fort, and into the entrance of the great arcaded marble reception room, the Diwan-i-Khas. 'Whilst stooping to remove my shoes,' Burnes continued, 'I suddenly found myself in the tight embrace of a diminutive, old-looking man.' This was none other than Ranjit Singh, the Lion of the Punjab himself. Taking Burnes by the hand, he brought him into the court where 'all of us were seated on silver chairs, in front of his Highness.'

The journey of Alexander Burnes up the Indus to Lahore, and then on to the then almost completely unknown Muslim emirates of Kabul and Bukhara, was one of the celebrated feats of Victorian travel and exploration, and later became the subject of one of the most famous travel books of the era – Burnes's *Travels into Bokhara*. It was also one of the defining opening moves of the Great Game. For Burnes was not really travelling as a diplomat, or for pleasure, or even out of scholarly curiosity. He had been sent by the Governor General of India, who himself was acting on orders from Downing Street, as an East India Company spy. Burnes was in fact one the most effective intelligence agents of his generation.

Alexander Burnes was an energetic, ambitious and resourceful young Highland Scot, the son of the Provost of Montrose. He was fluent in Persian, Arabic and Hindustani, and had an enviably clear and lively prose style. Like many others who would play the Great Game after him, it was Burnes's intelligence and above all his skill in languages that got him his promotion, and despite coming from a relatively modest background in a remote part of Eastern Scotland, he rose faster in the ranks than any of his richer and better-connected contemporaries. A small, broad-faced man, he had a high forehead, deeply inset eyes and a quizzical set to his mouth which hinted at both his enquiring nature and his sense of humour, something he shared with his cousin, the poet Robbie Burns.

His journey was part of a British plan to map the Indus and the passes of the Hindu Kush, and so gather intelligence on an increasingly crucial area of the world. Since seeing off Napoleon in 1812, the Russians had moved their frontier south and eastwards almost as fast as the East India Company had moved theirs north and westwards, and it was becoming increasingly evident that the two empires would at some point come into collision. British imperial strategists were beginning to fear that the armies of the Russian Empire were primed to march south through Central Asia to capture Afghanistan, before moving in for the checkmate: to wrest India from Britain. Lord Ellenborough, the hawkish President of the Company's Board of

Control, who was also the minister with responsibility for India in the Duke of Wellington's cabinet, was one of the first to turn this anxiety into policy: 'Our policy in Asia must follow one course only,' he wrote. 'To limit the power of Russia.'

By authorising a major new programme of intelligence gathering in Central Asia, Ellenborough effectively gave birth to the Great Game, creating an Anglo-Russian rivalry in the Himalayas where none had existed before. From this point on a succession of young Indian army officers and political agents would be despatched to the Hindu Kush and the Pamirs, sometimes in disguise, sometimes on 'shooting leave', to learn the languages and tribal customs, to map the rivers and passes, and to assess the difficulty of crossing the mountains and deserts.

Burnes was the trailblazer. As the dray horses looked out over the green grass of the Indus floodplains, Burnes and his companions began this process by discreetly taking soundings and bearings, measuring the flow of the river, and preparing detailed maps and flow charts, proving that the river Indus was navigable as far as Lahore. From Afghanistan and Bukhara they again produced maps and detailed notes on the roads threading through the Hindu Kush.

None of this, however, prevented Burnes enjoying himself and writing one of the great accounts of the region in between his official duties. For two months, Ranjit laid on a round of entertainments for Burnes. Dancing girls danced, troops were manoeuvred, deer were hunted, monuments visited and banquets were eaten. Burnes even tried some of Ranjit's home-made hell-brew, a fiery distillation of raw spirit, crushed pearls, musk, opium, gravy and spices, two glasses of which was normally enough to knock-out the most hardened British drinker, but which Ranjit recommended to Burnes as a cure for his dysentery. Burnes and Ranjit, the Scot and the Sikh, found themselves bonding over a shared taste for firewater.

At their final dinner, Ranjit agreed to show Burnes his most precious possession, the Koh-i-Nur: 'Nothing,' wrote Burnes, 'can be imagined more superb than this stone; it is of the finest water, about half the size of an egg. Its weight amounts to 3½ rupees, and if such a jewel is to be valued, I am informed it is worth 3½ millions of money.' Ranjit then presented Burnes with two richly carparisoned horses, dressed in costly

Kashmiri shawls, with their necks adorned with necklaces of agate, and with herons plumes rising from between their ears. While Burnes thanked Ranjit for the present, one of the dray horses was paraded for a final inspection, now decked in cloth of gold and saddled with an elephant's howdah.

Burnes clearly had immense charm and the normally watchful and suspicious Ranjit wrote to the Governor General the day of Burnes' departure to say how much he had enjoyed meeting this 'nightingale of the garden of eloquence, this bird of the winged words of sweet discourse.' When Burnes continued his journey into Afghanistan, the Afghans were no less delighted by him: the first chieftain he came across as he set foot on the Afghan bank of the Indus told him that he and his friends could 'feel as secure as eggs under a hen.' Burnes duly repaid the affection: 'I thought Peshawar a delightful place,' he wrote to his mother in Montrose a month later, 'until I came to Kabul: truly this is paradise . . . I tell them about steam ships, armies, ships, medicine, and all the wonders of Europe; and, in return, they enlighten me regarding the customs of their country, its history, state factions, trade &c . . . '

Burnes liked the place, liked its people, enjoyed its poetry and landscapes, and he admired its rulers. He went on to describe his warm reception by the Emir of Kabul, Dost Mohammad Khan, and described the sparkling intelligence of his conversation, as well as the beauties of the gardens and fruit trees of his palace, the Bala Hisar with its groves of 'peaches, plums, apricots, mulberries, pomegranates and vines... There were also nightingales, blackbirds, thrushes and doves... and chattering magpies on almost every tree.' If Burnes had charmed Dost Mohammad and his Afghans, they, in turn, had charmed him.

WILLIAM DALRYMPLE

PREFACE TO THE FIRST EDITION

In the year 1831 I was deputed in a political capacity to the Court of Lahore, charged with a letter from the King of England, and a present of some horses, to the ruler of that country. The principal object of my journey was to trace the course of the Indus, which had only been crossed at particular points by former travellers, and had never been surveyed but between Tatta and Hydrabad. My success in that undertaking, which was attended with many difficulties, and the sight of so many tribes hitherto little known, gave fresh strength to a desire that I had always felt to see new countries, and visit the conquests of Alexander. As the first European of modern times who had navigated the Indus, I now found myself stimulated to extend my journey beyond that river – the scene of romantic achievements which I had read of in early youth with the most intense interest.

The design received the most liberal encouragement from the Governor-General of India, Lord William Bentinck, whom I joined at Simla, in the Himalaya Mountains, after the termination of my mission to Lahore. His Lordship was of opinion that a knowledge of the general condition of the countries through which I was to travel, would be useful to the British Government, independent of other advantages which might be expected from such a journey.

The hazardous nature of the expedition, and the mode in which it could be best accomplished, required consideration. It would have been objectionable, and highly imprudent, to have entered the countries lying between India and Europe, as I had voyaged on the Indus, an accredited agent; and I was directed to appear (which I myself had suggested) as a private individual.

I was furnished with passports as a Captain in the British army returning to Europe, drawn out in French, English and Persian; and in such terms as would satisfy the people of my real character;

1

and show, at the same time, that Government was interested in my good treatment.

Every other arrangement regarding the journey was left to myself; and I received the sanction of the Governor-General to associate with me Ensign John Leckie – a young officer of the most buoyant disposition, who had been the companion of my voyage up the Indus. On the eve of departure, my fellow-traveller was recalled by the Government of Bombay. Believing that his place might be well supplied by a medical gentleman, which I thought would facilitate our progress through such countries, I gave to Mr James Gerard, a Surgeon of the Bengal army, the option to accompany me. That gentleman had passed most of his life in India, in traversing the Himalaya regions; and possessed an ardent desire for travel. I was also attended by a native Surveyor, Mahommed Ali, a public servant, who had been educated in the Engineer Institution of Bombay, under Captain G. Jervis, of the Engineers; and who had entitled himself to my utmost confidence by faithful and devoted conduct on many trying occasions during the voyage to Lahore. I also took a Hindoo lad, of Cashmere family, named Mohun Lal, who had been educated at the English Institution at Delhi, as he would assist me in my Persian correspondence, the forms of which amount to a science in the East. His youth and his creed would, I believed, free me from all danger of his entering into intrigues with the people; and both he and the Surveyor proved themselves to be zealous and trustworthy men, devoted to our interests. Being natives, they could detach themselves from us; and, by reducing our retinue, preserve our character as poor people, which I ever considered our best safeguard. We discharged the whole of our Indian servants but one individual, Ghoolam Hoosn, who demands my lasting gratitude for the hardships which he underwent on my account, and who is yet my faithful servant.

From the time I made up my mind to traverse the countries that lie between India and the Caspian, I determined to retain the character of an European, accommodating myself in dress, habits, and customs, to those with whom I should mingle. The sequel has proved that the design had much to recommend it, though the

2

character involved us in some difficulties. I adopted the resolution, however, in an utter hopelessness of supporting the disguise of a native; and from having observed that no European traveller has ever journeyed in such countries without suspicion, and seldom without discovery. From long intercourse with Asiatics, I had acquired some insight into their character, and possessed at the same time a fair colloquial knowledge of the Persian language, the *lingua franca* of the people I should meet. I did not, then, hesitate to appear among them in their own garb, and avow myself a foreigner. By all the accounts which I collected, it did not appear to me that there was any just cause for apprehending personal injury or danger; but I received little consolation from my friends in India, who referred to the fate of our predecessors, poor Moorcroft and his party, as our inevitable lot. [William Moorcroft, Superintendent of the East India Company's stud, who roamed Central Asia looking for a supply of suitable horses, died in mysterious circumstances, together with all his companions, in 1825 after visiting Bokhara.] I trust, however, that the happy termination of this journey will give a more favourable impression of the Asiatic character, and stimulate others (which I shall consider a high reward) to view and visit these lands.

[Burnes concludes his preface to the First Edition with acknowledgments to all those who helped and encouraged him, and begs the reader to bear in mind that it had been written while he was in 'constant employment' in India, and put together for publication very hurriedly. This evidently did not inhibit sales, for nearly 900 copies sold in a single day. A second impression was speedily brought out by his publisher, John Murray of Albemarle Street, and a corrected and slightly amended Second Edition appeared the following year.]

London, June 6th, 1834.

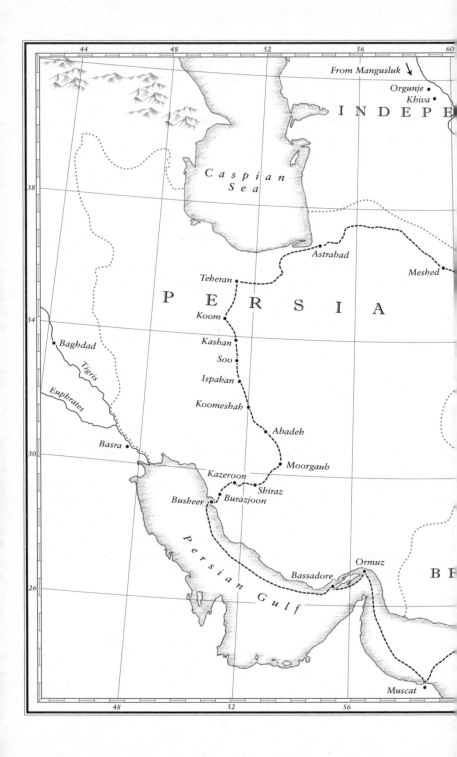

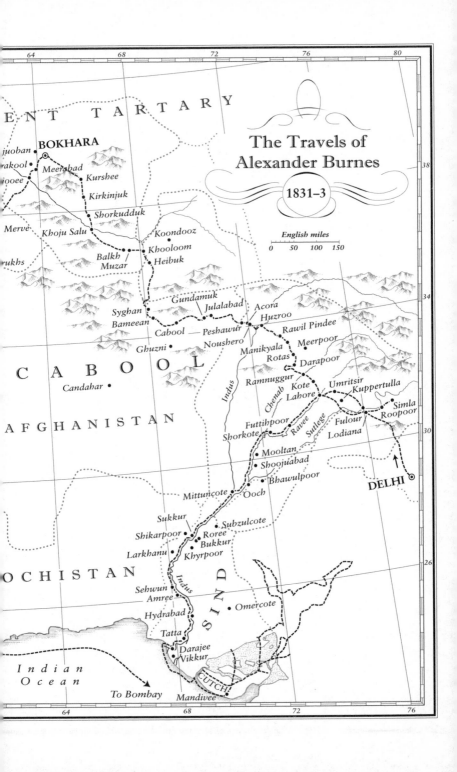

PART ONE

The Narrative of a Voyage
on the Indus

INTRODUCTION

I was employed as an officer of the Quartermaster-General's department for several years, in the province of Cutch [Kutch]. In the course of inquiries into its geography and history, I visited the eastern mouth of the Indus, to which the country adjoins, as well as that singular tract called the 'Run' [Rann], into which that river flows. The extension of our knowledge in that quarter served only to excite further curiosity, in which I was stimulated by Lieut-General Sir Thomas Bradford, then Commander-in-chief of the Bombay army. That officer directed his views, in a most enlightened manner, to the acquisition of every information regarding a frontier so important to Britain as that of North-western India. Encouraged by such approbation, for which I am deeply grateful, I volunteered my services, in the year 1829, to traverse the deserts between India and the Indus, and finally endeavour to descend that river to the sea. Such a journey involved matters of political moment; but the government of Bombay was then held by an individual distinguished above all others by zeal in the cause of Asiatic geography and literature. Sir John Malcolm despatched me at once, in prosecution of the design, and was pleased to remove me to the political branch of the service, observing that I should be then invested 'with influence with the rulers, through whose country I travelled, that would tend greatly to allay that jealousy and alarm which might impede, if they did not arrest, the progress of my enquiries'.

In the year 1830, I entered the desert, accompanied by Lieut. James Holland, of the Quartermaster-General's department, an officer ably qualified. After reaching Jaysulmeer, we were overtaken by an express from the Supreme Government of India, desiring us to return, since at that time, 'it was deemed inexpedient to incur the hazard of exciting the alarm and jealousy of the rulers of Sinde [Sindh], and other foreign states, by the prosecution of the design'. This disappointment, then most acutely felt, was dissipated in the following year, by the arrival of presents from the King of Great Britain for the ruler of Lahore, coupled, at the same time, with a desire that such an opportunity for acquiring correct information of the Indus should not be overlooked. This volume contains the narrative of the mission, which I conducted by the Indus to Lahore. My subsequent journey into Bokhara occupies the two last volumes of this work.

CHAPTER I

Voyage from Cutch to Tatta

In the year 1830, a ship arrived at Bombay with a present of five horses from the King of Great Britain to Maharaja Runjeet Sing [Ranjit Singh], the Seik [Sikh] chieftain at Lahore, accompanied by a letter of friendship from his majesty's minister to that prince. At the recommendation of Major-General Sir John Malcolm, then governor of Bombay, I had the honour of being nominated by the Supreme Government of India to proceed on a mission to the Seik capital, with these presents, by way of the river Indus. I held at that time a political situation in Cutch, the only portion of the British dominions in India which borders on the Indus.

The authorities, both in England and India, contemplated that much information of a political and geographical nature might be acquired in such a journey. The knowledge which we possessed of the Indus was vague and unsatisfactory, and the only accounts of a great portion of its course were drawn from Arrian, Curtius, and the other historians of Alexander's expedition. Sir John Malcolm thus minuted in the records of government, in August 1830:

> The navigation of the Indus is important in every point of view; yet we have no information that can be depended upon on this subject, except of about seventy miles from Tatta to Hydrabad [Hyderabad]. Of the present state of the Delta we have native accounts, and the only facts which can be deduced are, that the different streams of the river below Tatta often change their channels, and that the sands of all are constantly shifting; but, notwithstanding these difficulties, boats of a small draft of water can always go up the principal of them. With regard to the Indus above Hydrabad, there can be no doubt of its being, as it has been for more than two thousand years, navigable far up.

In addition, therefore, to the complimentary mission on which I was to be employed, I had my attention most specially directed to the acquisition of full and complete information regarding the Indus. This was a matter of no easy accomplishment, as the Ameers, or rulers of Sinde, had ever evinced the utmost jealousy of Europeans, and none of the missions which visited the country had been permitted to proceed beyond their capital of Hydrabad. The river Indus, likewise, in its course to the ocean, traverses the territories of many lawless and barbarous tribes, from whom both opposition and insult might be dreaded. On these matters much valuable advice was derived from Lieutenant-Colonel Henry Pottinger, political resident in Cutch, and well known to the world for his adventurous travels in Beloochistan. [Henry Pottinger, then a lieutenant, carried out a daring and perilous survey of Beluchistan in 1810, and his book *Travels in Beloochistan and Sinde* was published in 1816.] He suggested that it might allay the fears of the Sinde government, if a large carriage were sent with the horses, since the size and bulk of it would render it obvious that the mission could then only proceed by water. This judicious proposal was immediately adopted by the government; nor was it in this case alone that the experience of Colonel Pottinger availed me, as it will be seen that he evinced the most unwearied zeal throughout the difficulties which presented themselves, and contributed, in a great degree, to the ultimate success of the undertaking.

That a better colour might also be given to my deputation by a route so unfrequented, I was made the bearer of presents to the Ameers of Sinde, and at the same time charged with communications of a political nature to them. These referred to some excesses committed by their subjects on the British frontier; but I was informed that neither that, nor any other negotiation, was to detain me in my way to Lahore. The authorities in England had desired that a suitable escort might accompany the party; but though the design was not free from some degree of danger, it was evident that no party of any moderate detail could afford the necessary protection. I preferred, therefore, the absence of any of our troops, and resolved to trust to the people of the country; believing that, through their means, I might form a link of communication with the inhabitants. Sir John Malcolm observed, in his letter to the Governor-General, that 'the guard will be people of the country he visits, and those familiar with it. Lieut. Burnes prefers such, on the justest grounds, to any others; finding they facilitate his progress, while they disarm that jealousy which the appearance of any of our troops excites.' Nor were my sentiments erroneous; since a guard of wild Belooches protected us in Sinde, and allayed suspicion.

When these preliminary arrangements had been completed, I received my final instructions in a secret letter from the chief secretary at Bombay. I was informed that 'the depth of water in the Indus, the direction and breadth of the stream, its facilities for steam navigation, the supply of fuel on its banks, and the condition of the princes and people who possess the country bordering on it, are all points of the highest interest to government; but your own knowledge and reflection will suggest to you various other particulars, in which full information is highly desirable; and the slow progress of the boats up the Indus will, it is hoped, give you every opportunity to pursue your researches.' I was supplied with all the requisite surveying instruments, and desired to draw bills on honour for my expenses. In a spirit also characteristic of the distinguished individual who then held the government, I received the thanks of Sir John Malcolm for my previous services; had my attention drawn to the confidence now reposed in me; and was informed that my knowledge of the neighbouring countries and the character of their inhabitants, with the local impressions by which I was certain to be aided, gave me advantages which no other individual enjoyed, and had led to my selection; nor could I not be stimulated by the manner in which Sir John Malcolm addressed the Governor-General of India: 'I shall be very confident of any plan Lieut. Burnes undertakes in this quarter of India: provided a latitude is given him to act as circumstances may dictate, I dare pledge myself that the public interests will be promoted. Having had my attention much directed, and not without success, during more than thirty years, to the exploring and surveying countries in Asia, I have gained some experience, not only in the qualities and habits of the individuals by whom such enterprises can be undertaken, but of the pretexts and appearances necessary to give them success.' A young, active, and intelligent officer, Ensign J. D. Leckie, of the 22nd Regiment N.I., was directed to accompany me; a surveyor, a native doctor, and suitable establishments of servants were likewise entertained.

We sailed from Mandivee [Mandvi] in Cutch with a fleet of five native boats, on the morning of the 21st of January, 1831. On the day succeeding our departure, we had cleared the Gulf of Cutch. The danger in navigating it has been exaggerated. The eddies and dirty appearance of the sea, which boils up and bubbles like an effervescing draught, present a frightful aspect to a stranger, but the natives traverse it at all seasons. It is tolerably free from rocks, and the Cutch shore is sandy with little surf, and presents inducements for vessels in distress to run in upon the land. We passed a boat of fifty tons, which had escaped shipwreck, with a very valuable cargo from Mozambique, the preceding year, by this expedient.

Among the timid navigators of the East, the mariner of Cutch is truly adventurous: he voyages to Arabia, the Red Sea, and the coast of Zanguebar [Zanzibar] in Africa, bravely stretching out on the ocean after quitting his native shore. The 'moallim' or pilot determines his position by an altitude at noon or by the stars at night, with a rude quadrant. Coarse charts depict to him the bearings of his destination, and, by long-tried seamanship, he weathers, in an undecked boat with a huge lateen sail, the dangers and tornadoes of the Indian Ocean. This use of the quadrant was taught by a native of Cutch, who made a voyage to Holland in the middle of last century, and returned, 'in a green old age', to enlighten his country with the arts and sciences of Europe. The most substantial advantages introduced by this improver of his country were the arts of navigating and naval architecture, in which the inhabitants of Cutch excel. For a trifling reward, a Cutch mariner will put to sea in the rainy season, and the adventurous feeling is encouraged by the Hindoo merchants of Mandivee, an enterprising and speculating body of men.

On the evening of the 24th we had cleared the Gulf of Cutch and anchored in the mouth of the Koree [Kori], the eastern, though forsaken, branch of the Indus, which separates Sinde from Cutch. The Koree leads to Lucput [Lakhpat], and is the largest of all the mouths of the river, having become a branch of the sea as the fresh water has been turned from its channel. There are many spots on its banks hallowed in the estimation of the people. Cotasir and Narainseer are places of pilgrimage to the Hindoo, and stand upon the western promontory of Cutch. Opposite them lies the cupola of Rao Kanoje, beneath which there rests a saint, revered by the Mahommedans. To defraud this personage of frankincense, grain, oil, and money, in navigating the Koree, would entail, it is superstitiously believed, certain shipwreck. In this reverence we recognise the dangers and fear of the mariner. There is a great contrast between the shores of Sinde and Cutch; the one is flat and depressed, nearly to a level with the sea, while the hills of Cutch rise in wild and volcanic cones, which meet the eye long after the coast has faded from the view. We gladly exchanged this grandeur for the dull monotony of the shores of Sinde, unvaried as it is, by any other signs of vegetation than stunted shrubs, whose domain is invaded by each succeeding tide.

We followed the Sinde coast for four or five days, passing all the mouths of the Indus, eleven in number, the principal of which we entered and examined, without even the observation of the inhabitants. There was little indication of our being near the estuary of so great a river, for the water was only fresh a mile off shore from the Gora, or largest mouth of the Indus; and the junction of the river water with that of the sea was formed without violence, and might be now and then discovered by a small streak of foam and a gentle ripple. The number and subdivision of the branches diminish, no doubt, the velocity as well as the volume of the Indus; but it would be supposed that so vast a river would exercise an influence in the sea far from its embouchure; and I believe this is really the case in the months of July and August, during the inundation. The waters of the Indus are so loaded with mud and clay as to discolour the sea for about three miles from the land. Opposite its different mouths numberless brown specks are to be seen, called 'pit' by the natives. I found them, on examination, to be round globules, filled with water, and easily burst. When placed on a plate, they were about the size of a shilling, and covered by a brown skin. These specks are considered by the pilots to denote the presence of fresh water among the salt; for they believe them to be detached from the sand banks, by the meeting of the sea and the river. They give a particularly dirty and oily appearance to the water.

At nightfall on the 28th, we cast anchor in the western mouth of the Indus, called the Pittee. The coast of Sinde is not distinguishable a league from the shore. There is not a tree to be seen, though the *mirage* sometimes magnifies the stunted shrubs of the Delta, and gives them a tall and verdant appearance; a delusion that vanishes with a nearer approach. From our anchorage, a white fortified tomb, in the Bay of Curachee [Karachi], was visible north-west of us; and beyond it lay a rocky range of black mountains, called Hala, the Irus of Nearchus. I here read from Arrian and Quintus Curtius the passages of this memorable scene in Alexander's expedition, the mouth from which his admiral, Nearchus, took his departure from Sinde. The river did not exceed 500 yards in width, instead of the 200 stadia (furlongs) of Arrian, and the twelve miles which more modern accounts had assigned to it, on the authority of the natives. But there was still some resemblance to the Greek author; for the hills over Curachee form with the intervening country a semicircular bay, in which an island and some sand-banks might lead a stranger to believe, that the ocean was yet distant.

[Here Burnes quotes the Classical authors at length, as he does at intervals throughout his travels. Arrian – a Graeco-Roman soldier, philosopher and historian, who was also a Roman senator and friend of the emperor Hadrian – wrote his history of the campaigns of Alexander of Macedon in the early second century AD. Although this was nearly 400 years after Alexander's exploits, Arrian had access to writings by Ptolemy and Nearchus, both of whom were among Alexander's generals, and many of whose works have since been lost. Burnes, who had been fired by 'the most intense interest' in the 'romantic achievements' of Alexander the Great since his schooldays, now – at the age of twenty-six – found himself following in the footsteps of his namesake and hero. With his well-thumbed editions of the ancient texts always close to hand, he was able to compare his own observations of the land, its people and monuments with those of Alexander's officers during the conquest of Central Asia over 2,000 years previously. For reasons of space I have regretfully reduced or omitted many of these passages.]

I must not now dwell on these subjects, though eminently interesting; but, in the course of my narrative, I shall endeavour to identify the modern Indus with the features of remoter times. It is difficult to describe the enthusiasm which one feels on first beholding the scenes that have exercised the genius of Alexander.

The jealousy of the Sinde government had been often experienced, and it was therefore suggested that we should sail for the Indus, without giving any previous information. Immediately on anchoring, I despatched a communication to the agent of the Ameers at Darajee, signifying my plans; and, in the meanwhile, ascended the river with caution, anchoring in the fresh water on the second evening, thirty-five miles from the sea. Near the mouth of the river, we passed a rock stretching across the stream, which is particularly mentioned by Nearchus, who calls it 'a dangerous rock', and is the more remarkable, since there is not even a stone below Tatta in any other part of the Indus. We passed many villages, and had much to enliven and excite our attention, had we not purposely avoided all intercourse with the people till made acquainted with the fate of our intimation to the authorities at Darajee. A day passed in anxious suspense; but on the following morning, a body of armed men crowded round our boats, and the whole neighbourhood was in a state of the greatest excitement. The party stated themselves to be the soldiers of the Ameer, sent to number our party, and see the contents of all the boats, as well as every box that they contained. I gave a ready and immediate assent; and we were instantly boarded by about fifty armed men, who wrenched open everything, and prosecuted the most rigorous search for cannon and gunpowder. Mr Leckie and myself stood by in amazement, till it was at length demanded that the box containing the large carriage should be opened; for they pretended to view it as the Greeks had looked on the wooden horse, and believed that it would carry destruction into Sinde. A sight of it

17

disappointed their hopes; and we must be conjurors, it was asserted, to have come without arms and ammunition.

When the search had been completed, I entered into conversation with the head man of the party, and had hoped to establish, by his means, a friendly connection with the authorities; but after a short pause this personage, who was a Reis of Lower Sinde, intimated that a report of the day's transactions would be forthwith transmitted to Hydrabad; and that, in the meanwhile, it was incumbent on us to await the decision of the Ameer, at the mouth of the river. The request appeared reasonable; the more so, since the party agreed to furnish us with every supply while so situated. We therefore weighed anchor, and dropped down the river, but here our civilities ended. By the way we were met by several 'dingies' full of armed men, and at night were hailed by one of them, to know how many troops we had on board. We replied that we had not even a musket. 'The evil is done,' rejoined a rude Belooche soldier, 'you have seen our country; but we have four thousand men ready for action!' To this vainglorious observation succeeded torrents of abuse, and when we reached the mouth of the river, the party fired their matchlocks over us: but I dropped anchor and resolved, if possible, to repel these insults by personal remonstrance. It was useless: we were surrounded by ignorant barbarians, who shouted out, in reply to all I said, that they had been ordered to turn us out of the country. I protested against their conduct in the most forcible language; reminded them that I was the representative, however humble, of a great Government, charged with presents from Royalty; and added that, without a written document from their master, I should decline quitting Sinde. An hour's delay served to convince me that personal violence would ensue if I persisted in such a resolution and, as it was not my object to risk the success of the enterprise by such collision, I sailed for the most eastern mouth of the Indus, from which I addressed the authorities in Sinde, as well as Colonel Pottinger, the Resident in Cutch.

I was willing to believe that the soldiers had exceeded the authority which had been granted them; and was speedily put in possession of a letter from the Ameer, couched in friendly terms, but narrating, at great length, the difficulty and impossibility of navigating the Indus. 'The boats are so small,' said his Highness, 'that only four or five men can embark in one of them; their progress is likewise slow; they have neither masts nor sails; and the depth of the water in the Indus is likewise so variable as not to reach, in some places, the knee or waist of a man.' But this formidable enumeration of physical obstacles was coupled with no refusal from the Ruler himself, and it seemed expedient, therefore, to make a second attempt, after replying to his Highness's letter.

[The expedition made their second attempt on 10th February but were thwarted by a violent storm which buffeted them about for several days, splitting their sails and dismasting two of the vessels. Burnes sent a letter to the agents at Darajee protesting at their failure to honour their undertaking to keep the British party supplied while permission to proceed was being sorted out, but there was no reply. By now food and water were running low, and when Burnes sent a small boat to procure water, it was seized together with its occupants. There was no option now but to retreat from Sindh and return to Kutch, but on 22nd of February they were caught in an even worse storm in which all the flat-bottomed boats were engulfed by the racing tide. Miraculously they all survived and managed to limp back to Mandvi, with the carriage and dray horses unharmed.

Burnes was full of admiration for the zeal, bravery and loyalty of his crew, but he was forced to recognise that the Amir of Sindh was decidedly unfriendly and that a covert survey of the Indus was not going to be easy. The native agent who represented the interests of the British Government at Hyderabad confirmed with some amusement that the Amir feared that Burnes's little flotilla was the precursor of a full-scale invasion, and also pointed out that his pride was now involved: having said in his letter that the river was totally unnavigable, how could he allow the British to proceed? It would soon be obvious to them that the Indus was in fact full of boats. This was why the Amir had not replied to the Lieutenant's letter.

Finally, after an intervention by Colonel Pottinger in which he pointed out what an unfortunate impression the Amir's unhelpful conduct would make on the King of England, whose royal presents were being conveyed, Burnes and his party set out again on their third attempt to sail up the Indus.]

On the 10th of March we once more set sail for the Indus, and reached the Hujamree, one of the central mouths of the river, after a prosperous voyage of seven days. We could hire no pilot to conduct us across the bar, and took the wrong and shallow mouth of the river, ploughing up the mud as we tacked in its narrow channel. The foremost vessel loosened her red ensign when she had fairly reached the deep water, and, with the others, we soon and joyfully anchored near her. We were now met by an officer of the Sinde Government, one of the favoured descendants of the Prophet, whose enormous corpulence bespoke his condition. This personage came to the mouth of the river, for we were yet refused all admittance to the fresh water. He produced a letter from the Ameer, and repeated the same refuted arguments of his master, which he seemed to think should receive credit from his high rank. It would be tiresome to follow the Sindians through the course of chicanery which they adopted, even in this stage of the proceedings. An embargo was laid on all the vessels in the Indus and we ourselves were confined to our boats, on a dangerous shore, and even denied fresh water. The officer urged the propriety of our taking a route by land and, as a last resource, I offered to accompany him to the capital, by way of Tatta, and converse with the Ameer in person, having previously landed the horses.

[Many frustrating days of stalemate ensued, in which the Sindhians did their utmost to persuade Burnes to travel to Lahore by land, but he knew that he must not give way or the primary object of the expedition would be defeated. After exchanges of letters which tested Burnes's powers of diplomacy – and patience – to the full, he was finally given permission to proceed by water.]

I gladly quit the detail of occurrences which have left few pleasing reflections behind, except that success ultimately attended our endeavours, and that they elicited the approbation of Government. The Ameer of Sinde had sought to keep us in ignorance of the Indus, but his treatment had led to another and opposite effect, since we had entered, in the course of our several voyages, *all* the mouths of the river, and a map of them, as well as of the land route to Tatta, now lay before me. Our dangers on the banks and shoals had been imminent, but we looked back upon them with the pleasing thought that our experience might guide others through them.

CHAPTER II

Tatta to Hydrabad

A week's stay was agreeably spent in examining Tatta and the objects of curiosity which surround it. The city stands at a distance of three miles from the Indus. It is celebrated in the history of the East. Its commercial prosperity passed away with the empire of Delhi [i.e. the Mughal empire], and its ruin has been completed since it fell under the iron despotism of the present rulers of Sinde. It does not contain a population of 15,000 souls: and of the houses scattered about its ruins, one half are destitute of inhabitants. It is said that the dissensions between the last and present dynasties, which led to Sinde being over-run by the Afghans, terrified the merchants of the city, who fled the country at that time, and have had no encouragement to return. Of the weavers of 'loongees' (a kind of silk and cotton manufacture), for which this place was once so famous, 125 families only remain. There are not forty merchants in the city. Twenty money-changers transact all the business of Tatta; and its limited population is now supplied with animal food by five butchers. Such has been the gradual decay of that mighty city, so populous in the early part of last century, in the days of Nadir Shah. The country in its vicinity lies neglected, and but a small portion of it is brought under tillage. There is little in modern Tatta to remind one of its former greatness. A spacious brick mosque, built by Shah Jehan, still remains, but is crumbling to decay.

We quitted Tatta on the morning of the 10th of April, and retraced our steps to Meerpoor [Mirpur]; a distance of twenty-four miles, over roads nearly impassable from rain; thence crossed the Pittee by a ferry, at a thriving town called Bohaur, to Vikken. I observe in 'Hamilton's India' that this country is sometimes without rain for three years at a time; but we had very heavy showers and a severe fall of hail, though the thermometer stood at 86 degrees. The dews and mists about Tatta make it a disagreeable residence at this season, and the dust is described as intolerable in June and July.

Our road lay through a desert country along the 'Buggaur' (on which Meerpoor is built), one of the two large branches of the Indus, which separate below Tatta. It has its name from the destructive velocity with which it runs, tearing up trees in its course. It has been forsaken for a few years past, and had only a width of 200 yards where we crossed it below Meerpoor. The Indus itself, before this division takes place, is a noble river, and we beheld it at Tatta with high gratification. The water is foul and muddy but it is 2000 feet wide, and two fathoms and a half deep, from shore to shore. When I first saw it, the surface was agitated by a violent wind, which raised up waves that raged with great fury; and I no longer felt wonder at the natives designating so vast a river by the name of 'Durya', or the Sea of Sinde.

On our return, we saw much of the people, who were disposed from the first to treat us more kindly than the government. Their notions regarding us were strange: some asked us why we allowed dogs to clean our hands after a meal, and if we indiscriminately ate cats and mice, as well as pigs. They complained much of their rulers, and the ruinous and oppressive system of taxation to which they were subjected, as it deterred them from cultivating any considerable portion of the land. Immense tracts of the richest soil lie in a state of nature, between Tatta and the sea, overgrown with tamarisk shrubs, which attain, in some places, the height of twenty feet and, threading into one another, form impervious thickets. At other places we passed extensive plains of hard-caked clay, with remains of ditches and aqueducts, now neglected. We reached the sea in two days.

Arrian informs us, that, after Alexander returned from viewing the right branch of the Indus, he again set out from Pattala, and descended the other branch of the river, which conducted him to a 'certain lake, joined either by the river spreading wide over a flat country, or by additional streams flowing into it from the adjacent parts, and making it appear like bay in the sea.'

On the 12th of April, we embarked in the flat-bottomed boats, or 'doondees', of Sinde, and commenced our voyage on the Indus, with no small degree of satisfaction. Our fleet consisted of six of these flat-bottomed vessels, and a small English-built pinnace, which we had brought from Cutch. The boats of the Indus are not unlike China junks, very capacious, but most unwieldy. They are floating houses; and with ourselves we transported the boatmen, their wives and families, kids and fowls. When there is no wind, they are pulled up against the stream, by ropes attached to the mast-head, at the rate of a mile and a half an hour; but with a breeze, they set a large square-sail, and advance double the distance. We halted at Vikkur, which is the first port; a place of considerable export for grain, that had then fifty 'doondees', besides sea vessels, lying near it.

On the 13th, we threaded many small creeks for a distance of eight miles, and then entered the Wanyanee, or principal branch of the Indus, which is a fine river, 500 yards broad and 24 feet deep. Its banks were alternately steep and flat, the course very crooked, and the different turnings were often marked by branches running from this trunk to other arms of the delta. We had nothing but tamarisk on either bank, and the reed huts of a few fishermen alone indicated that we were in a peopled country.

As we ascended the river, the inhabitants came from miles around to see us. A Syud stood on the water's edge, and gazed with astonishment. He turned to his companion as we passed and, in the hearing of one of our party, said, 'Alas! Sinde is now gone, since the English have seen the river, which is the road to its conquest.' If such an event do happen, I am certain that the body of the people will hail the happy day; but it will be an evil one for the Syuds, the descendants of Mahommed, who are the only people, besides the rulers, that derive precedence and profit from the existing order of things. [Sindh was indeed annexed by the British, though not until 1843 – and very controversially. Major-General Sir Charles Napier admitted that 'we have no right to seize Scinde', but provoked the Sindhians into hostilities in order to do so. The British had recently suffered a calamitous defeat in the First Afghan War and were in the course of re-invading Afghanistan, taking brutal reprisals and reasserting British power. Although he had no orders to do so, Napier evidently felt this was an opportune moment to raise the

British flag in Sindh also. There was widespread indignation back in England, and Punch magazine published a cartoon of the general with the punning caption 'Peccavi' – 'I have sinned'.]

Nothing more arrests the notice of a stranger, on entering Sinde, than the severe attention of the people to the forms of religion, as enjoined by the Prophet of Arabia. In all places, the meanest and poorest of mankind may be seen, at the appointed hours, turned towards Mecca, offering up their prayers. I have observed a boatman quit the laborious duty of dragging the vessel against the stream, and retire to the shore, wet and covered with mud, to perform his genuflexions. In the smallest villages, the sound of the 'mowuzzun', or crier, summoning true believers to prayers, may be heard, and the Mahommedans within reach of the sonorous sound suspend, for the moment, their employment, that they may add their 'Amen' to the solemn sentence when concluded. The effect is pleasing and impressive but, as has often happened in other countries at a like stage of civilisation, the moral qualities of the people do not keep pace with this fervency of devotion.

On the evening of the 15th, we anchored at Tatta, after a prosperous voyage, that afforded a good insight into the navigation of the Indus which, in the Delta, is both dangerous and difficult. The water runs with impetuosity from one bank to another, and undermines them so, that they often fall in masses which would crush a vessel. During night they may be heard tumbling with a terrific crash and a noise as loud as artillery. In one place, the sweep of the river was so sudden that it had formed a kind of whirlpool, and all our vessels heeled round, on passing it, from the rapidity of the current. We had everywhere six fathoms of water, and in these eddies the depth was sometimes threefold; but our vessels avoided the strength of the current, and shifted from side to side, to choose the shallows.

We ascended the Indus in the season of the 'pulla,' a fish of the carp species, as large as the mackerel, and fully equalling the flavour of salmon. It is only found in the four months that precede the swell of the river from January to April, and never higher than the fortress of Bukkur. The natives superstitiously believe the fish to proceed there on account of Khaju Khizr, a saint of celebrity, who is interred at that town, from whence they are said to return without ever turning their tails on the sanctified spot, an assertion which the muddy colour of the Indus will prevent being contradicted. The mode of catching this fish is ingenious, and peculiar, I believe, to the Indus. Each fisherman is provided with a large earthen jar, open at the top, and somewhat flat. On this he places himself and, lying on it horizontally, launches into the stream, swimming or pushing forward like a frog, and guiding himself with his hands. When he has reached the middle of the river, where the current is strongest, he darts his net directly under him, and sails down with the stream. The net consists of a pouch attached to a pole, which he shuts on meeting his game; he then draws it up, spears it, and, putting it into the vessel on which he floats, prosecutes his occupation. There are some vessels of small dimensions, without any orifice, and on these the fishermen sail down in a sitting posture. Hundreds of people, old and young, may be seen engaged in catching pulla, and the season is hailed with joy by the people, as furnishing a wholesome food while it lasts, and an abundant supply of dry fish during the remainder of the year and for exportation to the neighbouring countries.

On the morning of the 18th, we moored opposite Hydrabad, which is five miles inland, having had a strong and favourable breeze from Tatta that brought us against the stream, at the rate of three miles an hour. The dust was intolerable every where, and a village might always be discovered by the dense clouds which hovered over it. This part of Sinde is well known: the country is devoted to sterility by the Ameers, to feed their passion for the chase. The banks are enclosed to the water's edge, and the interior of these hunting thickets is overgrown with furze, brushwood, and stunted babool trees, which always retain a verdant hue, from the richness of the soil. One or two solitary camels were to be seen raising water to fill the pools of these preserves, as the Ameer and his relatives had announced a hunting excursion, and the deer would be drawn by thirst to drink at the only fountain, and shot by an Ameer from a place of concealment. It is thus that the chiefs sport with their game and their subjects.

Immediately on our arrival, four different deputations waited on us, to convey the congratulations of Meer Moorad Ali Khan and his family, at our having reached the capital of Sinde, and at the same time to tender the strongest professions of friendship and respect for the British government; to all of which I returned suitable answers. In the evening we were conducted to Hydrabad, and alighted at the house, or 'tanda', of Nawab Wulee Mahommed Khan, the vizier of Sinde whose son, in the father's absence, was appointed our mihmandar [an official charged with looking after guests]. Tents were pitched, and provisions of every description sent to us; and it would, indeed, have been difficult to discover that we were the individuals who had so long lingered about the shore of Sinde, now the honoured guests of its jealous master. Great and small were in attendance on us: khans and Syuds, servants and chobdars brought messages and enquiries, till the night was far spent; and it may not be amiss to mention, as a specimen of conducting business in Sinde, that the barber, the water-cooler, and the prime minister were sent indiscriminately with errands on the same subject.

The ceremonial of our reception was soon adjusted, but not without some exhibition of Sindian character. After the time had been mutually fixed for the following afternoon, our mihmandar made his appearance at *daybreak*, to request that we would then accompany him to the palace. I spoke of the arrangements that had been made; but he treated all explanation with indifference, and eulogised in extravagant language, the great condescension of his master in giving us an interview so early, while the Vakeels, or representatives of other states, often waited for weeks. I informed the Khan that I entertained very different sentiments regarding his master's giving us so early a reception, and assured him that I viewed it as no sort of favour, and was satisfied that the Ameer himself was proud in receiving, at any time, an agent of the British Government. The reply silenced him, and he shortly afterwards withdrew, and sent an apology for this importunity which, he stated, had originated in a mistake. The pride of the Sindians must be met by the same weapons; and, however disagreeable the line of conduct, it will be found, in all matters of negotiation, to carry along with it its own reward: altercations that have passed will be succeeded by civility and politeness, and a shade of oblivion cast over all that is unpleasant.

In the evening we were presented to the Ameer of Sinde by his son, Nusseer Khan, who had previously received us in his own apartments to inform us of his attachment to the British Government, and the state secret of his having been the means of procuring for us a passage through Sinde. We found the Ameer seated in the middle of a room, attended by his various relatives: they all rose on our entrance, and were studiously polite. His Highness addressed me by name; said I was his friend, both on public and private grounds; for my brother (Dr James Burnes) had cured him of a dangerous disease. At the same time he caused me to be seated along with him on the cushion which he occupied; he begged that I would forget the difficulties and dangers encountered, and consider him as the ally of the British Government, and my own friend.

[Burnes was not much impressed by the Ameer, in spite of the superb jewels he and his family were wearing, nor by his somewhat scruffy palace. They met in an uncarpeted and dirty room, filled by a noisy rabble of soldiery who took no notice when the Ameer ordered them to be quiet. After the required civilities had been exchanged and the interview came to an end, Burnes sent the Ameer presents from the British government including a European gun and brace of pistols, a gold watch, two telescopes, a clock, and some cut-glass candlesticks, together with English shawls and cloths and a map of India and the world in Persian characters. However, the Vizier soon came to ask that the clock and the candlesticks be exchanged for something more to the Ameer's liking, from the store of official gifts which the British delegation doubtless had with them! Burnes managed to convey diplomatically that the presents had been specially chosen for the Ameer by the British authorities and he was unable to swap them – though the Vizier kept on hinting right up to the moment of departure.

All in all, though, Burnes was well satisfied with his reception at Hyderabad, for it was clear the Ameer was not going to hinder their onward passage to Lahore and had in fact put his royal barge at their disposal, together with servants, elephants, palanquins and anything else they might need as they sailed to the frontier.]

CHAPTER III

Voyage to Bukkur

On the morning of the 23rd of April, we embarked in the state barge of the Ameer, which is called a 'jumtee' by the natives of the country. They are very commodious vessels, of the same build as the other flat-bottomed boats of the Indus, and sadly gainsayed the beggarly account which his Highness, in his correspondence, had so often given of the craft in the river. It was about sixty feet long, and had three masts, on which we hoisted as many sails, made of alternate stripes of red and white cloth. There were two cabins, connected with each other by a deck; but contrary to the custom of other countries, the one at the bows is the post of honour. It was of a pavilion shape, coloured with scarlet cloth, and the eyes of intruders were excluded on all sides by silken screens. The jumtee was further decorated by variegated flags and pendants, some of which were forty feet long. We hoisted the British ensign at the stern of our pinnace, the first time, I suppose, it had ever been unfurled on the Indus; and the little vessel which bore it out-sailed all the fleet. I hope the omen was auspicious, and that the commerce of Britain may soon follow her flag. We moved merrily through the water, generally with a fair wind, anchoring always at night, and pitching our camp on the shore, pleased to find ourselves beyond the portals of Hydrabad.

We reached Sehwun on the 1st of May, a distance of 100 miles, in eight days. There was little to interest us on the banks of the river, which are thinly peopled, and destitute of trees or variety to diversify the scene. The Lukkee mountains, a high range, came in sight on the third day, running in upon the Indus at Sehwun. The stream itself, though grand and magnificent, was often divided by sand-banks, and moved sluggishly along at the rate of two miles and a half an hour. One of our boats had nearly sunk from coming in contact with a protruding stump; an accident of frequent occurrence on the Indus, and sometimes attended with fatal results, particularly to vessels descending the stream. Our escape from calamity gave the Sindians a topic for congratulation, and we daily heard the greatness of our fortune proclaimed. Every trivial incident, a slight breeze or any such occurrence, they did not hesitate to ascribe to our destiny.

Our crew consisted of sixteen men, and a happy set of beings they were: they waded through the water all day, and swam and sported about, as they passed along, with joyous hearts, returning occasionally to the boat to indulge in the hookah, and the intoxicating 'bang', or hemp, to which they are much addicted. They prepare this drug by straining the juice from the seeds and stalks through a cloth: when ready for use, it resembles green putrid water. It must be very pernicious. I do not know if I can class their pipes among the movables of the ship, for their stands were formed of a huge piece of earthenware, too heavy to be lifted, which remains at the stern, where the individuals retire to inhale the weed, made doubly noxious by its being mixed with opium. The sailors of Sinde are Mahommedans. They are very superstitious; the sight of a crocodile below Hydrabad is an evil omen which would never be forgotten, and in that part of the Indus these monsters certainly confined themselves to the deep.

*   *   *

The town of Sehwun stands on a rising ground, at the verge of a swamp, two miles from the Indus, close to a branch of that river called Arul, which flows from Larkhanu [Larkana]. It has a population of about 10,000 souls, and is commanded on the north side by a singular castle or mound of earth. Sehwun is sometimes called Sewistan, and is a place of antiquity. There are many ruined mosques and tombs which surround it, and proclaim its former wealth; but it has gradually gone to decay since it ceased to be the residence of a governor, who here held his court in the days of Moghul splendour. As it stands near the Lukkee mountains, I believe it may be fixed on as the city of Sambus, Raja of the Indian mountaineers, mentioned by Alexander. The Sindomanni cannot refer to the inhabitants of Lower Sinde, which is always called

Pattala, and its ruler the 'prince of the Pattalans'. Sindee is the modern term for the aboriginal inhabitants.

Sehwun has considerable celebrity and sanctity from the tomb of a holy saint of Khorasan, by name Lal Shah Baz, who was interred here about 600 years ago. The shrine stands in the centre of the town, and rests under a lofty dome at one end of a quadrangular building, which is handsomely ornamented by blue painted slabs, like Dutch tiles, that give it a rich appearance. A cloth of gold, with two other successive palls of red silk, are suspended over the sepulchre, and on the walls which surround it are inscribed in large Arabic letters the praises of the deceased, and extracts from the Koran. Ostrich eggs, peacocks' feathers, beads, flowers, &c. complete the furniture of this holy spot; and pigeons, the emblems of peace, are encouraged to perch on the cloths which shade the remains of departed virtue. The miracles of Lal Shah Baz are endless, if you believe the people. The Indus is subject to his commands, and no vessel dares to pass his shrine without making a propitiatory offering at his tomb. Thousands of pilgrims flock to the consecrated spot, and the monarchs of Cabool [Kabul] and India have often visited the sanctuary. The needy are daily supplied with food from the charity of the stranger; but the universal bounty has corrupted the manners of the inhabitants, who are a worthless and indolent set of men. The Hindoo joins with the Mahommedan in his veneration of the saint, and artfully insinuates 'Lal' to be a Hindoo name, and that the Mahommedans have associated with the faith of their prophet the god of an infidel creed. A tiger, once the tenant of the neighbouring hills, partakes of the general bounty in a cage near the tomb.

By far the most singular building at Sehwun, and perhaps on the Indus, is the ruined castle overlooking the town, which in all probability is as old as the age of the Greeks. It consists of a mound of earth sixty feet high, and surrounded from the very ground by a brick wall. The shape of the castle is oval, about 1200 feet long and by 750 in diameter. The interior presents a heap of ruins, strewed with broken pieces of pottery and brick. The gateway is on the town side, and has been arched; a section through it proves the whole mound to be artificial. At a distance this castle resembles the drawings of the Mujilebe tower at Babylon, described by Mr Rich in his interesting memoir. [Claudius Rich, the East India Company's Resident at Baghdad, had published *Memoir on the Ruins of Babylon* in 1815.]

The natives afford no satisfactory account of this ruin, attributing it to the age of Budur-ool-Jumal, a fairy, whose agency is referred to in everything ancient or wonderful in Sinde. It is to be observed that the Arul river passes close to this castle, and we are informed by Quintus Curtius that, in the territories of Sabus Raja (which I imagine refers to Sehwun), 'Alexander took the strongest city by a tunnel formed by his miners.' A ruin of such magnitude, standing, as it therefore does, on such a site, would authorise our fixing on it as the very city 'where the barbarians, untaught in engineering, were confounded when their enemies appeared, almost in the middle of the city, rising from a subterraneous passage of which no trace was previously seen'. So strong a position would not, in all probability, be neglected in after-times; and in the reign of the Emperor Humaioon [Humayun, son of Babur], AD 1541, we find that monarch unable to capture Sehwun, from which he fled on his disastrous journey to Omercote [Umarkot]. His son Acbar [Akbar the Great] also invested Sehwun for seven months, and after its capture seems to have dismantled it. There are many coins found in the castle of Sehwun, but among thirty I could find no trace of the Greek alphabet. They were Mahommedan coins of the sovereigns of Delhi.

About eighteen miles below Sehwun, and on the same side of the river, is the village of Amree [Amri], believed to have been once a large city, and the favourite residence of former kings. It is said to have been swept into the Indus. Near the modern village, however, there is a mound of earth, about forty feet high, which the traditions of the country point out as the halting-place of a king, who ordered the dung of his cavalry to be gathered together, and hence the mound of Amree. There are some tombs near it, but they are evidently modern. We halted four days at Sehwun. The climate was most sultry and oppressive: the thermometer stood at 112 degrees in a tent, and did not fall below 100 at midnight, owing to scorching winds from the west, where the country is bleak and mountainous.

The lofty range which runs parallel with the Indus from the sea-coast to the centre of Asia, is joined by the Lukkee mountains south of Sehwun, and thus excludes the refreshing breezes of the ocean.

We quitted Sehwun on the 4th with difficulty, for we could not procure men to drag our boats. The mihmandar, though he was the vizier's son, and acted under the seal of the Ameer, could not prevail on the Calendar, or priest of the tomb, who said that no such order had ever been given, and he would not now obey it. Some persons were seized: his people drew their swords, and said that, when no longer able to wield them, they might go. We knew nothing of the matter till it was over, as it was entirely a private arrangement of Syud Tukkee Shah, the mihmandar. When the men heard that they were to be remunerated for their trouble, they came of their own accord before we sailed. Every thing in Sinde being effected by force under despotism, the watermen of Sehwun fled the town, or took up their abode in the sanctuary, when they saw the 'jumtee' approach, believing, as usual, that services would be required of them gratuitously.

On the day after quitting Sehwun we were met by Mahommed Gohur, a Belooche chief, and a party, the confidential agents of Meer Roostum Khan, the Ameer of Khyrpoor [Khairpur], who had been sent to the frontier, a distance of eighty miles, to congratulate us on our arrival, and declare their master's devotion to the British Government. We hardly expected such a mark of attention in Sinde, and were therefore gratified. The deputation brought an abundant supply of sheep, flour, fruit, spices, sugar, butter, ghee, tobacco, opium &c. &c., on which our people feasted. Sheep were slain and cooked; rice and ghee were soon converted into savoury viands; and I believe all parties thanked Meer Roostum Khan as heartily as we did, nor did I imagine that this was but the commencement of a round of feasting which was daily repeated so long as we were in his country, a period of three weeks. Mahommed Gohur was a decrepit old man, with a red beard. He wore a very handsome loongee round his waist. He did not recover from his surprise throughout the interview, for he had never before seen an European.

In return for Meer Roostum Khan's kindness, I addressed to him a Persian letter in the following terms, which will serve as a specimen of the epistolary style used by the people of this country, which I imitated as closely as possible:

(After compliments:) I hasten to inform your Highness that I have reached the frontiers of your country in company with the respectable Syud Tukkee Shah, who has accompanied me on the part of Meer Moorad Ali Khan from Hydrabad. As I have long since heard of your Highness from those who pass between Cutch and Sinde, it forms a source of congratulation to me that I have arrived in your dominions, and brought along with me in safety the presents which have been graciously bestowed on Maha Raja Runjeet Sing by His Majesty the King of England, mighty in rank, terrible as the planet Mars, a monarch great and magnificent, of the rank of Jemshid, of the dignity of Alexander, unequalled by Darius, just as Nousherwan, great as Fureedoon, admired as Cyrus, famed as the Sun, the destroyer of tyranny and oppression, upright and generous, pious and devout, favoured from above, &c. &c.: may his dominion endure for ever!

It is well known that when a friend comes to the country of a friend it is a source of much happiness, and I have therefore written these few lines; but when I have the pleasure of seeing you, my joy will be increased. I had written thus far, when the respectable Mahommed Gohur, one of those enjoying your Highness's confidence, arrived at this place, to acquaint me with your professions of respect and friendship for the British Government, bringing along with him many marks of your hospitality. Need I say I am rejoiced? Such civilities mark the great.

A voyage of ten days brought us to Bukkur, but we landed a few miles from that fortress, to prepare for a visit to Khyrpoor and its chief, who had made us so welcome in his country. We saw much of the Sindians on our way up the river, and did everything to encourage their approach by granting free admission on board to the commonest villager who wished to view the horses. The body of the people are little better than savages, and extremely ignorant; their spiritual guides and Syuds, or the followers of the prophet, however, showed knowledge and independence. I happened to ask a party of Syuds to what Ameer they were subject: they replied, 'We acknowledge no master but God, who gives us villages and all we desire.' I was struck with the family likeness that prevails throughout this class in Sinde, for it is not to be supposed that a tribe so numerous has lineally descended from the prophet of Arabia. The beggars of Sinde are most importunate and troublesome. They practise all manner of persuasion to succeed in their suit for alms: tear up grass and bushes with their mouths, and chew sand and mud to excite compassion.

With the better orders of society we had frequent intercourse and conversation. Some of them felt interested about the objects of our mission to Lahore. They did not give us much credit for sincerity in sending it by a route which they believed never to have been passed since the time of Noah. They were full of enquiries regarding our customs. Our Khyrpoor friend, Mohammed Gohur, was particularly horrified at our arrangements for getting a wife, and begged me in future to let my beard grow. The knowledge of this individual I may describe, when he asked me if London were under Calcutta: he was, however, a pleasant man; I delighted to hear him sing the praises of the soldiers of Sinde, who, he said, differed from all the world in thinking it an honour to fight on foot. The feelings of pity which some of the people displayed for us were amusing: they were shocked to hear that we cleaned our teeth with hogs' bristles. I was frequently asked to lay aside the English saddle, which they considered quite unworthy, and worse than a seat on the bare back of the horse.

The Indus in this part of its course is called Sira, in distinction from Lar, which is its appellation below Sehwun. These are two Belooche words for north and south; and of the name of Sirae, or Khosa, a tribe inhabiting the desert on the east, we have thus a satisfactory explanation, as these people originally spread from Sira, in the upper course of the Indus. Mehran, a name of this river, familiar to Indians and foreigners, is not used by the natives of the country. The water of the Indus is considered superior, for every purpose of life, to that drawn from the wells of Sinde. When taken from the river it is very foul, but the rich keep it till the mud with which it is loaded subsides. There are few ferry-boats on the Indus, and it is a curious sight to see the people crossing it on skins and bundles of reeds. A native will often float down to a distance of fifteen or twenty miles, accompanied by a whole herd of buffaloes, preferring this mode of travelling to a journey on the banks. From Sehwun upwards they kill the 'pulla' fish by nets suspended from the bow of small boats, which are, at the same time, the habitations of the fisherman and his family. The wife, who is generally a sturdy dame, pulls the stern oar to keep the vessel in the middle of the stream, often with a baby in her arms, while the husband kills the fish. One would not have expected to find porpoises so far from the sea, but they are to be observed sporting in the river as high as Bukkur; they are more grey than those in the salt water.

I should have mentioned that, before reaching Bukkur, we were visited by the Nawab Wulee Mahomed Khan Lugharee, one of the viziers of Sinde, who had travelled from Shikarpoor to meet us. We found an old man of seventy-two, on the verge of the grave. He treated us with particular kindness, and quite won our hearts by his attentions. He gave me a horse and a rich loongee. He said in the plainest terms that the Ameer had had evil counsel to detain us so long in Sinde, and that he had written urgently to his Highness not to commit himself by such a step. We had now a good opportunity of seeing a Belooche chief on his native soil. He came with a splendid equipage of tents and carpets, accompanied by three palankeens [covered sedan chairs carried on poles by four men], and about 400 men. A set of dancing-girls were among his suite; and in the evening we were compelled, against our inclination, to hear these ladies squall for a couple of hours and, what added to the disgust of the scene, they drank at intervals of the strongest spirits, to *clear their voices*, as they said, until nearly intoxicated. It was impossible to express any displeasure at this exhibition, since the gala, however much out of taste, was got up in the hope of adding to our amusement. The people with us, who now amounted to 150, were sumptuously entertained by the Nawab, who kept us with him for two days.

On the morning of the 14th we disembarked near the small village of Alipoor, and were met by the vizier of Meer Roostum Khan, who had come from Khyrpoor to receive us. His name was Futteh Khan Ghoree, an aged person of mild and affable manners, and of peculiar appearance from a snow-white beard and red hair. Our reception was cordial and kind; the vizier assured us of the high satisfaction with which his master had heard of our arrival, for he had long desired to draw closer to the British government, and had never yet had the good fortune to meet any of its agents. He said that Meer Roostum Khan did not presume to put himself on an equality with so potent and great a nation, but hoped that he might be classed among its wellwishers, and as one ready to afford his services on all occasions. Futteh Khan added that Khyrpoor formed a separate portion of Sinde from Hydrabad, a fact which he begged I would remember. I was not altogether unprepared for this communication, for I judged from his previous efforts to please that the ruler had some object in view. I assured the vizier of my sense of his master's attentions, and promised to talk on these matters after our interview. He brought a palankeen to convey me in state to Khyrpoor, a distance of fourteen miles, to which city we marched on the following day.

After what I have already stated, our interview with Meer Roostum Khan may be well imagined. He received us under a canopy of silk seated on a cushion of cloth of gold. He was surrounded by the members of his family, forty of whom (males), descended in a right line from his father, are yet alive. There was more state and show than at Hydrabad, but as little attention to order or silence. We exchanged the usual complimentary speeches of like occasions. I thanked his Highness for the uniform attention and hospitality which we had received. Meer Roostum Khan is about fifty; his beard and hair were quite white, and the expression of his countenance, as well as his manners, peculiarly mild. He and his relatives were too much taken up with our uniforms and faces to say much, and he begged us to return in the evening, when there would be less bustle and confusion; to which we readily assented. I gave him my watch before leaving, and sent him a brace of pistols and a kaleidoscope, with various articles of European manufacture, with which he was highly delighted. The crowd was hardly to be penetrated, but very orderly:

they shouted as we approached, and nothing seemed to amuse them so much as the feathers of our hats. 'Such cocks!' was literally the expression. For about 200 yards from the palace (if I can use such a term for the mud buildings of Sinde), there was a street of armed men, and among them stood thirty or forty persons with halberds, the foresters or huntsmen of the household.

In the evening we again visited the Ameer, and found him seated on a terrace spread with Persian carpets, and surrounded, as before, by his numerous relatives. He made a long address to me regarding his respect for the British government, and said that I had of course learned his sentiments from his vizier. He looked to our Mihmandar from Hydrabad, who I found had been doing everything in his power to prevent our meeting at all, and then changed the conversation. The Ameer asked innumerable questions about England and its power, remarking that we were not formerly so military a nation, and he had heard that a few hundred years ago we went naked and painted our bodies. On our religion he was very inquisitive, and when I informed him that I had read the Koran, he made me repeat the 'Kuluma', or creed, in Persian and Arabic, to his inexpressible delight. He said that our greatness had risen from a knowledge of mankind, and attending to other people's concerns as well as our own. He examined my sword, a small cavalry sabre, and remarked that it would not do much harm; but I rejoined, that the age of fighting with this weapon had passed, which drew a shout and a sigh from many present. There was so much mildness in all that the Ameer said, that I could not believe we were in a Belooche court. He expressed sorrow that we could not stay a month with him; but since we were resolved to proceed, we must take his state barge, and the son of his vizier, to the frontier, and accept the poor hospitality of a Belooche soldier, meaning himself, so long as we were in the Khyrpoor territory. I must mention that the hospitality, which he so modestly named, consisted of eight or ten sheep, with all sorts of provisions for 150 people daily; and that while at Khyrpoor, he sent for our use, twice a day, a meal of seventy-two dishes. They consisted of pillaos, and other native viands. The cookery was rich, and some of them delicious. They were served up in silver. We quitted Khyrpoor

with regret, after the attentions which we had received. Before
starting, the Ameer and his family sent to us two daggers, and two
beautiful swords with belts ornamented by large masses of gold. The
blade of one of them was valued at £80. To these were added many
cloths and native silks; also a purse of a thousand rupees, which I did
not accept, excusing myself by the remark, that I required nothing
to make me remember the kindness of Meer Roostum Khan.

Mr Elphinstone has remarked, 'that the chiefs of Sinde appear to
be barbarians of the rudest stamp, without any of the barbarous
virtues'. [The Hon. Mountstuart Elphinstone was a distinguished
scholar/administrator who left the East India Company to write *A
History of India*.] I fear that there is too much truth in the character,
though the Khyrpoor family exhibited little to show themselves
deserving of the stigma; but the chiefs of this country live entirely for
themselves. They wallow in wealth, while their people are wretched.
Professing an enthusiastic attachment to the religion of Mahommed,
they have not even a substantial mosque in their territories; and at
Hydrabad, where the town stands on a rock, and indeed every where,
they pray in temples of mud, and seem ignorant of elegance or comfort
in all that concerns domestic arrangements. The Beloochees are a
particularly savage race of people, but they are brave barbarians.
From childhood they are brought up in arms; and I have seen some of
the sons of chiefs who had not attained the age of four or five years
strutting about with a shield and a sword of small size, given by the
parents to instil into them, at that early period, the relish for war.
This tribe composes but a small portion of the Sindian population;
and while they are execrated by the peaceable classes of the community
for their imperious conduct, they, on the other hand, hate the princes
by whom they are governed. It would be difficult to conceive a more
unpopular rule, with all classes of their subjects, than that of the
Ameers of Sinde: nor is the feeling disguised; many a fervent hope did
we hear expressed, in every part of the country, that we were the
forerunners of conquest, the advance-guard of a conquering army.
The persons of the Ameers are secure from danger by the number of
slaves which they entertain around their persons. These people are
called 'Khaskelees', and enjoy the confidence of their masters, with a

considerable share of power: they are hereditary slaves, and a distinct class of the community, who marry only among themselves.

We marched to Bukkur on the morning of the 19th, which is a fortress fifteen miles from Khyrpoor, situated on an insulated rock of flint on the Indus, with the town of Roree [Rohri] on one side and Sukkur on the other. It was not to be supposed that the Ameer would give us permission to visit this fancied bulwark of his frontier, and I did not press a demand which I saw was far from agreeable; but we had good opportunities of examining the place while passing it, both on shore and on the river. The island is about 800 yards long, of an oval shape, almost entirely occupied by the fortification, which looks more European than most Indian works: it is a beautiful object from the banks of the Indus; its towers are mostly shaded by large full-grown trees, and the tall date drops its weeping leaves on the mosques and walls. There are several other islets near it, on one of which stands the shrine of Khaju Khizr, a holy Mahommedan, under a dome that contributes to the beauty of the scene. The Indus rolls past Bukkur in two streams, each of 400 yards wide, and the waters lash the rocks which confine them with noise and violence. During the swell, the navigation of this part of the river is dangerous, though the boatmen of Bukkur are both expert and daring. The town of Roree, which faces Bukkur, stands on a precipice of flint forty feet high, and some of its houses, which are lofty, overhang the Indus. The inhabitants of these can draw up water from their windows, but a cut road in the rock supplies the citizens with this necessary of life without risking their lives. The opposite bank of Sukkur is not precipitous like that of Roree. A precious relic, the lock of Mahommed's hair, enclosed in a golden box, attracts the Mahommedan pilgrim to Bukkur, though the inhabitants are chiefly Hindoos.

On the banks of the Indus we had a curious interview in the evening after our arrival with the vizier from Khyrpoor, who had been sent by Meer Roostum Khan to escort us thus far, and see that we were furnished with boats. After requesting to be received privately, he renewed the subject of our first conversation, and said that he had been instructed by his master to propose a solemn treaty of friendship with the British government on any terms that might be named: he then ran over the list of neighbouring states which owed their existence to an alliance – the Chief of the Daoodpootras [Daudputras], the Rawul of Jaysulmeer [Jaisalmer], and the Rajah of Beecaneer [Bikaner], &c. &c., and then concluded with a peroration full of gravity, that it was foretold by astronomers, and recorded in his books, that the English would in time possess all India; a prediction which both Meer Roostum and himself felt satisfied would come to pass, when the British would ask why the chiefs of Khyrpoor had not come forward with an offer of allegiance. I tried to remove, but without effect, the sad prognostications of the minister, and declared my incompetency to enter on such weighty matters as a treaty between the states, without authority and before receiving a written statement under the Ameer's seal. I said that I would make known the wishes that had been expressed to my government, which would be gratified to hear they had such friends, which seemed to please the diplomatist; he begged that I would bear in mind what had passed, and exacted a promise that I would write to him when gone and so water the tree of friendship, that the object might be ultimately effected – 'for the stars and heaven proclaimed the fortune of the English!'

This was not the only incident of interest that occurred at Bukkur: we had a visit from an Afghan nobleman of rank, who had been on a mission to the Governor-General from the late Shah Mahmood of Herat, and was now on his return to his native country, by way of Sinde and Mekran [Makran], the dissensions of the dismembered Cabool preventing his passing by the usual route. He was one of the finest natives I ever saw, and had a flowing beard reaching to his waist: he was full of Calcutta and its wonders, and had adopted many of our customs. He rode on an English saddle; but as he had just found out that it was partly made of hog's skin, he begged my acceptance of it, for he dared not take such a thing to his country, and would not again use it. I civilly declined the offer, and regretted that the information regarding the materials of the saddle had been traced to me; for, as he liked our fashions, it was a pity he could not carry them to his own country. Previous to the envoy's leaving us, he begged I would give him an English brush, which I did with pleasure; but I

41

did not consider it necessary to add that, in addition to the skin of the unclean beast, he would now have the bristles. He went away in great good humour with the gift, for which he offered me his palankeen.

I was sorry that I should have been the means of giving uneasiness to the Afghan, for it seems that he acquired his knowledge regarding the construction of his saddle from our Sindian Mihmandar, Tukkee Shah, who had taunted him with uncleanness. This person was a Syud, one of the strictest Mohammedans I ever met. He was a son of Meer Ismael Shah, and of Persian descent. We found him intelligent and learned, and his polished manners made us regret the loss of so agreeable a companion. He left us at Bukkur, to take temporary charge of the Shikarpoor district during the absence of his brother, the Nawab.

While at Bukkur, I visited the ruins of Alore, which is said to have been once the capital of a mighty kingdom, ruled by the Dulora Rae, and on which Roree, Bukkur, and Sukkur have risen. It extended from the ocean to Cashmere, from Candahar to Kanoje, and was divided into four vast viceroyalties: the harbour of Diu, in Kattywar, is expressly mentioned as one of its sea-ports. It sunk under the Mahommedan arms so early as the seventh century of the Christian era, when subdued by the lieutenant of the Caliph of Bagdad, Mahommed bin Cassim, who invaded India, according to a Persian manuscript, in search of ornaments for the seraglio of the Caliph.

The particulars of its history are to be found at great length in the Chuchnamu, a history of Sinde in Persian, believed to be authentic, and so called from the ruler of Alore, a Brahmin, by name Duhr bin Chuch. The ruins of Alore are yet to be discovered in a rocky ridge four miles south-east of Bukkur, and are now marked by an humble hamlet, with some ruined tombs. A low bridge with three arches, named the 'Bund of Alore or Arore', constructed of brick and stone, alone remains of all its greatness. It is thrown across a valley, which in by-gone years formed the bed of a branch of the Indus, from which the waters fertilised the desert, and reached the sea by Omercote and Lucput – a channel through which they still find egress in a great inundation.

CHAPTER IV

The Country of Bhawul Khan

On the 21st May, we set sail from Bukkur, having exchanged our boats for another description of vessel, called 'zohruk', not in use in Lower Sinde. They are of an oblong square shape, rounded fore and aft, and built of the *talee* tree, clamped with pieces of iron instead of nails, an operation which is performed with great neatness. Some of the vessels exceed eighty feet in length and twenty in breadth. They are flat-bottomed, and pass quicker through the water than the *doodee*, though they have but one mast.

The curiosity of the people on the banks of the Indus was intense. One man in the crowd demanded that we should stop and show ourselves, since there had never been a *white-face* in this country before, and we were bound to exhibit, from the welcome which we had received: he had seen Shah Shooja, the ex-king of Cabool, but not an Englishman. Need I say we gratified him and the crowd, of which he was the spokesman? 'Bismilla,' 'in the name of God,' was their usual exclamation when we appeared, and we daily heard ourselves styled kings and princes. The ladies were more curious than their husbands. They wear earrings of large dimensions, with turquoises suspended or fixed to them; for these stones are of little value in the vicinity of Khorasan. Among the women, I should note the Syudanees, or Bebees, the female descendants of Mahommed: they go about veiled, or rather with a long white robe thrown over their entire body, having netted orifices before the eyes and mouth. They are all beggars, and very vociferous in their demands for alms: one set of them (for they go about in troops), when they found I did not readily meet their demands, produced a written paper from the shrine of Lal Shah Baz, at Sehwun, to hasten my charity! Father Manrique, in his journey by the Indus some centuries ago, complains 'of the frail fair ones' who molested him on the way. In the present age, the dress of the courtezans, who are to be met with in every place of size in the country, would give a favourable idea of the wealth of Sinde, and it is one of the few, if not the only, amusements of the inhabitants to listen to the love songs of these people. They are a remarkably handsome race, and carry along with them a spirit of enthusiasm in their performances unknown to the ladies of Hindoostan.

Three days after quitting Bukkur, we came in sight of the mountains of Cutch Gundava, distant about a hundred miles from the right bank of the Indus; the most remarkable peak was named Gendaree. We here entered a country inhabited by various Belooche tribes, long addicted to piracy and plunder, but their spirit has been destroyed by the growing power of the Khyrpoor chiefs. They offered no opposition or insult, and many came to pay us a friendly visit.

*   *   *

A very few days brought us beyond the reach of these Belooches, and the dominions of Sinde; for we anchored thirty miles north of Subzulcote, the frontier town, on the evening of the 26th, on the line of boundary between the Khan of the Daoodpootras and the Ameers of Sinde. Our progress had been exceedingly rapid, for we had a favourable breeze, and often followed the lesser branches of the Indus to escape the violence of the stream. The boats sailed with celerity, for we came one hundred and twenty miles by the course of the river in six days against the stream. We here had a farewell feast from the Khyrpoor Ameer and Meer Nusseer Khan the son of the principal Ameer, who had shown us marked civility throughout the journey. After the people had fared sumptuously, our boats were crowded like sheepfolds. I addressed valedictory letters to both the Ameers and their chief ministers, besides several replies to other persons. In my epistles, I told the Khyrpoor chief that his friendship and kindness had brought us without an accident, and with un-precedented speed, against the mighty stream of the Indus; and I thought it as well, for the edification of the Hydrabad Ameer, to add, that *the Indus was a navigable river* from the ocean, and had abundance of water everywhere! I did not quit Sinde favourably

44

impressed, either with his character or policy; but we should not try such a man by an European standard, and he doubtless opposed our choice of the route by the Indus on sufficiently good grounds. I parted from our Khyrpoor friends with reluctance, for their hospitality and kindness had been great, and it was with difficulty that I was permitted to reward the boatmen. The Mihmandar said that he had been ordered to prohibit it, and his master only desired to please the British Government. This person was very inferior to our former companion the Syud, but, if less learned and intelligent, he had the more sterling qualities of sincerity and honesty: his name was Inayut Khan Ghoree.

We here dismissed, and with regret, our Sindian escort, which had followed us from the mouths of the Indus. They seemed to have become attached to us, and followed us in our walks and rides with unusual alacrity; as we were leaving, they accompanied us to the water's edge with loud cries of thanks for our kindness and prayers for our welfare. Some of them begged to accompany us to Lahore; but, on the same principle that they had been hired in Sinde, it would be proper to enlist natives of the new country we were entering, and I declined their request. These men used to kill game for us, and were ever ready to anticipate our wishes. Their honesty was unimpeachable; we never lost any thing in our progress through a strange country, protected by strangers on whom we had no tie, and who had been brought from the fields to enter our service.

The natives of the neighbouring countries, and the higher class of people in Sinde, have a singular notion regarding the fish diet of the inhabitants. They believe it prostrates the understanding; and, in palliation of ignorance in any one, often plead that 'he is but a fish-eater'. The lower order of the Sindians live entirely on fish and rice, and I certainly remarked the prolific nature of the food in the number of children on the banks of the Indus. The greatest fault which an European would find with the people of Sinde is their filthy habits. They always wear dark-coloured garments from religious motives, but the ablutions of the Prophet are little attended to. People must be in easy circumstances, I believe, or cease to feel want, before they adopt habits of cleanliness. The change of costume in the people, announced already a change of country. Since leaving Bukkur, we had met many Afghans and natives of the kingdom of Cabool. The boots of some of these strangers, made of variegated leather, ribbed, in some instances, not unlike the skin of the tiger, formed an extraordinary dress for a long-bearded old man.

In the evening of the 27th we quitted Sinde, and ascended the river for a few miles, where we were met by Gholam Kadir Khan, a Nuwab [Nawab] and person of high rank, who had been sent to welcome us by Bhawal Khan, the chief of the Daoodpootras, in whose country we had now arrived. He was a little pot-bellied man, with a happy expression of countenance, and said that he was sent to communicate the delight with which his master hailed our approach. He brought a most kind message – that a fleet of fifteen boats had been collected, and was now in readiness to convey us through the Daoodpootra country, while the Khan had fitted up a boat expressly for our accommodation. He brought likewise a purse of a hundred rupees, which he had been desired to send me daily: this I declined, saying, that money was useless where every necessary and luxury of life was furnished by his master's hospitality. We soon got on easy terms with our new hosts, and weighed anchor next evening for the frontier village, where we halted. Many Daoodpootras came to see us: they differ in appearance from the Sindians, and wear turbans formed of tight and round folds of cloths. On the 30th of May our fleet, now swelled to eighteen boats, quitted the Indus at Mittuncote, where it receives the united waters of the Punjab rivers: as if to remind us of its magnitude, the stream was here wider than in any other part of its course, exceeding 2000 yards. We took a last farewell of its waters, and entered the Chenab.

In Lower Sinde the pastoral tribes live in reed houses, and rove from one place to another. In these parts of the Indus they dwell in habitations elevated eight or ten feet from the ground, to avoid the damp and the insects occasioned by it. These are also built of reeds, and entered by a ladder. They are small neat cottages, and occupied by wandering tribes, who frequent the banks of the river till the season of inundation. We reached Ooch [Uch], where the joint streams of the Sutlege and Beas, here called the Garra, fall into the

Chenab. The name of Punjnud, or Five Rivers, is unknown to the natives; and we now navigated the Chenab, or Acesines of the Greeks, the name of the five rivers being lost in that of the greater stream. [The word 'Punjab' clearly comes from the same root: panj=five, ab=water. The rivers are the Jhelum, Chenab, Ravi, Beas and Sutlej.] These united rivers form a noble stream, and the banks of the Chenab are free from the thick tamarisk jungles of the Indus. They were studded with innumerable hamlets, particularly towards the Indus, for the rich pasture attracts the shepherd.

Our arrival at Ooch had been so much earlier than was anticipated as to give rise to an incident which might have proved serious. The troops of Bhawul Khan were encamped on the banks of the river, and in a dusky day our numerous fleet was mistaken for the Seik army, which had been threatening to invade his territories. A discharge of a cannon and some musketry arrested the progress of our advanced boat. The mistake was readily discovered, and the chagrin and vexation that followed afforded us some amusement. I thought that apologies and regrets would never have ceased.

The town of Ooch stands on a fertile plain at a distance of four miles from the Acesines, beautifully shaded by trees. It is formed of three distinct towns, a few hundred yards apart from each other, and each has been encompassed by a wall of brick, now in ruins. The population amounts to 20,000. The streets are narrow, and covered with mats as a protection from the sun, but it is a mean place. We were accommodated in a garden well stocked with fruit trees and flowers, which was an agreeable change from our confined boats. When preparing for a journey to visit the Khan – who was absent at Dirawul, in the desert – we were surprised by the arrival of a messenger, with the information that he had reached Ooch from a distance of sixty miles, that he might save us the trouble of coming to him, and evince his respect for the British Government. The messenger brought us a deer, which the Khan had shot, and of which he begged our acceptance, with forty vessels of sherbet, and as many of sweetmeats and preserves; also a bag containing 200 rupees, which he requested I would distribute in charity, to mark the joyful event of our arrival.

On the morning of the 3rd of June we visited Bhawul Khan, who had alighted at a large house outside the town, a mile distant: he sent an escort of his regular troops, with horses, palankeens, and various other conveyances – one of which deserves description. It was a sort of chair, covered with a red canopy of cloth, supported by two horses, one in front and the other behind, and the most awkward vehicle that can be imagined, for it could be turned with difficulty, and the horses did not incline to such a burden. We passed a line of soldiers, about 600 in number, dressed in uniforms of red, blue, white, and yellow, and then entered the court yard, under a salute of eighty guns. The passages were lined with officers and chiefs, and we found the Khan seated in an area spread with carpets, attended only by about ten persons: he rose and embraced us. He made particular enquiries regarding Mr Elphinstone, who, he said, had been the means of raising up a sincere and lasting friendship between his family and the British Government.

Bhawul Khan is a handsome man, about thirty years of age, somewhat grave in his demeanour, though most affable and gentleman-like. During the interview he held a rosary in his hand, but the telling of the beads did not interrupt his conversation. He dilated at length on the honour which Runjeet Sing had had conferred upon him in receiving presents from the King of Great Britain; nor did he, in any way, betray his feelings towards the Lahore chief, though they are far from friendly. The Khan, unlike most natives, seemed to avoid all political subjects. He produced his matchlock, and explained to us his manner of hunting deer, his favourite sport, and expressed a strong wish that we should accompany him to his residence in the desert. We left him quite charmed with his kindness, and the sincere manner in which he had shown it. In the evening the Khan sent for our perusal the testimonials that had been given to his grandfather by Mr Elphinstone, which are preserved with great pride and care in the archives of his government. For my own part, I felt equal satisfaction to find the English character stand so high in this remote corner of India, and the just appreciation of the high-minded individual who had been the means of fixing it.

During our stay at Ooch, we were visited by some of the principal merchants of Bhawulpoor [Bahawalpur], who had followed the Khan. The intelligence of these people, and extent of their travels, surprised me. Most of them had traversed the kingdom of Cabool, and visited Balkh and Bokhara: some had been as far as Astracan [Astrakhan], and they used the names of these towns with a familiarity as if they had been in India. They had met Russian merchants at Bokhara, but assured me that they never came to the eastward of that city. The intervening countries they represented as perfectly safe, and bestowed the highest commendations on Dost Mahommed, of Cabool, and the Uzbeks, who encouraged commercial communication. These merchants are chiefly Hindoos, whose disposition peculiarly adapts them for the patient and pains-taking vocation of a foreign merchant. Some of them are Jews, who retain the marks of their nation in all countries and places. It was my conversation with these men which made me decide on under-taking the journey to Central Asia, that I afterwards performed.

We continued at Ooch for a week. The place is ancient, and highly celebrated in the surrounding countries from the tombs of two saints of Bokhara and Bagdad. The Ghorian emperors [A Turko-Afghan dynasty which conquered Punjab in the 12th century] expelled the Hindoo Rajas of Ooch, and consigned the surrounding lands to pious Mahommedans. The tombs of the two worthies I have named are handsome, and held in much reverence by the people; they are about five hundred years old, and tradition is silent regarding the history of the place beyond that period. The town of Ooch stands on a mound of earth or clay, like the city of Tatta, which I judge to have been formed by the ruins of houses. The Chenab has swept away a portion of the mound, and the section of it which has been thus exposed seems to support the conjecture which I have stated.

On the 5th of June we had a visit from Bhawul Khan. He insisted on coming in person to see us, and sent a large tent to be pitched by our garden, in which we received him. He sat for about an hour, and put numerous questions regarding the manufactures of Europe. The chief is of a mechanical turn of mind; he produced a detonating gun, which had been made under his directions from an European pattern, and certainly did credit to the artificer; he had also manufactured the necessary caps and fulminating powder. He expressed, at this interview, much satisfaction with the presents which we had sent him; they consisted of a brace of pistols, a watch, and some other articles. The Khan came in an open sort of chair, to which we conducted him on his departure. He was attended by about a thousand persons, and I observed that he distributed money as he passed along.

After the visit, our Mihmandar brought us presents from the Khan; they consisted of two horses richly caparisoned with silver and enamel trappings, a hawk, with shawls and trays of the fabrics made at Bhawulpoor, some of which were very rich; to these were added a purse of 2000 rupees, and a sum of 200 for the servants; and, last of all, a beautiful matchlock, which had its value doubled by the manner in which it was presented. 'The Khan,' said the messenger, 'has killed many a deer with this gun, and he begs you will accept it from him and, when you use it, remember that Bhawul Khan is your friend.' In the evening we had a parting interview with Bhawul Khan. I gave him a handsome percussion gun and assured him, what I felt most sincerely, that we should long remember his kindness and hospitality. He embraced us on our leaving him and entreated us to write to him and command his services. The courtiers and people were as polite as their chief. We left Ooch on the following morning and pitched our camp at the junction of the Chenab with the Garra, or united streams of the Beas and Sutlege.

The country about Ooch is flat and exceedingly rich; there are many signs of inundation between the town and the river. The dust was most intolerable; but it always cleared up towards evening, and we saw the sun set in splendour behind the mountains of Sooliman [Suleiman ranges] across the Indus, eighty miles distant. They did not appear high, and were not distinguished by any remarkable peaks. It is a little below the latitude of Ooch that they assume a direction parallel to the Indus, which they afterwards preserve. We lost sight of the range on our voyage to Mooltan [Multan] the day after leaving Ooch.

On the morning of the 7th we passed the mouth of the Sutlege, and continued our voyage on the Chenab to the frontiers of Bhawul

Khan, which we reached on the evening of the 8th. The Chenab receives the Sutlege without turmoil, and appears quite as large above as below the conflux. The waters of either river are to be distinguished some miles below the junction by their colour: that of the Chenab is reddish, and when joined by the Sutlege, the waters of which are pale, the contrast is remarkable. For some distance the one river keeps the right, and the other the left, bank; the line of demarcation between the two being most decided.

We parted with our Mihmandar, Gholam Cadir Khan, before passing into the Seik territory. We had seen a great deal of him, and found him well informed on all such subjects as he could be supposed to know. He carried four or five historical works with him, among which was the Chuchnamu, or History of Sinde, to which I have alluded, one or two books on medicine, and some volumes of poetry: yet he made a most particular request, at our last interview, that I would tell him the secret of magic, which he was certain we possessed. I assured him of the error under which he laboured: 'But,' said he, 'how is it that you have had a favourable wind ever since I met you, and performed a twenty days' voyage in five, when a breath of air does not sometimes stir in this country for months?' I told him that such was the good fortune of the English. There is little cordiality subsisting between the Seiks and Bhawul Khan, and it was with the utmost difficulty that I prevailed on the Nawab to let us proceed to the Seik camp, a distance of six miles, in the boats belonging to his master. 'The Seiks,' he said, 'are my master's enemies, and no boat of ours shall cross their frontier.' He at last assented, on my becoming answerable for the return of the vessels.

A few hours' sail brought us to the place of rendezvous late at night, and the fires of the soldiers blazing in the darkness only increased our anxiety to meet our new friends. It was the camp of the party which had been sent from Lahore to await our arrival, and had long expected us. Immediately on landing we were received by Sirdar Lenu Sing, who came with considerable state on an elephant, and was attended by a large retinue. The Sirdar [a title originally used to denote *feudal princes*, *noblemen*, and other *aristocrats*] was richly dressed, and had a necklace of emeralds and armlets studded with diamonds. In one hand he held a bow and in the other two Persian letters in silken bags. He congratulated us, in the name of Maharaja Runjeet Sing, on our arrival, and had been desired by his Highness to communicate that he was deeply sensible of the honour conferred upon him by the King of England, and that his army had been for some time in readiness on the frontier, to chastise the barbarians of Sinde, who had so long arrested our progress. He then delivered to me the letters which appointed himself as our Mihmandar, in conjunction with two other persons; presenting at the same time a bow, according to the custom of the Seiks. On the ceremony being terminated, the Sirdar and several others placed bags of money at my feet, amounting to about 1400 rupees, and then withdrew.

The first intercourse with a new people can never be destitute of interest, and the present was far from being so. These Seiks are tall and bony men, with a very martial carriage: the most peculiar part of their dress is a small flat turban, which becomes them well; they wear long hair, and from the knee downwards do not cover the leg. When the deputation had withdrawn, an escort of regular troops attended to receive orders, and sentries were planted round our camp. It was novel to hear the words of command given in the French language, and to be attended by a party of cavalry, who unfurled the tricolor flag at the end of their lances.

No sooner had the day broke than the Maharaja's people evinced much anxiety to view the dray horses, and we had them landed for exhibition. Their surprise was extreme, for they were little elephants, said they, and not horses. Their manes and tails seemed to please, from their resemblance to the hair of the cow of Tibet [i.e. yak]; and their colour, a dappled grey, was considered a great beauty. It was not without difficulty that I replied to the numerous questions regarding them, for they believed that the presents of the King of England must be extraordinary in every way; and for the first time, a dray horse was expected to gallop, canter, and perform all the evolutions of the most agile animal. Their astonishment reached its height when the feet of the horses were examined, and a particular request was made of me to permit the despatch of one of the shoes to

Lahore, as it was found to weigh 100 rupees, or as much as the four shoes of a horse in this country. The curiosity was forthwith despatched by express, and accompanied by the most minute measurement of each of the animals, for Runjeet Sing's special information. The manner in which this rarity was prized, will be afterwards seen, when it is gravely recorded, *that the new moon turned pale with envy on seeing it!*

Our own comforts were not forgotten among their wonder and admiration, for the attentions of the people were of the most marked description. Our Mihmandar said that he had the strictest injunctions regarding our reception; and he rigidly acted up to the spirit of the following document, that will best show the distinguished and kind manner in which we were treated in the territories of Maharaja Runjeet Sing. [Burnes then quotes in full the detailed instruction from the Maharaja about how he was to be treated, including the provision of an elephant for his personal use, the provision of liberal quantities of money, sweetmeats and rich food, all necessary provisions for his party, excursions to the forts along the way should he wish to inspect them, gun salutes at his arrival in the major cities, thus displaying the 'great friendship which subsists between the two states'.]

There is at all times much display and hyperbole in affairs of this description throughout the East; but in the present instance it will be observed that the Maharaja not only evinced his liberality in other matters, but in throwing open to our inspection the strong holds of his country, which can be duly appreciated by those only who have experienced the extreme jealousy of most Indian governments. The Seik Sirdars in attendance on us were likewise most communicative; and this is the more remarkable, as it could not have escaped the Maharaja, that in taking the unfrequented tract which we had followed on the Indus we were seeking for new information, after the spirit of our country.

CHAPTER V

Voyage in the Country of the Seiks

By the 12th of June our preparations for the voyage were completed, and we again embarked on the Chenab. The boats here were of a very inferior description, still called 'zohruk'; they had no sails, and hoist a mat on a low mast instead: their waists are scarcely a foot above water, and those which they could collect for us, were but the different ferry boats of the river. There is no trade carried on by water in this country, and there are in consequence no boats. A sail of a few hours brought us to the ferry opposite Shoojuabad [Shujaabad], where we halted. The country is of the richest and most fertile description, and its agricultural resources are much increased, by conducting water to the remoter parts, in large canals and aqueducts.

In the evening of the 13th we visited the town of Shoojuabad, which stands four miles eastward of the river. It is a thriving place, surrounded by a fine wall of brick, about thirty feet high. The figure of the place is that of an oblong square, and the wall is strengthened by octagonal towers, at equal distances. The interior is filled up with houses, which are built in streets, at right angles to one another, and a suburb of huts surrounds the walls. Shoojuabad fort was built by the Nuwab of Mooltan in the year 1808, and the public spirit of that person raised it, in the course of ten years, to great opulence. It is situated in a most beautiful country and is watered by two spacious canals for many miles, both above and below the town. It was captured by the Seiks, along with Mooltan, and now forms the frontier fortress of the Lahore chief. We were accompanied to Shoojuabad by our Mihmandar, who appeared in state for the occasion; he sat on an elephant in a chair of silver, two horses were led before him, with saddles of red and yellow velvet, his bow and quiver were borne by one menial, and his sword by another; while he himself was decorated with precious jewels. At the palace of the town, we were met by many of the respectable inhabitants, before whom the '*zyafut*', or money gift, and sweetmeats of the Maharaja, were presented to us. We afterwards were conducted through the principal street, and welcomed in a gratifying manner, wherever we went. On quitting the fortress the garrison fired a salute.

On the 15th we came in sight of the domes of Mooltan, which look well at a distance, and alighted in the evening at the Hoozooree Bagh, a spacious garden enclosed by a thin wall of mud, a mile distant from the city. The ground is laid out in the usual native style: two spacious walks cross each other at right angles, and are shaded by large fruit trees, of the richest foliage. In a bungalow, at the end of one of these walks, we took up our quarters, and were received by the authorities of the city in the same hospitable manner as at Shoojuabad. They brought a purse of 2500 rupees, with a hundred vessels of sweetmeats, and an abundant supply of fruit: we felt happy and gratified at the change of scene, and civilities of the people.

The city of Mooltan is upwards of three miles in circumference, surrounded by a dilapidated wall, and overlooked on the north by a fortress of strength. It contains a population of about 60,000 souls, one third of whom may be Hindoos; the rest of the population is Mahommedan, for though it is subject to the Seiks, their number is confined to the garrison, which does not exceed 500 men. The Afghans have left the country, since they ceased to govern. Many of the houses evidently stand on the ruins of others: they are built of burnt brick, and have flat roofs: they sometimes rise to the height of six stories, and their loftiness gives a gloomy appearance to the narrow streets. The inhabitants are chiefly weavers and dyers of cloth. The silk manufacture of Mooltan is called '*kais*', and may be had of all colours, and from the value of 20 to 120 rupees per piece. It is less delicate in texture than the 'loongees' of Bhawulpoor. Runjeet Sing has with much propriety encouraged this manufacture, since he captured the city, and by giving no other cloths at his court, has greatly increased their consumption; they are worn as sashes and scarves by all the Seik Sirdars. They are also exported to Khorasan and India, and the duties levied are moderate.

The fortress of Multoon merits a more particular description; it stands on a mound of earth, and is an irregular figure of six sides, the longest of which, towards the north-west, extends for about 400 yards. The wall has upwards of thirty towers, and is substantially built of burnt brick, to the height of forty feet outside; but in the interior, the space between the ground and its summit does not exceed four or five feet, and the foundations of some of the buildings overtop the wall, and are to be seen from the plain below. The interior is filled with houses, and till its capture by the Seiks in 1818, was peopled, but the inhabitants are not now permitted to enter, and a few mosques and cupolas, more substantially built than the other houses, alone remain among the ruins. The fortress of Mooltan has no ditch; the nature of the country will not admit of one being constructed; and Runjeet Sing has hitherto expended great sums without effect. The inundation of the Chenab, and its canals, together with rain, render the vicinity of Mooltan a marsh, even in the hot weather, and before the swell of the river has properly set in, the waters of last year remain.

The walls of the fortress are protected in two places by dams of earth. The modern fort of Mooltan was built on the site of the old city, by Moorad Bukhsh [Murad Baksh], the son of Shah Jehan, about the year 1640, and it subsequently formed the jagheer of that prince's brothers, the unfortunate Daro Shikoh, and the renowned Aurangzebe. [Under the Mughals a *jagir* assigned revenue rights – usually over an area of land, though here a particular fortress, and the holder of these rights was called the *jagirdar*.] The Afghans seized it in the time of Ahmed Shah, and the Seiks wrested it from the Afghans, after many struggles, in 1818. The conduct of its governor during the siege, deserves mention; when called on to surrender the keys, and offered considerate treatment, he sent for reply, that they would be found in his heart, but he would never yield to an infidel: he perished bravely in the breach. His name, Moozuffur Khan, is now revered as a saint, and his tomb is placed in one of the holiest sanctuaries of Mooltan. The Seiks threw down the walls of the fort in many places, but they have since been thoroughly renewed or repaired; they are about six feet thick, and could be easily breached from the mounds that have been left in baking the bricks, which are within cannon range of the walls.

At Mooltan we first saw the practice of religion amongst the Seiks. In a veranda of the tomb of Shumsi-Tabreezee, a 'Gooroo' or priest of that persuasion, had taken up his abode since the conquest of the city. We found him seated on the ground, with a huge volume in front of him, and a place covered with cloth, like an altar, at one end of the apartment: he opened the book at my request, and repeating the words 'wa gooroojee ka futteh' ('May the Gooroo be victorious', the national war-cry of the Seiks), touched the volume with his forehead, and all the Seiks in attendance immediately bowed to the ground: he then read and explained the first passage that he turned up, which was as follows: 'All of you have sinned; endeavour there- fore to purify yourselves: if you neglect the caution, evil will at last overtake you.' I need hardly mention that the volume was the 'Grinth', or holy book of the Seiks: their reverence for it amounts to veneration, and the priest waves a '*choury*', or a Tibet cow's tail, over it, as if he were fanning an emperor. The Gooroo was free from pomp and pride, and gave a willing explanation to our enquiries: he opened his holy book to acknowledge the gift of a few rupees, that I made in due form, and requested my acceptance of some confections in return.

The presence of a Seik priest, and the paraphernalia of his order, under the roof of a Mahommedan tomb, will furnish a good com- mentary on the state of that religion in this country: it is barely tolerated. In this city, which held for upwards of 800 years so high a Mahommedan supremacy, there is now no public '*numaz*'; the true believer dare not lift his voice in public. The '*Eeds*' and the Mohuram pass without the usual observances, and the '*Ullaho Acbar*' of the priest is never heard; the mosques are yet frequented, but the pious are reduced to offering up their orisons in silence. Such has been the state of things since Mooltan fell in 1818, and yet the number of Seiks is confined to that of the garrison, from four to five hundred men. The Mahommedans, who amount to about 40,000 souls, suffer no other inconvenience from their new masters, who afford every protection to their trade. The Seiks excuse themselves, by alleging that they have not inflicted, in retribution, one fourth of their own sufferings at the hands of the Mahommedans. They are, I believe, correct in the averment, but religious persecution is always revolting, and exercises a baneful influence in every age and country.

The climate of Mooltan differs from that of the countries lower down the Indus: showers of rain are common at all seasons, and yet the dust is intolerable. For nine successive evenings, we had a tornado of it from the westward, with lightning, and distant thunder. Such storms are said to be frequent; they appear to set in from the Sooliman mountains, between which and the Indus the sand or dust is raised. The heat and dust of Mooltan have grown into a proverb, to which have been added, not unmeritedly, the prevalence of beggars, and the number of the tombs, in the following Persian couplet:

> Chuhar cheez hust, toohfujat-i-Mooltan.
> Gird, Guda, gurma wu goristan.

As far as I could judge, the satire is just: the dust darkened the sun: the thermometer rose in June to 100 degrees of Fahrenheit, in a bungalow artificially cooled: the beggars hunted us every where, and we trod on the cemeteries of the dead, in whatever direction we rode.

The country around Mooltan is highly cultivated: the Acesines sends the water of its inundation to the very walls of the city, and there is a large canal that extends it, at other seasons, through Mooltan itself. The plain that lies between the river and city has the appearance of a rich meadow, and is overgrown with date trees, which form here a productive source of revenue. It is a popular belief in the country that this tree was introduced from Arabia by Mahommed-bin-Cassim, who brought the fruit as a provision for his army. It is a curious fact that they are principally found in the track of that invader, who marched from Alore to Mooltan. If the tradition be true, the destroying Moslem compensated in some degree for the evils and scourge of his inroad. There are many ruined hamlets around Mooltan, the remains of Jagheers, held by the Afghans, but though these are deserted, their inhabitants have only changed their residence, and occupy houses in the city. We removed our camp on the 20th to the banks of the Acesines, which is four miles distant. The river is about 650 yards wide, but at the ferry itself it is expanded to 1000 at this season. We here found ten boats, laden with mineral salt, from Pind Dadun Khan; they exceeded eighty feet in length. These boats drop down to Mooltan in twelve days, from the mines, when fully laden.

We embarked on the 21st of June, in a boat which the Maharaja had fitted up for our reception with two wooden bungalows, and, along with the rest of our fleet, prosecuted our voyage. We did not again exchange our boats, in the way to Lahore. On quitting the ferry at Mooltan, we came in sight of the desert that lies between the Chenab and the Indus. It does not commence so low as Ooch, as has been represented in our maps, but near the latitude of Mooltan, and runs parallel with the river, at a distance of about two miles, leaving a stripe of cultivated land. The sand-hills resemble those of the sea-shore, and have a scanty covering of bushes, I cannot call it verdure: they do not exceed twenty feet in elevation, but from refraction often appeared much higher. There is a great contrast between the sterile tract, and the champaign plains of the eastern bank, which we found everywhere irrigated. The villages lie at a distance of about two miles from the river, and have their fields fertilised from canals, by the Persian wheel. On the banks of the Indus, wells are common, but on the Chenab they are only to be seen on the verge of canals that branch from it.

The arrangements made for our progress through the Seik territories were very complete. We sailed from sunrise to sunset and found thirty or forty villagers alongside by day-break to drag each boat. The fatigue and exertion which these people underwent in a hot sun was excessive. When they passed a field of melons, but few were left to the owner, and many an old lady scolded loudly as they invaded her property. The people of this country are treated with little consideration by the government; they are not oppressed, yet considered its servants since the conquest. But for our interference, these villagers, who had waded through the water and quicksands, would have been dismissed empty-handed at night. The bounty of the Maharaja enabled us daily to entertain sumptuously, with flour and ghee, 300 hungry villagers; and the Mihmandar further assured me that due remission would be made for the destruction of the fields in our progress. While we ourselves advanced by water, the elephants, camels, and escort seconded our motions on shore; and we always found them drawn up in parade array on the ground fixed for our night's encampment, as we slept on shore. Before dusk we rode out on elephants to the neighbouring villages, and conversed with the people, who are lamentably ignorant; they consist mainly of Juts, a tribe of Mahommedans engaged in agriculture.

On the 24th we quitted the Acesines, and entered on the navigation of the Ravee. At the point of union, the former river has a breadth of three quarters of a mile, though the deep part does not extend for 500 yards. The Ravee throws itself into the Chenab by three mouths, close to each other. This river is very small, and resembles a canal, rarely exceeding 150 yards in breadth in any part of its course. Its banks are precipitous, so that it deepens before it expands. Nothing can exceed the crookedness of its course, which is a great impediment to navigation, for we often found ourselves, after half a day's sail, within two miles of the spot from which we started.

On 27th of June we reached the small town of Tolumba [Tulamba], which is situated in a grove of date trees, nearly three miles south of the Ravee. Sheriff-o-Deen, the historian of Timour, informs us that that conqueror crossed the Ravee at Tolumba, on his route to Delhi, so that we now found ourselves on the track of another invader. The Tartar is yet remembered by his offerings at the shrines in this neighbourhood. Below the town, the Ravee assumes a straight course for twelve miles, and presents a vista of beautiful scenery, as the banks are fringed with lofty trees, that overhang the river. The natives attribute this peculiarity to divine influence. The clothes of a saint, when bathing, were washed into the stream, and the eyes of the holy man, when turned in search of them, straightened the river!

The Hydaspes was now at hand; the spot where it unites with the Acesines was only forty-five miles distant: here the fleet of Alexander encountered its disasters in the rapids, and the hordes of Timour were terrified by the noise of the waters. Much to the surprise of our Seik friends, who could not comprehend the motives of our curiosity, we set out on a galloping expedition for the scene of these memorable events, and found ourselves on the second evening on the banks of the Hydaspes. Our anxiety to behold the 'fabulous Hydaspes' was heightened by the belief that this spot, so famous in ancient history, had never been visited by an European since the days of the Greeks. The river joins the Acesines with a murmuring noise, but the velocity of the current is inconsiderable, and vessels pass it without danger, except in July and August. There are no eddies or rocks, nor is the channel confined, but the ancient character is supported by the noise of the confluence, which is greater than that of any of the other rivers. The boatmen at the ferry said that during the swell of the river, they placed themselves under the protection of a saint, whose tomb stands at the fork of the two rivers. The superstitious reliance bespeaks danger.

In the space which intervenes between the Hydaspes and Ravee, and about equidistant from either river, stand the ruins of Shorkote, near a small town of that name. They occupy a considerable space, being much larger than Sehwun, and of the same description; viz. a mound of earth, surrounded by a brick wall, and so high as to be seen for a circuit of six or eight miles. The traditions of the people state that a Hindoo Rajah of the name of Shor ruled in this city, and was attacked by a king from 'Wulayut', or the countries westward, about 1300 years ago, and overcome through supernatural means. Shorkote is mentioned by Timour's historian, and its locality leads me to fix on it as the place where Alexander received his wound, for he crossed to the west bank of the Hydraotes in pursuit of the Malli, who had retired to 'a fortified city not far off', the walls of which were of brick. The story of the King of the West is, to say the least of it, a very probable tradition of Alexander of Macedon. The construction of the place throws some light on the fortresses which were captured by Alexander. Ancient cities on the Indus appear to have been mounds of earth surrounded by brick walls. At Shorkote I had the good fortune to procure a variety of coins, which I long believed to be Hindoo; but my surmise regarding the antiquity of the spot received a strong and satisfactory confirmation through the intelligence of the able secretary to the Asiatic Society of Bengal –

Mr James Prinsep. That gentleman discovered it to be a Bactrian coin, resembling that of an Appolodotus, and shaped like Menander – two coins of the Bactrian monarchs, found by Colonel J. Tod, and engraved in the Transactions of the Royal Asiatic Society. The Greek word Bazileos may be read, and I had, therefore, to congratulate myself on having, in my journey to the Hydaspes, found the first Grecian relic in the Punjab.

We returned to Tolumba on the 1st of July, jaded from the excessive heat, but highly gratified with our journey. We immediately embarked, and prosecuted our voyage. During our absence the river had risen two feet, from a fall of rain in the mountains, but it did not appear much wider. We saw more aquatic birds in the Ravee than in our whole voyage; they consisted of cranes, storks, pelicans, ducks, teal, &c. Among the inhabitants of the river itself, a creature called 'bolun' was the most remarkable. We saw several of them in the mouth of the Ravee, which were of a black colour, and rolled like the porpoise. The natives class this fish with the alligator, and say it has four small paws, and a long snout like a pig. Its habits do not lead it on shore, and it lives on small fish. The large alligator is unknown here but the long-nosed reptile called 'ghuryal' abounds. There is said to be a singular creature, called 'thundwa', in this river, which is described as of the turtle species, and to have a string in its mouth, by which it can entangle a man, or even an elephant.

The heat now became oppressive, and gave indication of the monsoon, according to the natives. In the afternoon of the 3rd of July we had the thermometer in the shade so high as 110 degrees at 4 pm; and at sunset a storm set in from the north-west, which was really sublime. Clouds appeared to approach us for about half an hour, gradually rising from the horizon, and looking more like mountains in motion. When it came upon us, we found it to be one of those tornadoes that we experienced near Mooltan, and unaccompanied by rain. The wind was hot and sultry, and bore clouds of fine dust along with it. It passed over in an hour, and was succeeded by vivid flashes of lightning from the same quarter. Six days after the phenomenon the rain set in with great violence, and till then we had a continuance of the dust every evening.

Our Mihmandar waited on us at the village of Cheechawutnee [Chichawatni] with an enormous elephant, and said that he had been instructed by the Maharaja to place it at our disposal, as he feared the native houda [a covered seat on the back of an elephant] did not suit our taste: he was right in his conjectures, and we appreciated the civility. The animal was richly caparisoned, and bore a large chair, ornamented with silver and enamel work, lined with red velvet. He was accompanied by six of the Maharaja's own Orderlies, in dresses of scarlet faced with yellow, which had a good appearance. The Seiks, in all the various military costumes that they have adopted, never lay aside the small turban of their tribe which, I must say, becomes them.

It was a source of no small amusement to watch the love of gossip among the natives of our suite. We had a reporter sent purposely from the Court, who daily despatched an account of our employment and rides: the news-writer of Mooltan followed us from that city, and every day transmitted a Gazette; I had also letters from the news-writer at Lahore, giving me a *précis* of local news, and asking for a *morceau* in return. Nothing, however, could exceed the politeness of all the people towards us, and the ready and happy manner they acceded to our wishes made us careful to wish for anything. The polite natives of this quarter view with dread the barbarity and customs of Sindees and Beloochees.

About fifty miles eastward of Tolumba, I passed inland for four miles to examine the ruins of an ancient city called Harapa [Harappa]. The remains are extensive, and the place, which has been built of brick, is about three miles in circumference. There is a ruined citadel on the river side of the town, but otherwise Harapa is a perfect chaos, and has not an entire building: the bricks have been removed to build a small place of the old name hard by. Tradition fixes the fall of Harapa at the same period as Shorkote (1300 years ago), and the people ascribe its ruin to the vengeance of God on Harapa, its governor, who claimed certain privileges on the marriage of every couple in his city, and in the course of his sensualities was guilty of incest.

As we ascended the Ravee, and cleared the country of the Kattias, the population increased, and their hamlets, though small, were numerous. Crowds of people flocked to the banks of the river as we approached, and evinced the most intense curiosity to see us. One man would call out that he was a Syud, another that he was a Zemindar [a rural official or revenue collector], a third that he was a Peer, or Saint, and a fourth, that he was a Seik, while the ladies themselves were not backward in expressing their anxiety for a sight of us. On such occasions we always moved out of our cabin, or bungalow, but this ready exhibition only attracted another concourse of spectators. The notions which they entertained of us were most extravagant: we were believed to be under the guardian care of two pigeons, who shaded us from the sun and rain. One individual asked us seriously to impart to him the secret of converting shreds of onions into gold ducats, which he had understood we had been practising!

The bravery of our Seik friends had been already exhibited to us by their attacking the wild hog with a sword, on foot; but a nobler specimen of their courage was displayed in the death of a tiger. We disturbed the animal in a thicket of tamarisk close to our boats, and the Mihmandar immediately invited us to see the sport. Mr Leckie accompanied the party but our elephant was not at hand, and I did not go. The party was entirely composed of horsemen. The monster was speedily wounded by some one, and several riders were unhorsed from the fright of their steeds. The Seiks then advanced on foot, sword in hand, to attack the tiger: he sprang at one man most furiously, and, as he fixed on his left shoulder, the poor fellow bravely struck his head by a well-directed blow: the contest was unequal, and the man fell, horribly lacerated. His comrades instantly ran up and, with cuts and wounds, the tiger was soon killed. He was a huge animal, and measured ten feet: his thigh was as large as that of a full-grown man. The coolness and courage of the Seiks surpass belief; they have great encouragement from their chiefs. To all my enquiries regarding the unfortunate man that had been wounded, they replied, with an ostentation of indifference, that he was but a Seik, would be well rewarded, and had already received a horse, and his annual pay had been increased an hundred rupees. The skin, head, and paws of the tiger were immediately despatched to the

Maharaja, whose bounty will be further extended to the wounded. This encouragement makes these people the bravest of the Indians.

The [medical] faculty will be surprised at the Seik mode of curing a wound received from a tiger, at variance as it is with European practices. They entertain an opinion that, if a person who has been so wounded be allowed to sleep, he will see the tiger in his dreams, and thus lose his heart, and inevitably die. They therefore furnish the patient with the strongest stimulants, and set people to prevent his falling asleep for five or six days. By that time the wounds assume a certain appearance and they then permit the man to rest. In the instance which I have mentioned, I can answer for the copious use of stimulants, as we supplied the brandy. The patient recovered.

The intelligence of the Seik Sirdar Lenu Sing, our Mihmandar, had more than once arrested my attention. From a perusal of translations, he had acquired some knowledge of our astronomical system, and of the astrolabe, with several other such instruments. He expressed his doubts on some parts of the theory, and asked me to explain the continuance of the pole star in one place when the earth was said to move so many miles daily in its orbit round the sun. Among other information that I was enabled to impart to him, I showed him the thermometer, and explained the nature of the instrument. He immediately had the whole particulars committed to writing: and, where such avidity, and so laudable a thirst for knowledge, were displayed, I could not withhold making him a present of the instrument. This Sirdar was equally expert in the martial exercises of his nation: he handled the bow with grace and dexterity; he was an excellent horseman, and could hit a mark at full speed; and I have seen him touch the ground with both feet at the gallop and regain his seat. I must mention that his curiosity did not always take a scientific turn, for his wonder had been excited by our art in preserving meat, fish &c. A ham, which I showed him, was calculated to satisfy his doubts, and he was only contented when he had got a complete recipe for curing it. The Seiks are very fond of hog; and ham bids fair to be a standing dish in the Punjab.

By the 11th July we had left the country of the Kattias, and reached Futtihpoor [Fatehpur], where the land is cultivated. Our

approach to Lahore seemed to facilitate every arrangement: a detachment of fifty lancers had been stationed in the intervening villages,
to assemble the inhabitants, to drag the boats the moment we
approached. Our own suite was now increased to about 500 people;
and to a drum and fife, which had always been with us, a bugle was
added. Such dissonance as was now produced was never heard 'at
tattoo or reveille o' and they played at both hours. We also had a
Cashmere boat sent for our accommodation, called the 'purinda' or
bird. It was a complete skiff, about sixty feet long, and pointed at
both ends, so that half of the boat did not even touch the water. I
am informed that this style of build, not unlike the gondola of
Venice, is general in the lake of Cashmere. The crew were natives
of that country and they impelled their vessel by small green-
painted paddles, with which they struck the water in a peculiar
manner. They were very handsome and athletic men, dressed in red
jackets. The boat itself had a square bungalow in the centre, with a
flat roof, where we sat during the cool of the evening. She was flat-
bottomed and had her planks clamped with iron. Her motion through
the water was tremulous, and by no means agreeable, but the celerity
with which vessels of this kind move is acknowledged.

On the 13th of July, a deputation from the Kardar of Kot Kamalia
waited on us with presents of fruit, &c., and a sum of 1100 rupees. A
letter was brought, at the same time, from the Maharaja, expressive
of his great satisfaction at our approach. The epistle was flowery to
a degree seldom met with even in the Persian language, and filled
with similes about gardens, roses, zephyrs, and fountains. Every
word of a letter which I had addressed to his Highness was declared
to be a bud of everlasting friendship, and every letter of every word
was a blown rose! But the document would require a translation,
and that, perhaps, it does not deserve.

*   *   *

At noon, on the 17th of July, we came in sight of the lofty minarets
of the King's mosque at Lahore, and might have reached the ancient
capital of the Moghul empire, and the termination of our protracted
voyage; but the ceremonial of our *entrée* required arrangement, and

we halted three or four miles from the city, at the earnest request of our conductors. As the sun set, I saw, for the first time, the massy mountains which encircle Cashmere, clothed in a mantle of white snow. I felt a nervous sensation of joy as I first gazed on the Himalaya, and almost forgot the duties which I owed to our conductors, in contemplating these mighty works of nature.

CHAPTER VI

Lahore

On the morning of the 18th of July we made our public entrance into Lahore. The Maharaja's minister, Uzeez-o-Deen, and Raja Goolab Sing, with the principal men of the state, met us at a distance of three miles from the city, escorted by a guard of cavalry and a regiment of infantry. We were introduced to these personages by Captain Wade, the political agent of government at Lodiana [Ludhiana], who had been deputed to Lahore on the occasion, and was accompanied by Dr A. Murray. The sight of these gentlemen, after our long absence from European society, excited the most pleasurable feelings. Our reception was also most gratifying, heightened as it was, by the reflection that our undertaking had been this day brought to a safe and successful issue. We alighted at a garden about a mile from Lahore, the residence of M. Chevalier Allard, whose manners and address were engaging and gentleman-like. We here parted with the deputation, after receiving a large sum of money and a profusion of sweetmeats in the name of the Maharaja.

The Chevalier then conducted us to an upper room, where we sat down to a *dejeuner a la fourchette* of the richest cookery. Another French gentleman, M. Court, was of our party. The scene was novel to us: the walls and roof of the apartment were entirely inlaid with small pieces of mirror. Champagne usurped the place of tea and coffee. M. Allard is the Maharaja's General of cavalry – and we had the trumpets of his division in attendance during breakfast. We continued with our worthy host during the following day, which passed in preparations for our introduction at Court, which had been fixed for the 20th of July.

About 9 a.m., when the Maharaja had reached the ancient palace that stands within the walls of Lahore, he sent a deputation of his nobles to conduct us to Court. All the Sirdars and officers who had been from time to time sent to us were previously in attendance at our residence, besides a numerous escort, and the pageant was further swelled by a detachment of Bengal sepoys which Captain Wade had brought from Lodiana.

The coach, which was a handsome vehicle, headed the procession; and in rear of the dray-horses we ourselves followed on elephants, with the officers of the Maharaja. We passed close under the walls of the city, between them and the ditch, and entered Lahore by the palace gate. The streets were lined with cavalry, artillery, and infantry, all of which saluted as we passed. The concourse of people was immense; they had principally seated themselves on the balconies of the houses, and preserved a most respectful silence. On entering the first court of the palace, we were received by Raja Dihan Sing, a fine soldier-like looking person, dressed in armour, by whom we were conducted to the door of the palace. While stooping to remove my shoes at the threshold, I suddenly found myself in the arms and tight embrace of a diminutive old-looking man – the great Maharaja Runjeet Sing. He was accompanied by two of his sons, who likewise embraced Mr Leckie and myself; when the Maharaja conducted me by the hand to the interior of his court; our reception was of the most distinguished nature, and he had advanced that distance to do us honour.

We found Captain Wade and Dr Murray in the Durbar, and all of us were seated on silver chairs, in front of his Highness. The Maharaja made various complimentary remarks; asked particularly after the health of his Majesty the King of Great Britain; and, as we had come from Bombay, enquired for Sir John Malcolm. When we had been seated a short time, I informed his Highness that I had brought along with me in safety to Lahore five horses, which his most gracious Majesty the King of England had conferred upon him, in consideration of the relations of amity and concord subsisting between the states, as also a carriage from the Right Honourable the Governor-General of India in token of his Lordship's esteem. I then added, that the horses were accompanied by a most friendly letter from his Majesty's minister for the affairs of India, which I held in my hand in a bag of cloth of gold, sealed with the arms of England. On this the Maharaja and his Court, as well as ourselves, rose up, and his Highness received the letter, and touched his forehead with the seal. The letter was then handed to his minister, Uzeez-o-Deen, who read a Persian translation of it in the presence of the whole Court. The envoys from the surrounding states were present.

[The text of Lord Ellenborough's official letter is given here.]

As the contents of the document were unfolded, the Maharaja gave evident symptoms of his satisfaction, and when the letter was half read, he said that he would greet its arrival by a salute; and a peal of artillery from sixty guns, each firing twenty-one times, announced to the citizens of Lahore the joy of their King. His Highness then expressed his intention of viewing the presents, and we accompanied him. The sight of the horses excited his utmost surprise and wonder: their size and colour pleased him: he said they were little elephants and, as they passed singly before him, he called out to his different Sirdars and officers, who joined in his admiration.

Nothing could exceed the affability of the Maharaja: he kept up an uninterrupted conversation for the hour and a half which the interview lasted: he enquired particularly about the depth of water in the Indus, and the possibility of navigating it, and put various questions regarding the people who occupy its banks, and their political and military importance. I alluded to the riches of Sinde, which seemed to excite his utmost cupidity. He introduced us to all the representatives of the neighbouring states, and concluded by asking if we should like to see his own stud. About thirty horses were immediately brought, and passed in review order before us. They were caparisoned in the richest and most superb manner, and some of them were adorned with very valuable jewels: he named each horse, and described his pedigree and points, as he was brought up. They were of all countries, and from their necks being tightly reined up, certainly looked well; but they were not the stud which one would have expected at Lahore – all the horses appeared to be under-limbed.

The exertion which his Highness underwent seemed to exhaust him, and we withdrew. Nature has, indeed, been sparing in her gifts

Maharaja Runjeet Sing

to this personage, and there must be a mighty contrast between his mind and body. He has lost an eye, is pitted by the small pox, and his stature does not certainly exceed five feet three inches. He is entirely free from pomp and show, yet the studied respect of his Court is remarkable; not an individual spoke without a sign, though the throng was more like a bazar than the Court of the first native Prince in these times.

The hall of audience, in which the interview took place, was built entirely of marble, and is the work of the Moghul emperors: part of the roof was gorgeously decorated by a pavilion of silken cloth studded with jewels. The Maharaja himself wore a necklace, armlets, and bracelets of emeralds, some of which were very large. His sword was mounted with the most precious stones. The nobles were likewise dressed for the occasion with jewels, and all the Court appeared in yellow, the favourite colour of the nation, which has a gaudy but striking effect.

On the following morning, the Maharaja intimated his wish for our presence, at a military review in honour of passing events. We found his Highness on the parade ground, seated on a terrace, a short distance from the walls of Lahore. Five regiments of regular infantry were drawn up in line, three deep. Runjeet requested we would pass down the line and inspect them. They were dressed in white, with black cross-belts, and bore muskets, the manufacture of Cashmere or Lahore: there was a mixture of Hindoostanees and Seiks in every corps. After the inspection, the brigade manoeuvred under a native general officer, and went through its evolutions with an exactness and precision fully equal to our Indian troops: the words of command were given in French.

We took up our abode in the garden-house of M. Chevalier Ventura, another General, who was absent on the Indus with his legion. Our intercourse with the French officers was on the most friendly footing and it continued so during our residence at Lahore. Among these gentlemen, M. Court struck me as an acute and well-informed person; he is both a geographer and an antiquarian. M. Court, as well as his brother officers, was formerly in the service of one of the Persian Princes, and travelled to India as a native, which gave him an opportunity of acquiring the best information regarding the intervening countries. He showed me the route from Kermenshah, by Herat, Candahar, Ghuzni, and Cabool, to Attock, constructed topographically with great care; and he informed me, at the same time, that he had been less anxious to obtain a complete map of that part of Asia, than to ascertain one good route with its detours, and the military and statistical resources of the country. The French have much better information of these countries than ourselves and M. Court, in explaining his map to me, pointed out the best routes for infantry and cavalry. This gentleman has likewise employed a residence of four years in the Punjab to illustrate its geography: he has encountered jealousy from Runjeet Sing, but still managed to complete a broad belt of survey from Attock to the neighbourhood of our own frontier. I doubt not but the antiquities as well as the geography of the Punjab will be illustrated by this intelligent gentleman who, to his honour be it said, adds to a zeal in the pursuit, the strongest desire to disseminate his own knowledge and stimulate others. The fruit of M. Court's labours, I believe, will ere long be given to the public by the Geographical Society of Paris, or some other of the learned bodies in that capital.

[Burnes goes out of his way to stress the good relations he had with the French officers, possibly because this might have come as quite a surprise to his readers. There had been extreme rivalry, and at times outright war, between the Compagnie des Indes and the East India Company in the previous century, not to mention an attempt by Napoleon to co-opt the Tsar of Russia in an abortive invasion of India in 1801. Anti-French feeling was still rife in England.]

In our evening rambles at Lahore, we had many opportunities of viewing this city. The ancient capital extended from east to west for a distance of five miles and had an average breadth of three, as may be yet traced by the ruins. The mosques and tombs, which have been more stably built than the houses, remain in the midst of fields and cultivation as caravanserais for the traveller. The modern city occupies the western angle of the ancient capital, and is encircled by a strong wall. The houses are very lofty and the streets, which are narrow, offensively filthy, from a gutter that passes through the centre. The bazars of Lahore do not exhibit much appearance of wealth, but the commercial influence of the Punjab is to be found at Umritsir [Amritsar], the modern capital. There are some public buildings within the city that deserve mention. The King's mosque is a capacious building of red sandstone, which had been brought by Aurungzebe from near Delhi. Its four lofty minarets still stand, but the temple itself has been converted into a powder magazine. There are two other mosques, with minarets, to proclaim the falling greatness of the Mahommedan empire, where the 'faithful,' as every where else in the Punjab, must offer up their prayers in silence.

But the stranger must cross the Ravee to behold the finest ornament of Lahore – the 'Shah Dura', or tomb of the Emperor Juhangeer, which is a monument of great beauty. [Jahangir, who died in 1627, was the son of Akbar the Great.] It is a quadrangular building, with a minaret at each corner, rising to the height of seventy feet. It is built chiefly of marble and red stone, which are alternately interlaid in all parts of the building. The sepulchre is of most chaste workmanship, with its inscriptions and ornaments arranged in beautiful mosaic; the shading of some roses and other flowers is even preserved by the different colours of the stone. Two lines of black letters, on a ground of white marble, announce the name and title of the 'Conqueror of the World', Juhangeer, and about a hundred different words in Arabic and Persian, with the single signification of God, are distributed on different parts of the sepulchre. The floor of the building is also mosaic. The tomb was formerly covered by a dome, but Bahadoor Shah threw it down, that the dew and rain of heaven might fall on the tomb of his grandfather Juhangeer. It is probable that this beautiful monument will soon be washed into the river Ravee, which is capricious in its course near Lahore, and has lately overwhelmed a portion of the garden wall that environs the tomb. [Happily, Burnes's prediction turned out to be over-pessimistic.]

The next, though by no means the least, object of interest at Lahore, is the garden of Shah Jehan [Jahangir's son and successor] – the Shalimar. It is a magnificent remnant of Moghul grandeur, about half a mile in length, with three successive terraces, each above the level of the other. A canal, which is brought from a great distance, intersects this beautiful garden, and throws up its water in 450 fountains to cool the atmosphere. The marble couch of the Emperor yet remains, but the garden suffered much injury before Runjeet Sing obtained his present ascendancy. The Maharaja himself has removed some of the marble houses, but he has had the good taste to replace them, though it be by more ignoble stone.

As we were proceeding one morning to examine the tomb of Juhangeer, we found Runjeet Sing seated on the plain, and surrounded by his troops. He sent one of his officers to call us and we passed about half an hour with him. He gave us an account of the inroads of the Afghans into the Punjab, and told us that we now sat on their ground of encampment. Zuman Shah, the blind king at Lodiana, he said, had thrice sacked the city of Lahore; he also talked of his designs on India, and the vicissitudes to which kings are subject. The Maharaja was the plainest dressed man at his Durbar; his clothes were shabby and worn.

On the evening of the 25th, his Highness gave us a private audience, in which we saw him to great advantage, for he directed his Court to withdraw. On our arrival, we found him seated on a chair, with a party of thirty or forty dancing girls, dressed uniformly in boys' clothes. They were mostly natives of Cashmere or the adjacent mountains, on whom grace and beauty had not been sparingly bestowed. Their figures and features were small, and their Don Giovanni costume of flowing silk most becoming, improved as it was by a small bow and quiver in the hand of each. The 'eyes of Cashmere' are celebrated in the poetry of the East, of which these Dianas now furnished brilliant specimens, in gems black and bright, disfigured, however, by a kind of sparkling gold dust glued round each organ. 'This,' said Runjeet Sing, 'is one of my regiments (pultuns), but they tell me it is one I cannot discipline' – a remark which amused us, and mightily pleased the fair. He pointed out two of the ladies, whom he called the 'Commandants' of this arm of his service, to whom he had given villages, and an allowance of five and ten rupees a day. He shortly afterwards called for four or five elephants to take these, his *undisciplined* troops home.

Runjeet then commenced on more important subjects and ran

over, among other things, the whole history of his connection with the British government. It had, at first, he said, excited great suspicion and discontent among the Seik Sirdars, but he himself was satisfied of its advantage from the outset. Sir John Malcolm, he continued, had first stood his friend in 1805, and Sir Charles Metcalfe had completed his happiness. Sir David Ochterlony had further cemented the bonds of friendship, and the letter which I had now delivered to him from the minister of the King of England partook more of the nature of a treaty than a common epistle, and had gratified him beyond his powers of expression.

[Sir John Malcolm, the East India Company's Governor of Bombay from 1827–31, had always supported Ranjit, and wrote a book called *A Sketch of the Sikhs*. Sir Charles Metcalfe had been sent by the Company as envoy to the court of Ranjit Singh in 1808 at the age of twenty-three, and more recently had been Resident at Hyderabad. Ochterlony, as a Major-General in Ludhiana in 1808, was instrumental in the signing of the Treaty of Amritsar the following year, which established friendly relations between Ranjit Singh and the British government.]

He here recurred to the riches of Sinde, expressing an earnest desire to appropriate them to his own use, and put the most pointed questions to me regarding the feelings of Government on such a subject. Runjeet is very fond of comparing the relative strength of the European nations, and, on this occasion he asked whether France or England were the greater power. I assured him they were both great; but he had only to remember our power in India, to be satisfied of the military character of Britain. Runjeet Sing is, in every respect, an extraordinary character. I have heard his French officers observe that he has no equal from Constantinople to India; and all of them have seen the intermediate powers.

We continued at Lahore as the guests of the Maharaja till the 16th of August, and had many opportunities of meeting him, but I do not think I can add any thing to the history of his rise, drawn up by the late Captain William Murray, political agent at Ambala. The most creditable trait in Runjeet's character is his humanity; he has never been known to punish a criminal with death since his accession to power; he does not hesitate to mutilate a malefactor, but usually banishes him to the hills. Cunning and conciliation have been the two great weapons of his diplomacy. It is too probable, that the career of this chief is nearly at an end; his chest is contracted, his back is bent, his limbs withered, and it is not likely that he can long bear up against a nightly dose of spirits more ardent than the strongest brandy.

On the 16th of August we had our audience of leave with Runjeet Sing, but my fellow traveller was unable to attend from indisposition. Captain Wade accompanied me. He received us in an eccentric manner, under an open gateway leading to the palace. A piece of white cloth was spread under our chairs instead of a carpet, and there were but few of his Court in attendance. In compliance with a wish that I had expressed, he produced the 'Koh-i-Noor', or mountain of light, one of the largest diamonds in the world, which he had extorted from Shah Shooja, the ex-King of Cabool. Nothing can be imagined more superb than this stone; it is of the finest water, and about half the size of an egg. Its weight amounts to $3\frac{1}{2}$ rupees, and if such a jewel is to be valued, I am informed it is worth $3\frac{1}{2}$ millions of money, but this a gross exaggeration. The 'Koh-i-Noor' is set as an armlet, with a diamond on each side about the size of a sparrow's egg.

Ranjeet seemed anxious to display his jewels before we left him, and with the diamond was brought a large ruby, weighing 14 rupees. It had the names of several kings engraven on it, among which were those of Aurungzebe and Ahmed Shah. There was also a topaz of great size, weighing 11 rupees, and as large as half a billiard ball: Runjeet had purchased it for 20,000 rupees.

[The farewell audience ended with the Maharaja conferring many magnificent presents on the British party, together with a letter to Lord Ellenborough, the Minister for India, expressed in the customary flowery style. He thanks the Minister for the dray horses 'of superior quality, of singular beauty, of mountainous form, and elephantine stature' and for the 'large and elegant carriage', and refers to Burnes as 'that nightingale of the garden of eloquence, that bird of the winged words of sweet discourse . . . ' Even allowing for oriental hyperbole, the youthful Burnes must have felt pleased by this fulsome acknowledgement of his diplomatic skills.]

On presenting this letter his Highness embraced me and begged I would convey his high sentiments of regard to the Governor-General of India. I then took leave of Maharaja Runjeet Sing, and quitted his capital of Lahore the same evening in prosecution of my journey to Simla, on the Himalaya Mountains, where I had been summoned to give an account of my mission to Lord William Bentinck [the Governor-General], then residing in that part of India.

We reached Umritsir, the holy city of the Seiks, on the following morning – a distance of thirty miles. The intervening country, called Manja, is richly cultivated. The great canal, or '*nuhr*', hich was cut from the Ravee by one of the Emperors of Hindoostan, and brings the water for a distance of eighty miles, passes by Umritsir, and runs parallel with the Lahore road. It is very shallow, and sometimes does not exceed a width of eight feet: small boats still navigate it. We halted a day at Umritsir, to view the rites of Seik holiness, and our curiosity was amply gratified. In the evening we were conducted by the chief men of the city to the national temple. It stands in the centre of a lake, and is a handsome building, covered with burnished gold. After making the circuit of it, we entered, and made an offering to the '*Grinth Sahib*' or holy book, which lay open before a priest, who fanned it with the tail of a Tibet cow, to keep away impurity, and to add to its consequence. When we were seated, a Seik arose and addressed the assembled multitude. He invoked Gooroo Govind Sing, and every one joined hands; he went on to say, that all which the Seiks enjoyed on earth was from the Gooroo's bounty; and that the strangers now present had come from a great distance, and brought presents from the King of England, to cement friendship, and now appeared in this temple with an offering of 250 rupees. The money was then placed on the Grinth, and a universal shout of '*Wagroojee ka futtih!*' closed the oration. We were then clad in Cashmere shawls and, before departing, I begged the orator to declare our desire for a continuance of friendship with the Seik nation, which brought a second shout of '*Wagroojee ka futtih*'; '*Khalsajee ka futtih!*' May the Seik religion prosper!

From the great temple, we were taken to the Acali [Akhali] boonga, or house of the Immortals, and made a similar offering. We were not allowed to enter this spot, for the Acalis or Nihungs are a wrong-headed set of fanatics, not to be trusted. In reply to the offering, the priest sent us some sugar. The Acalis are clothed in turbans of blue cloth, which runs into a peak: on this they carry several round pieces of iron, weapons of defence, which are used like the quoit. These bigots are constantly molesting the community by abuse and insult, or even violence; a week does not pass in the Punjab without a life being lost: but Runjeet suppresses their excesses with a firm and determined hand, though they form a portion of the establishment in a religion of which he himself is a strict observer. He has attached some of the greatest offenders to his battalions, and banished others. Our conductor, Desa Sing Majeetia, father of our Mihmandar, a Seik of the confederacy, and a kind old man, was very solicitous about our safety, and led us by the hand, which he grasped firmly, through the assembled crowd. From the temple we made the tour of Umritsir, which is a larger city than Lahore. This place is the great emporium of commerce between India and Cabool. The traders are chiefly Hindoos, before whose door one wonders at the utility of large blocks of red rock-salt being placed, till informed that they are for the use of the sacred city cows, who lick and relish them.

At a distance of twenty-three miles from Umritsir, we came on the Beas, or Hyphasis of Alexander. The country is varied by trees, but not rich, and the soil is gravelly. On the 21st we crossed the Beas at Julalabad, where it was swollen to a mile in width by rain. Its current exceeded in rapidity five miles an hour; we were nearly two hours in crossing, and landed about two miles below the point from which we started. The greatest depth was eighteen feet. The boats used in this river are mere rafts with a prow; they bend frightfully, and are very unsafe, yet elephants, horses, cattle, and guns are conveyed across on them. We passed in safety, but an accident, which might have proved serious, befell us in one of the small channels of this river. It was about thirty yards wide, and eighteen feet deep, and we attempted the passage on an elephant. No sooner had the animal got out of his depth, than he rolled over, and precipitated Mr Leckie and myself head-foremost into the water, wheeling round at the same time to gain the bank he had quitted. Dr Murray alone retained his seat: but we were not long in regaining terra firma, without any other inconvenience than a ducking. We did not again attempt the passage on an elephant, but crossed on inflated buffalo skins supporting a framework.

Our halting-place was Kuppertulla [Kapurthala], ten miles from the Beas, the estate of Futtih Sing Aloowala, one of the Seik chiefs who was present with Lord Lake's army in 1805, when encamped in this vicinity. [Britain's eventual success in the Maratha Wars in 1804 had brought Company troops very close to Sikh territory. The Sikh leader – the young Ranjit Singh – prudently avoided a military confrontation and negotiated a treaty of friendship.] He is yet a young man. He received us with great respect and kindness, and sent his two sons to meet us as we approached. He came himself in the evening on a visit and on the following day, when we returned it, he gave us a grand fete in his garden-house, which was illuminated. The display of fireworks was varied, and we viewed it with advantage from a terrace.

Futtih Sing is the person whom Sir John Malcolm describes in his 'Sketch of the Seiks' as requiring his dram, and years have not diminished his taste for liquor. Immediately we were seated he produced his bottle, drank freely himself, and pressed it much upon us: it was too potent for an Englishman; but he assured us, that whatever quantity we drank, it would never occasion thirst. We filled a bumper to the health of the Sirdar and his family, and were about to withdraw, when he produced most expensive presents, which could not in any way be refused: he gave me a string of pearls, and some other jewels, with a sword, a horse, and several shawls. Futtih Sing is an uncouth-looking person, but he has the manners of a soldier, and when we left him, he urgently requested that we would deliver his sincere sentiments of regard to his old friend Sir John Malcolm.

We made three marches from Kuppertulla to Fulour, on the banks of the Sutlege, a distance of thirty-six miles. The town of Fulour is the frontier post of the Lahore Chief; and here we left our escort and Seik friends, who had accompanied us from Mooltan. We distributed cloths to the commissioned and non-commissioned officers, and a sum of 1000 rupees among the men, which gratified all parties. The Maharaja continued his munificence to the last, and before crossing the Sutlege, he had sent us no less than 24,000 rupees in cash, though we had declined to receive the sum of 700 rupees, which had been fixed for our daily allowance after reaching Lahore.

[Burnes and his companions left Fulour on 26 August and made their way to Ludhiana in 'British India', where Captain Wade was stationed.]

At Lodiana, we met two individuals who have exercised an influence on the Eastern world, now pensioners of the British – the ex-Kings of Cabool, Shah Zuman and Shah Shooja-ool-Moolk [Shuja-ul-Mulk]. The ceremonial of our introduction to Shah Shooja corresponded nearly with that described by Mr Elphinstone; for, in his exile, this fallen monarch has not relinquished the forms of royalty. The officers of his court still appear in the same fanciful caps, and on a signal given in Turkish (*ghachan*, begone), the guards run out of the presence, making a noise with their high-heeled boots. The person of the Shah himself has been so correctly described, that I have little to say on that subject. In his misfortunes, he retains the same dignity and prepossessing demeanour as when king. We found him seated on a chair in a shady part of his garden, and stood during the interview. He has become somewhat corpulent, and his expression is melancholy, but he talked much, and with great affability. He made many enquiries regarding Sinde, and the countries on the Indus, and said that 'he had rebuked the Ameers for their suspicion and jealousy of our intentions in coming to Lahore. Had I but my kingdom,' continued he, 'how glad should I be to see an Englishman at Cabool, and to open the road between Europe and India!'

The Shah then touched upon his own affairs, and spoke with ardent expectations of being soon able to retrieve his fortunes. In reply to one of his questions, I informed him that he had many well-wishers in Sinde. 'Ah!' said he, 'these sort of people are as bad as enemies; they profess strong friendship and allegiance, but they render me no assistance. They forget that I have a claim on them for two crores [crore = ten million] of rupees, the arrears of tribute.'

Shah Shooja was plainly dressed in a tunic of pink gauze, with a green velvet cap, something like a coronet, from which a few emeralds were suspended. There is much room for reflection on the vicissitudes of human life while visiting such a person. From what I learn, I do not believe the Shah possesses sufficient energy to seat himself on the throne of Cabool and that if he did regain it, he has not the tact to discharge the duties of so difficult a situation.

The brother of Shah Shooja, Shah Zuman, is an object of great compassion, from his age, appearance, and want of sight. We visited him also, and found him seated in a hall with but one attendant, who announced our being present, when the Shah looked up and bade us 'Welcome.' He is stone blind, and cannot distinguish day from night; he was as talkative as his brother, and lamented that he could not pass the remainder of his days in his native land, where the heat was less oppressive.

Shah Zuman has lately sunk into a zealot: he passes the greater part of his time in listening to the Koran and its commentaries. Poor man! He is fortunate in deriving consolation from any source. When taking leave, Shah Zuman begged I would visit him before quitting Lodiana, as he was pleased at meeting a stranger. I did not fail to comply with his wishes, and saw him alone. I had thought that age and misfortunes made him indifferent to all objects of political interest; but he asked me, in a most piteous manner, if I could not intercede with the Governor-General in behalf of his brother, and rescue him from his present exile. I assured him of the sympathy of our government, and said, that his brother should look to Sinde and the other provinces of the Dooranee empire for support, but he shook his head, and said that the case was hopeless. After a short silence, the Shah told me that he had inflammation in the eyes, and begged I would look at them. He has suffered from this ever since his brother caused him to be blinded with a lancet. As he has advanced in years, the organ seems to have undergone a great change, and the black part of the eye has almost disappeared. It is impossible to look upon Shah Zuman without feelings of the purest pity and, while in his presence, it is difficult to believe we behold that king, whose name, in the end of last century, shook Central Asia, and carried dread and terror along with it throughout our Indian possessions. Infirm, blind, and exiled, he now lives on the bounty of the British Government.

[The founder of the Durrani dynasty, Ahmad Khan Abdali, who was elected Shah of Afghanistan by his fellow chieftains after the demise of Nadir Shah in 1747, was a powerful leader who extended the empire from Meshed to Kashmir and Delhi, and from the Oxus to the Arabian Sea. But after his death in 1772 the empire began to fragment as the various chiefs jostled for power. His grandson Shah Zaman seized power in 1793 (making some of his half-brothers into deadly enemies) and announced his ambition to claw back as much of Ahmad's empire as possible. This alarmed not only the British but also the Shah of Persia, who helped Mahmud of Herat – one of the disaffected brothers – to overthrow Zaman and take his place. Mahmud had his brother blinded and thrown into prison in 1800. Three years later another brother, Shuja, threw out Mahmud but the latter eventually ousted Shah Shuja and regained the throne, while Shuja and the blinded Zaman were given sanctuary by the British in Ludhiana in 1815.]

After ten days' recreation at Lodiana, where we mingled once more with our countrymen, we prosecuted our journey to Simla, on the Himalaya mountains, a distance of about 100 miles, which we reached in the course of a few days. We here beheld a scene of natural sublimity and beauty, that far surpassed the glittering court which we had lately left. At Simla we had the honour of meeting the Right Honourable Lord William Bentinck, the Governor-General of India; and his Lordship evinced his satisfaction at the result of our mission, by entering at once into negotiations for laying open the navigation of the Indus to the commerce of Britain – a measure of enlightened policy, considered both commercially and politically. I had the honour of receiving the following acknowledgment of my endeavours to elucidate the geography of that river, and the condition of the princes and people who occupy its banks.

[The Governor-General's detailed letter was what any ambitious young subaltern would have died for. He praises Burnes's prudence and discretion in his dealings with the local chieftains, mentions the great value of his painstaking geographical work, expresses his 'entire and unqualified approbation' of the successful completion of the important duty which had been assigned to him, and concludes by promising that his 'zeal, diligence and intelligence' would be speedily brought to the attention of the powers-that-be in England.

* * *

The First Edition of Burnes's book, published in 1834, concludes the *Narrative of a Voyage on the Indus* on this gratifying note, before moving on to the account of his journey to Central Asia. But the book sold so well that a Second Edition was produced the following year, enabling Burnes to make some amendments and improvements. Among these was a new chapter covering the interval between the two expeditions, which he spent mainly in Upper India. The highlight was a ceremonial meeting between the Governor-General of India and Maharaja Ranjit Singh at Rupur in October 1831, which he likens to the Field of the Cloth of Gold between Henry VIII and François I in the 16th century. The chapter consists mainly of a letter written at the time, for Burnes frankly admits that later events had obliterated some of the detail from his memory.]

CHAPTER VII

Upper India – Delhi

In the former edition, I did not think it necessary to trouble the reader with an account of my residence in Upper India, for the few months which elapsed between the termination of my voyage on the Indus and departure for Central Asia. The country in which I was then moving, however interesting, is pretty well known, and has been frequently described; yet the time of my visit was eventful, since it was marked by the splendid interview of the 'Lion of the Punjab', Maharaja Runjeet Sing, with Lord William Bentinck, the Governor-General of India. I have been urged by numerous friends in this country to convey some notion of that spectacle, and fill up at the same time the blank which separated the volumes, by giving a brief account of what I saw in Upper India, and during my visit to the imperial city of Delhi.

After a six weeks' residence in the Himalaya, I descended from the mountains in the end of October, along with the suite of the Governor-General, and accompanied his Lordship to Roopoor [Rupur], a village on the banks of the Sutlege, at which the meeting took place. The following is a hurried sketch of what passed: The Governor-General's camp was formed at Roopur by the 22nd of October, and on the following day the escort of his Lordship arrived from the different military stations in the neighbourhood. We had lancers and horse artillery, with European and native infantry, to exhibit on this occasion the different arms of a British force.

The 24th passed in suspense and expectation; and there were not wanting politicians to doubt the sincerity of the Maharaja, and circulate reports that he never intended to cross the Sutlege. The following morning dissipated these fears, and a cannonade of some quarter of an hour's duration, from the other side of the river, announced the presence of Maharaja Runjeet Sing. His Highness' s approach, which but few had the good fortune to witness, is described as most imposing. His troops received him in a broad street, lengthened out to nearly two miles by irregular cavalry.

Preparations were immediately made, by both parties, for a reciprocal welcome: the deputations passed each other on the way, and a salute on both sides of the river intimated their arrival. On the part of Lord William Bentinck, General John Ramsay, Mr H. T. Prinsep, the Political Secretary of the Governor-General, Majors McLachlan, Caldwell, and Benson, A.D.C., congratulated his Highness. On that of the Maharaja, his eldest son, Kurruck Sing, with his suite, paid a like compliment. Runjeet received his Lordship's mission with great affability: the conversation turned on various subjects, but was chiefly confined to observations on the increase of friendship that must follow such appropriate marks of good will.

[Presents were ceremonially exchanged, the British band played 'God save the King' – much to the delight of Prince Kurruck Singh – and the initial welcoming ceremony was concluded. Early next morning General Ramsay and a number of other officers, including Burnes and Wade (the political agent from Ludhiana), crossed the Sutlej and escorted the Maharaja and his entourage to the first formal meeting with the Governor-General. The party travelled mainly by elephant – those of the Sikh leader being noticeably more splendid than those of the British! – and Burnes shared a howdah with General Ramsay and acted as interpreter between him and Ranjit Singh, whose elephant travelled alongside.]

His Highness himself, with his son, and a favourite son of one of his chiefs, occupied the centre; his nobles, in gold and silver houdas, preceded and followed; his generals and commanders, seated on horses richly caparisoned, arranged the troops; and a body of four thousand cavalry, uniformly dressed in yellow, formed the wings of this magnificent procession. The Maharaja himself directed every movement with the eye and confidence of a soldier; he conversed freely with the gentlemen near him; commanded silence among his troops, and was readily obeyed; his every word seemed talismanic and one could not but confess, that, in even this ceremonial display, he exhibited the energies of his mind, and wonderful talents for command. The *coup d'oeil*, as the troops debouched from the bridge of boats, was picturesque and striking; the bodyguard spread on both sides, to swell the pageant of their king, and each chevalier, on his fierce and fiery steed, seemed only anxious to leave more lasting impressions of the ruler of the Punjab.

A few minutes brought the cortege within the line of British troops; a royal salute announced the event. His Highness, undismayed by the crowd, or the approach of the suite of the Governor-General, advanced steadily, and asked the names of each regiment as he passed. The appearance of His Majesty's 31st regiment of foot particularly arrested his notice. The lancers were obscured by the approach of the procession, which drew up in front of them to receive the Maharaja. The elephants closed with one another; the doorways of both houdas were opened and Runjeet sprung, with some agility, into his Lordship's arms, when the Governor-General of the East and the 'King of the Five Rivers', seated together, advanced to the state tents. His Lordship assisted his Highness in descending from the elephant, and conducted him to the audience tent, where he was received by Lady William Bentinck, and the other ladies in camp. After some complimentary remarks, Runjeet was conducted, with his own suite and that of the Governor-General, into the next tent. The party sat and conversed for an hour, when the presents, served up in fifty-one trays, were placed before the Maharaja. He saw them carefully packed, and then proceeded to examine the horses and an elephant, which formed part of the gift. He exhibited his own led horses to the Governor-General, and begged his acceptance of one of them; he then remounted his elephant, under a royal salute, and left the British camp. To judge by general report, he left it not without instilling a most favourable impression on the minds of all who saw him throughout the ceremony.

Early in the morning of the 26th, Kurruck Sing again crossed the Sutlege, to conduct the Governor-General to his father's camp. His Lordship departed under a royal salute, accompanied by his personal staff, all the public functionaries, and the principal European gentlemen present. Runjeet Sing advanced to the water's edge, about a mile from camp, where his Lordship left his own elephant, and proceeded in the same houda with the Maharaja. The spectacle which now presented itself was truly grand. There were seventy elephants advancing with Seik chiefs and European gentlemen in full uniform. It would be impossible to give a description of the magnificence exhibited at the Seik encampment on this occasion. Two regiments of infantry were drawn up at right angles to one another; at the apex of the triangle was a spacious and lofty triumphal arch, covered with red cloth and gilded ornaments, lined with yellow silk. Another arch, more splendid than the first, was erected a short distance in advance, and proceeding through both of these we reached the court-yard. His Highness's suite of tents occupied a rising ground overlooking the Sutlege, and inside the screen that entirely surrounded them the troops of the household were drawn up in order, forming a perfect wall of soldiers: there was a silence among this mass of men that made the scene most imposing. On alighting from the elephants, Runjeet conducted the Governor-General to a pavilion where the court was held, and seated his Lordship between himself and his son. The chiefs occupied the space immediately behind his Highness, and the European gentlemen sat on two rows of chairs that formed a street for the approach of the different personages of rank who were to be introduced. The whole court was shaded by a lofty arcade of yellow silk: on the floor were spread out the richest carpets and shawls of Cashmere, and behind the Maharaja stood a spacious tent glittering with every ornament; it was composed partly of crimson velvet, yellow French satin, and Cashmere shawls. It realised every notion of Eastern grandeur. But the Maharaja himself was a greater object of attraction than this magnificence: he was robed in green satin; on his right arm he wore that splendid diamond the 'Koh-i-noor', and his wrist and neck were encircled by superb pearls.

After the arrangement of being seated, the different European gentlemen were introduced, and the pertinent remarks of Runjeet to each individual regarding his particular calling marked the mind of the man. His Highness conversed with Lord William through Captain Wade upon various subjects, and then introduced his nobles. Kishen Singh, his commander-in-chief, and others of his favourites, performed the part of masters of the ceremonies, and as the different names were announced, the parties withdrew in great regularity. Who could have expected such civilisation among the 'republican and besotted Seiks'? The fact is, they have changed their nature: they are now subject to a monarch of martial habits. About three hundred chiefs were introduced: some appeared in chain armour, and one individual, Soojet Sing, a raja, and high in favour, wore a casque surmounted by a white plume, splendidly adorned with pearls and diamonds: he was the handsomest man at court, and on this day the admiration of both Europeans and natives. On a golden footstool in front of the Maharaja sat a youth, the nephew of this person, and the only individual in the Punjab who is allowed the honour of a seat. He wore the largest necklace of pearls which I have ever seen, and the intelligent physiognomy of the little fellow seemed to speak favourably for Runjeet's choice.

The appearance of the Seiks is most warlike, and I question if a body of nobler-looking heroes than graced this court has ever been exhibited since the dismemberment of the Moghul empire. When the chiefs had withdrawn, the Maharaja gave a signal, which brought a detachment *of his regiment of Amazons*, about seventy in number, richly attired in yellow silk, and uniformly dressed: they drew up in front of the Governor-General, under the orders of a favourite commandant, who controlled the division with a long cane. Some of the ladies were very beautiful; nor did they seem to regret that on such an occasion so many eyes were turned towards them. The ladies succeeded in making an impression, and were desired to withdraw after chanting a few Persian odes on love and beauty. From this music the Maharaja passed to sounds less dissonant in the band of His Majesty's 16th lancers, which at his particular request was introduced into the court. He equally admired the instruments and the soldier-like looking men who used them. His questions were incessant, and his gratification was announced by ordering three thousand rupees for distribution among the different bands of music which were in attendance.

His Highness next produced his own stud of riding horses for the inspection of the Governor-General. The housings and trappings of all the animals were rich and splendid: one of the dray horses, even, was brought forward to swell the pageant, but his rough hairy legs, and coarse appearance, ill became the glittering gold and crimson velvet with which his back was ornamented. Runjeet said that he had at last got paces out of him, and had frequently ridden him; he further added, that he had given a village and five hundred rupees to the man who had succeeded in training him! Rose water and *uttur* sprinkled on the assembly signified its close, and Runjeet conducted Lord William to a boat on the banks of the Sutlege, where he embarked under a salute. The high road to the bridge of boats passed through a garden, which was fantastically laid out in different-shaped parterres. The seed had only been sown on the day before Runjeet Sing arrived, and now presented to view various figures of peacocks, horses &c. It had grown up thus suddenly from constant irrigation; being, I presume, water-cresses, or something of that description.

[Next day Ranjeet Singh made a formal visit to the British, and inspected the assembled troops with great enthusiasm, seated on his favourite horse.]

His activity was as usual very great; he was here, there, and everywhere; he rode round the infantry squares, and called to his commander in chief to note the number that knelt down. He rode between the ranks of the lancers, and begged to examine a lance, which he considered too heavy. When the review was finished, he expressed great satisfaction, and produced three mules laden with money, requesting it might be divided among the troops. The sum amounted to about 11,000 rupees. He said that he wished to give the Europeans a dram, but he had no other way of doing so than in money. His Highness had an interview with the officer commanding, General Adams, before he left the ground. He had been misinformed, he said, regarding our manoeuvres, which he understood were performed with rapidity; but he now saw that the British moved like elephants, slow and steadily.

On the following morning, the Governor-General and his suite crossed the river to witness a review of the Seik army. There were about 10,000 men on the ground, more than one half of which were irregulars. Four infantry battalions manoeuvred in brigade, and at the termination of the field-day there seemed to be but one opinion regarding their efficiency. Many indeed (and some of them high judges) believe that they surpass the company's army; but, be this as it may, their state reflects great credit on the Maharaja and his French officers. Before the Governor-General left the field, he made a like present to the Maharaja's troops as had been given to our own.

[The Maharaja next gave a – literally – glittering reception for the European ladies and their husbands, at which his bevy of dancing girls scattered gold dust all over the guests. Burnes noted that even two days later those who had attended the soiree could be identified by their 'glittering and bespangled faces'. The highlight of the evening came when the Koh-i-Nor diamond was handed around for the guests to examine. After a couple more days of fireworks and horse-artillery displays, the festivities came to an end and both sides withdrew well satisfied with this new and strategically important friendship.

Burnes, however, had a lot of work to complete before setting out on his next expedition and he hurried to Ludhiana to stay with his friend Captain Wade. In this relatively quiet hill-station he was able to sort out the mass of information he had collected about the Indus, its many tributaries, complicated delta, the distances between settlements and varying depths and currents and so on. The remainder of Volume I is devoted to this geographical data – which was to contribute later to his being awarded the Gold Medal of the Royal Geographical Society.

Just before setting out for Central Asia, Burnes took the opportunity to visit the Mughal ruins at Delhi, redolent with the legendary splendour of Shah Jehan. In the 16th and 17th centuries the Mughals had dominated the sub-continent, but after the death of Aurangzeb in 1707, power gradually slipped away from them as warlike neighbours eroded their dominions (not to mention the East India Company, ever ready to 'keep the peace' or step into a vacuum). In time-honoured fashion, Delhi itself had been sacked in 1739 by hordes of Turko-Mongols under Nadir Shah, who poured down from the Hindu Kush mountains. Nadir had already usurped the throne of Persia, seized Kandahar, Kabul and then the Punjab. When he left Delhi, after a terrible massacre, he carried with him the Peacock Throne of Shah Jehan and the Koh-i-Nor diamond. The latter, as we have seen, was later snatched back, along with the Punjab, by Maharaja Ranjit Singh. The penultimate 'Great Mughal' was Akbar Shah II, an emperor without an empire and confined to a crumbling palace in Delhi. Burnes paid him a visit before returning to Ludhiana.]

Dec. 15ᵗʰ 1831. – I paid my obeisance to the Great Mogul this morning, in company with the Resident, Mr Martin. I made my *kotou* to the fifteenth in descent from Timour, was clothed in a dress of honour, and had the other insignia given by oriental princes tied on my head by his majesty. He is a decrepit, toothless old man, with a venerable expression of countenance. The mummery of the ceremony was absurd, and I could not suppress a smile, as the officers mouthed, in loud and sonorous solemnity, the titles of the king of the world, the ruler of the earth – a monarch now realmless, a prince without even the shadow of power!

Dec. 19ᵗʰ 1831. – I visited the tomb of Humaioon this morning. It is a most elegant structure, and in a great state of preservation. In pacing its handsome terrace, I was led into many a reflection regarding the departed king: his dethronement, his exile, his dreary and calamitous journey into the desert, were all before me. On my return from the tomb, I went to the Hindoo college, and was surprised to find Indian children versed in the geography and political state of Europe. I heard of the dismemberment of Poland from the native youths of Delhi: the march of intellect appeared to advantage in this capital. I selected one of these young lads to accompany me to Tartary. [This was Mohan Lal, who did not disappoint.]

Dec. 20ᵗʰ 1831. – I have great reason to feel delighted with my visit to Delhi, and with such feelings I departed for Lodiana. There is nothing ancient in the appearance of this capital: its houses are modern, and of small dimensions; its streets are spacious, and give one an idea of late improvements, though really the original design of Shah Jehan. The abundant supply of water makes it a convenient residence to its numerous population; and it is certainly the cleanest city I have seen in India. The surrounding country is beautifully interspersed with the ruins of mosques and caravanserais, which the stranger may visit with facility by good roads, that alone point out the supremacy of an European nation.

Dec. 21st 1831. – I came on the plains of Panniput early in the morning, and stopped to view its fields of glory. Timour, Babur and Ahmed Shah here fought three great battles. The last, which over-threw the Mahrattas commanded by the Bhow, is well remembered; but the plough has for years past effaced all traces of the eventful day. In passing through the streets, two cocks were fighting with great spirit; to remind the stranger, no doubt, of the warlike scene. I reached Lodiana on the 23rd.

[The remainder of Volume 1 is concerned with detailed geo-graphical information on the Indus valley, and has been omitted.]

PART TWO

An Account of a Journey from India to Cabool, Tartary and Persia

CHAPTER I

Lahore

In the end of December, 1831, I had the honour to obtain the final sanction of the Governor-General of India to proceed to Central Asia. I received my passports from his lordship at Delhi on the 23rd of that month, and proceeded by express to Lodiana on the frontiers, where I had the pleasure of meeting my fellow-traveller Mr James Gerard, of the Bengal Army. We here experienced many acts of kindness and assistance from Capt. C. M. Wade, the political agent, whose good offices I have to acknowledge with gratitude. The society of this, the most remote station of British India, also evinced an interest in our welfare which was truly gratifying. We took leave of it at a convivial party given for the occasion on 2nd of January, and on the following day bade a long farewell to such scenes, and plunged into the solitude of an Indian desert. We took the route that leads along the left bank of the Sutlege, till that river is joined by the Beas, or Hyphasis.

Before crossing the boundaries of India it was both prudent and necessary to receive the permission of Maharaja Runjeet Sing, the ruler of the Punjab. It was suggested to me that a private application was in every respect preferable to an official letter from government, since the most favourable reception which I had already experienced from his highness left no doubt of his ready compliance. I consequently addressed his highness, and solicited the indulgence of again entering his territories. I gave him a brief outline of the objects which I had in view, and congratulated myself on having to traverse, at the outset, the territories of so friendly an ally. In the course of three days we were joined by a small escort of cavalry sent to welcome us, and their commandant brought a most friendly reply from the Maharaja, expressive of his pleasure at our approach. It was also intimated to us that we should receive presents of money and gifts as

97

we advanced; but, as it would better suit our character to pass without these attentions, I civilly declined them. Reports would precede us, and doubtless in an exaggerated enough shape, which made it desirable to shun all pomp and show, and the more so since we had really no right to them.

As we descended the banks of the Sutlege, we gradually lost sight of the Himalaya mountains. For the first twenty miles they could be seen in great grandeur, clothed in snow from base to summit, without an inferior ridge to hide their majesty. They were about 150 miles distant, and not so peaked in their outline as the same range of mountains to the eastward. The hoary aspect of this stupendous chain formed a striking contrast with the pleasing verdure of the plains of the Punjab. In the morning these, indeed, were covered with hoar-frost, but it disappeared under the first rays of the sun, and left, in this alternation of heat and cold, a hard green sward, which is not often seen in tropical countries.

On the banks of the river we passed innumerable villages, the houses of which were terrace-roofed, and formed of sun-dried brick on a wooden framework. They had a clean and comfortable look, and the peasantry appeared well clad and happy. They consist of Juts, both Hindoo and Mahommedan, and a few Seiks. All the Mahommedans have been converted from Hindooism; and it is a curious fact that the Moslems predominate on the southern bank, where, from the vicinity to the Hindoo world, one would have expected to find those of that persuasion. In the upper parts of the Sutlege, near Lodiana, the inhabitants are exclusively agricultural; but after that river has been joined by the Beas, or Hyphasis, the habits of the people are predatory. There they are known under the various denominations of Dogur, Julmairee, Salairee, &c. and by the general designation of Raat, and live in a perpetual state of opposition to one another.

*   *   *

On the 11th we crossed by the ferry boats at Huree ka Puttun, and landed in the Punjab at the village of that name. There are twenty-three boats at this ferry; and it is protected by a party of 400 horse, whom the ruler of the Punjab has stationed here to prevent the fanatics of the Seik creed from passing into the British territories. As we entered the village, we were met by a crowd of females and children, who approached to chant our welcome. They are the poorer peasantry and, of course, actuated by the hope of reward; but the custom has something pleasing in it. The boys of the village had also assembled to gratify their curiosity; while we approached, they were silent, and looked with attention: when we had passed, all was bustle and uproar, running and falling, jumping and laughing, till the head man and his troopers called the urchins to order. I remember well when no one more delighted in such scenes than myself. Human nature is the same everywhere.

We had no sooner set foot on the Punjab than a sirdar, or chief, of the name of Sham Sing, appeared by order of his master. He presented me with a bow, according to the custom of the Seiks, and two bags of money; which latter I declined, being amply satisfied at the readiness with which we had received permission to enter the country. I wished also to dispense with this personage and his cavalcade; but it was impossible, since he had been deputed from Lahore to escort us, and the road was described as not altogether safe for a small party. It was well we did not separate ourselves from the chief, as we afterwards passed a village on fire, and in possession of the Seik fanatics, to whom I have already alluded. We met a body of 500 horse, with two field-pieces, proceeding to chastise these 'wrong-headed and short-sighted' men, as they are styled in the language of the Punjab cabinet.

At Puttee we visited one of the royal studs of Runjeet Sing. We found about sixty brood mares, chiefly of the Dunnee breed, from beyond the Hydaspes, where the country is dry and elevated. May not this aridity, as resembling the soil of Arabia, where the horse attains such perfection, have something to do with its excellence? These animals are exclusively fed on barley, and a kind of creeping grass called '*doob*', which is considered most nutritive. The horses at this stud were lately attacked by an epidemic disease, of which a Mahommedan, who resides in a neighbouring sanctuary, is believed to have cured them. Though a Mahommedan, the Seiks have in gratitude repaired and beautified his temple, which is now a conspicuous white building, that glitters in the sun. The Seik people are tolerant in their religion; and I have remarked in India generally much more of this virtue than the people receive credit for. It may be superstition which induces this general respect of all religions; but, however originating, it is a sound and wholesome feeling. The Mahommedans have, no doubt, been overbearing in their conquests; (and what conquerors have not been overbearing?) but, as they settled among the people, their prejudices disappeared, to the mutual benefit of themselves and their subjects.

In our progress to Lahore, we entered the great road of Juhangeer, which was once shaded with trees, and studded with minarets and caravanserais. It conducted the traveller 'From Agra to Lahore of the Great Mogul', and has been celebrated in Lalla Rookh, in the royal procession to Cashmere. In the lapse of time the trees have disappeared; but many minarets and superb caravanserais still mark the munificence of the Mogul emperors. The road itself is yet a broad and beaten way; nor was it possible to tread upon it without participating in the excitement which the author of Lalla Rookh has raised, and I may almost say gratified.

On the morning of the 17th we entered the imperial city of Lahore, which once rivalled Delhi. We wound among its ruins; and when yet three miles distant, were met by Monsieur Allard, and two natives of rank sent to welcome us. The Chevalier came in his carriage drawn by four mules, into which the Doctor and myself stepped, and drove to his hospitable mansion, where we alighted and took up our quarters. After the ceremony of receiving various friendly and formal messages from Runjeet, the native part of the deputation withdrew, leaving a profusion of the fruits of Cashmere and Cabool as an earnest of the condescension of their master. In the evening, a purse of 1100 rupees was sent to us; nor was it possible to refuse the money without giving offence.

We next morning paid our respects to the Maharaja, and were received with marked affability in a garden about two miles from the city. We found him in great spirits, and continued with him for about two hours. His conversation ranged from points of the utmost importance to mere trifles. Runjeet made the most particular enquiries regarding our intended journey; and, since it was no part of my object to develop the entire plans in view, we informed his highness that we were proceeding *towards* our native country. On taking leave, he requested that we would continue as long as possible at his court, since he wished to show us some tiger-hunting, and give an entertainment in his palace – honours which we duly appreciated. We meanwhile returned to enjoy the friendly society of M. Allard and his brother officers. I shall make no further mention of Lahore, since it is described in my first visit to the court, and was now no longer a scene of curious novelty.

Near midnight on the 22nd, we were much alarmed by an earthquake, which continued for about ten seconds with great violence. The atmosphere had indicated nothing unusual; the barometer underwent no variation either before or after it; and the thermometer stood so low as 37 degrees, and fell four degrees under the freezing point before sunrise. In July last it had risen to 102 degrees. I was informed that earthquakes were of frequent occurrence at Lahore, particularly during winter. In Cashmere they are still more common; and appear to be more usual on approaching the mountains. The lofty minarets of Lahore afford, however, the most convincing proof that there can have been no very violent commotion of nature since they were built – nearly two hundred years ago. The shock on the present occasion appeared to run from south-east to north-west; and it was singular to discover, after crossing Hindoo Koosh, that this was the exact direction of its course. In the valley of Badukhshan [Badakhshan], and the whole upper course of the Oxus, the greater portion of the villages had been overthrown, which had buried some thousands of people in their ruins. The shock had occurred there at the same time and, as far as I could judge, at the same hour, since they mentioned the midnight horrors of the sad event.

[The next couple of weeks were passed in feasting and amusements on the Maharaja's customary spectacular scale – including the promised tiger-hunt.]

During these gay and festive scenes, we were not forgetful of the difficulties which awaited us; and availed ourselves of the experience of Messrs Allard and Court, who had travelled overland from Persia through a part of the countries we were now about to traverse. These gentlemen seemed to vie with each other in every act of kindness. They furnished us with various letters to their acquaintances in Afghanistan, and gave us many hints to guide our conduct. Monsieur Court, indeed, drew up a précis of them, the result of his own experience, which I annex since it conveys, at the same time, most valuable information to a traveller, and gives me an opportunity of expressing my gratitude both to him and M. Allard, and the reasons on which I found it. These gentlemen did not disguise from me the many apprehensions which they entertained for our safety; but our visit to Lahore had not been made to discuss the chances of our success, but only in prosecution of the journey.

[Monsieur Court's helpful advice is contained in a 4-page letter, beginning with a French proverb: If you want to travel in peace, you must howl like the wolves among whom you find yourself. In other words, always conform to the manners and dress of the local population. He warns the Englishmen to avoid displaying any object which might be coveted, for the 'barbarians' would not hesitate to murder in the course of stealing it. They should never make the natives lose face, nor try to make friends with them, for they lacked European concepts of good faith, honesty and loyalty – in spite of their flattering tongues. He emphasises that they must bid an absolute farewell to alcohol until they reach Europe; they should avoid any sort of conspicuous consumption and on no account give any presents, for fear of appearing rich and thereby inviting robbery. He counsels them to keep indoors as much as possible, speak little and avoid getting into discussions, to be discreet in asking for information and in recording it. Finally, they should avoid all areas infested with Turkman slave raiders – and always be armed to the teeth.]

On the evening of the 10th of February, we took our leave of Maharaja Runjeet Sing on the parade-ground, where he again exhibited to us, with apparent pride, the progress which his troops had made in throwing shells. On this occasion he asked for my opinions on opening the Indus; and remarked that, as that river and its five great tributaries passed through his territories, he ought to derive greater advantages than the British government. He spoke of the scheme as might have been expected from a man of his enlightened views; but said that he did not relish the idea of vessels navigating all parts of his territories. He fears collision with the British government. His Highness then proceeded to dictate letters in our behalf to the chiefs of Peshawur and Cabool, as well as several other personages beyond the Indus. He also issued orders to all the chiefs and agents between his capital and the frontier; and stretching his hand from the elephant, gave each of us a hearty shake, and said farewell. He particularly requested me to write to him frequently, and give an account of the countries I traversed, with their politics and customs, and never forget him in whatever region I might be placed. We received letters from Runjeet Sing himself in the deserts of Tartary and in Bokhara; nor did we fail to comply with his request when far from his territories. I never quitted the presence of a native of Asia with such impressions as I left this man: without education, and without a guide, he conducts all the affairs of his kingdom with surpassing energy and vigour, and yet he wields his power with a moderation quite unprecedented in an Eastern prince.

CHAPTER II

Across the Punjab to the Indus

After taking an affectionate farewell of Messrs Allard and Court, we quitted Lahore in the forenoon of the 11th of February and alighted at the tomb of Juhangeer, a splendid mausoleum across the Ravee. Without any depression of spirits, or diminution of zeal, I felt no small degree of solitude at being separated from our hospitable friends; and I now look back on the few weeks which I passed at Lahore as some of the happiest of my life. Nor was there much in our first night's lodging to cheer us – the wreck of a royal cemetery, which the *manes* [revered remains] of a king had once rendered sacred, but lately converted into a barrack for a brigade of infantry, who had further contributed to its desolate appearance. We put up for the night in one of the garden-houses which surround it, and listened to the puerile stories of the people, who assured us that the body of the emperor, like the fabled tale of that of Mahommed, was suspended by loadstones. One has only to enter a chamber underneath to see it resting on the ground.

It now became necessary to divest ourselves almost of every thing which belonged to us, and discontinue many habits and practices which had become a second nature; for the success of our enterprise depended upon these sacrifices. We threw away all our European clothes, and adopted, without reserve, the costume of the Asiatic. We exchanged our tight dress for the flowing robe of the Afghans, girt on swords and *'kummur-bunds'* (sashes); and with our heads shaved, and groaning under ponderous turbans, we strutted about slip-shod; and had now to uncover the feet instead of the head. We gave away our tents, beds, boxes, and broke our tables and chairs. A hut, or the ground, we knew, must be our shelter, and a coarse carpet or mat our bed. A blanket, or *'kummul'*, served to cover the native saddle, and to sleep under during night; and the greater portion of my now limited wardrobe found a place in the '*khoorjeen*', or saddle-bags, which were thrown across the horse's quarter. A single mule for each of us carried the whole of our baggage, with my books and instruments; and a servant likewise found a seat upon the animal. A pony carried the surveyor, Mohammed Ali; and the Hindoo lad had the same allowance. These arrangements took some time and consideration; and we burned, gave away, and destroyed whole mule-loads of baggage – a propitiatory offering, as I called it, to those immortal demons the Khyberees, who have plundered the traveller, from time immemorial, across the Indus. Of what use would it have been to have adopted the costume and customs of the country, and to be yet burdened with the useless paraphernalia of civilisation? It is, nevertheless, a curious feeling to be sitting cross-legged, and to pen a journal on one's knees. Custom soon habituated us to these changes; and we did not do the less justice to our meals because we discarded wine and spirits in every shape, and ate with our fingers from copper dishes without knives and forks.

Half-way across to the Chenab, we halted in a garden at Kote [Kot], the residence of one of Runjeet Sing's colonels, and an agreeable place. It was not 100 yards square, but well stored with fruit-trees and flowers: most of the former were now in blossom, and an enumeration of them would give a favourable idea of this climate. They consisted of the peach, apricot, greengage, fig, pomegranate, quince, orange sweet and bitter, lime, lemon, guava, grape, mango, jamboo, bair, date, cardamom, almond, and the apple; with seven or eight other kinds, of which I can only give the native names – the *gooler, sohaujna, goolcheen, umltass, bell, bussoora*. The walks of the garden were lined with beautiful cypresses and weeping willows; and in the flower-beds were the narcissus, and rose-bushes of the '*sidburg*', or an hundred leaves. Most of the trees and flowers are indigenous; but many had been introduced from Cashmere, and a native of that valley was the gardener. The proprietor of this pleasant spot was absent: his villa was in disorder, and neglected, since he is suffering from the avarice of his ruler. His son, a sharp boy of nine years old, paid us a visit, and repeated some lines of a Persian poet which he was reading at school. Little fellow! he is growing up to witness scenes of blood, at all events of alteration, in this land.

*   *   *

We reached the banks of the Chenab, or Acesines, at Ramnuggur [Rabwah], a small town, the favourite resort of Runjeet Sing, and where he has often mustered his army when proceeding on his campaigns beyond the Indus. It stands on a spacious plain where he can exercise his troops. We crossed the Chenab by the usual ferry and a journey of forty-five miles brought us to the banks of the Jelum, or the famous Hydaspes of the Greeks. It winds its way through an alluvial plain, at the base of a low rocky range of hills. We embarked upon this fine river, and sailed down with the stream for a distance of five miles. On the voyage we disturbed several crocodiles from the different islands, which are more numerous than in the other Punjab rivers.

[Near the town of Pind Dadun Khan the British party came upon the 'Salt Range', stretching from the Indus to the Jhelum, which contains numerous salt-mines, one of which they visited. While admiring the 'bright and beautiful' crystals of red salt, they were appalled by the 'spectacle of misery' presented by the women, children and old men who dragged the salt to the surface. All of them had breathing problems and 'cadaverous looks'. Burnes was glad to distribute among them some of the money which Runjeet Sing had insisted on giving him. The mines can still be visited today: Khewra is the second-biggest salt-mine in the world.]

At Jelum [the town of Jhelum] the river is divided into five or six channels, and is fordable at all times, except in the monsoon. About fifteen miles below Jelum, near the modern village of Darapoor, we hit upon some extensive ruins called Oodeenuggur, which seem to have been a city that extended for three or four miles. The traditions of the people are vague and unsatisfactory, for they referred us to the deluge, and the time of Noah. Many copper coins are found, but those which were brought to me bore Arabic inscriptions. A slab, with an inscription in that language, which had lately been dug up, was also shown to us; and I learn from M. Court that he found a fluted pillar near this site with a capital very like the Corinthian order. It, however, had a Hindoo figure on it. At present there are no buildings standing; but the ground is strewed with broken pieces of kiln-burnt bricks and pottery, the latter of a superior description. On the opposite side of the Hydaspes to Darapoor stands a mound said to be coeval with Oodeenuggur, where the village of Moong is built, at which I procured two Sanskrit coins. There are likewise some extensive ruins beyond Moong, near Huria Badshapoor. I do not conceive it improbable that Oodeenuggur may represent the site of Nicae, and that the mounds and ruins on the western bank mark the position of Bucephalia. We are told that these cities were built so close to the river that Alexander had to repair them on his return from the Punjab campaign, since they stood within the influence of the inundation. It is to be observed that towns which have an advantageous locality are seldom deserted and, if so, that others rise near them, which will account for the Arabic coins found in the neighbourhood. Alexander is said to have pitched his camp at a distance of 150 stadia from the river, on a plain; and there is an extensive champaign tract behind this very site.

In our search for the remnants of Alexander's cities, we are led into reflections on the state of the country in those days, and it is curious to compare them with our own times. We are informed that Porus, with whom Alexander fought on the banks of this river, maintained a force of 30,000 infantry and 4000 cavalry, with 200 elephants and 300 war chariots, and that he had subdued all his neighbours. Now, if we change the war chariots into guns, we have precisely the regular force of Runjeet Sing, *the modern Porus*, who has likewise overwhelmed all his neighbours. The same country will generally produce the same number of troops, if its population be not reduced by adventitious circumstances.

We quitted the banks of the Jelum, and entered the country of Potewar, inhabited by a tribe of people called Gukers, famed for their beauty, and claiming a Rajpoot origin [Rajput denotes a Hindu military caste from north India]. Our approach to the Mahommedan countries became evident daily, and showed itself in nothing more than the costume of the women, many of whom we now met veiled.

One girl whom we saw on the road had a canopy of red cloth erected over her on horseback, which had a ludicrous appearance. It seemed to be a framework of wood; but as the cloth concealed every thing as well as the countenance of the fair lady, I did not discover the contrivance. The costume of the unveiled portion of the sex had likewise undergone a change; they wore wide blue trousers, tightly tied at the ankle, which taper down, and have a graceful appearance. A narrow web of cloth sixty yards long is sometimes used in a single pair, for one fold falls upon the other.

On the 1st of March we reached the celebrated fort of Rotas [Rohtas], considered to be one of the great bulwarks between Tartary and India. As we wound through the dismal defiles, and might be ruminating on the various expeditions which had traversed this very road, the fort burst upon our view like the scene of a magic lantern. It had been hidden from us by towering precipices. We approached its ponderous walls by a straggling path which time had chiselled in the rock, and soon reached its lofty gateway. The black hoary aspect of the fort, and the arid sterility of the surrounding rocks, inspired us with no favourable idea of the neighbourhood, which has been the resort of many a desperate band. We had omitted to provide ourselves with Runjeet Sing's order for admission into this fortress; but we proceeded to the gateway, as a matter of course, and after a parley the doors were thrown open. The official permission arrived from Lahore on the following day.

We soon found ourselves among friends, and listened to the tales of the veterans without any fear of witnessing the scenes of their ancestors. The Afghan officers of the Mogul empire under the Emperor Humaioon dethroned that monarch, and fortified themselves in Rotas, in the year 1531. Shere Shah was its founder. Twelve years, and some millions of rupees, are said to have been wasted in its construction; yet it was betrayed and fell. Humaioon returned from his wanderings with the auxiliaries of Iran, and recovered the kingdom of his forefathers. He commanded that the fort of Rotas should be levelled; but so massy are its walls, and so strong is the whole edifice, that his Ameers and Oomrahs [grandees] ventured to ask his majesty, whether he came to recover his throne, or destroy a single fort, since the one undertaking would require as much energy as the other. Humaioon contented himself with levelling a palace and a gateway as the monument of his conquest, and prudently marched to Delhi. We examined its walls and outworks, its gateways and bastions; and the people pointed out to us the orifices for pouring oil on the besiegers. We viewed with admiration the elaborate loopholes for the matchlock, the deep wells cut in the live rock, and the bomb-proof magazines of the fortification. From one of the towers we had a commanding view of the plain, in which we could distinguish a spacious caravanserai, the work of the generous and tolerant Akbar. He here eclipsed his father Humaioon as much as he did in all the acts of his protracted reign. The son raised an edifice to shelter the weary traveller in his pilgrimage; the parent, full of wrath, wasted a greater sum in the demolition of a palace. These caravanserais have been erected at every stage as far west as the Indus; and the traveller cannot pass them without a pleasurable feeling at the enlightened design of their founder. The Emperor Akbar was a philanthropist.

[Burnes's party then pressed on towards Rawalpindi through magnificent scenery, stopping to examine an archaeological site at Manikyala which had been partially excavated by some of Ranjeet's French officers. Burnes himself found some small antiquities and carried them away with him, though they were subsequently lost.]

We reached Rawil Pindee on the 7th, and alighted at the house which the ex-King of Cabool built in his exile. It was a miserable hovel. The town of Rawil Pindee is agreeable; and we were pleased to find the mountains covered in snow, and but twelve miles distant. We were now fast leaving Hindoostan and its customs behind us. The dandelion had become a common weed. At Manikyala, we halted next door to a bakery, where the whole bread of the village is baked. How much more sensible is this custom, than that every family should prepare it separately, as in India, and live in perpetual terror of defilement from one another! We were glad to be considered customers of the village oven.

On our road we met a numerous body of Afghans, and also Hindoo pilgrims, crowding from beyond the Indus to the great religious fair of

Hurdwar: they looked more like Mahommedans than the followers of Brahma. The festival occurs every twelve years, and distance serves to increase the devotion of the pilgrim. The sight of these people from beyond the Indus gave rise to many curious sensations. We wore their dress, and they knew us not; we received their salutations as countrymen, and could not participate in their feelings. Some of them would ask, as we passed, whether we were going to Cabool or Candahar; and from their looks and questions, I found many a secret and doubtful thrill pass across me. This I found to arise from the novelty of our situation, for it soon wore off after we mingled familiarly with the people; and, in course of time, I gave and returned the usual salutations with all the indifference of a practised traveller.

About fifteen miles from Rawil Pindee, we passed the defile of Margulla, and descried with joy the mountains beyond the Indus. This is a narrow pass over the low hills, and paved with blocks of stone for 150 yards. A Persian inscription, let into the rock, commemorates the fame of the civilised Emperor who cut the road. The defiles continue for about a mile; when a bridge across a rivulet conducts the traveller to the next caravanserai. A bridge, a caravanserai, and a road cut through a hill, within a distance of two miles, bespeak a different rule from that of the Punjab in modern times. [The Margalla hills are now a national park.] We continued our march to Osman, about twenty miles from Rawil Pindee. It stands on a plain, at the mouth of a valley, close to the base of the outlying hills. Its meadows are watered by the most beautiful and crystal rivulets, that flow from the mountains. Some of them are conducted by artificial means through the village, and turn little water-mills that grind flour. Up the valley stands the fort of Khanpoor, with some beautiful gardens; and over it snow-clad mountains rear their peaks. The fields of this fruitful valley lie neglected, from the exorbitant assessment of the person who farms it. The peasants have no hope of redress but by such an expedient; and this entire suspension of the labours of the husbandmen may open the understanding of the misguided governor.

We visited Osman, which is about four miles from the King's road, at the base of the lower Himalaya, to examine a mound or 'tope', like that of Manikyala, which stands on the nook of a range of hills near the ruined village of Belur, about a mile beyond Osman. The construction of the building gives it to the same era as that of Manikyala. It is fifty feet high, or about two thirds of the height of Manikyala. It has also been opened, and the square aperture formed of cut stone has descended into the building. The small pilasters are likewise to be recognised, but the mouldings are more numerous, and the general outline of the building is somewhat different. The 'tope' of Belur is a conspicuous object, from its elevated situation, but I could not gather a tradition regarding it from the numerous population. Like one in search of the philosopher's stone, I was led from place to place, and now learned that there were two buildings similar to these 'topes', beyond the Indus, between Peshawur and Cabool. We also discovered the ruins of another tope, three miles eastward of Rawil Pindee. The few coins which I found at the tope of Belur were of the same type as those already described. Seeing that both the structures of Manikyala and Belur are pierced by a shaft that descends into the building, I incline to a belief that in these topes we have the tombs of a race of princes who once reigned in Upper India, and that they are either the sepulchres of the Bactrian kings, or their Indo-Scythic successors, mentioned in the Periplus of the second Arrian. The rudeness of the coins would point to the latter age, or second century of the Christian era. [Burnes was not far from the ancient Gandharan capital of Taxila. A century later the surrounding plain – between Rawalpindi and Peshawar – was found to abound with Buddhist sites of enormous archaeological importance.]

From the beautiful rivulets of Osman we passed down the valley, and, after a march of seven miles, found ourselves in the garden of Hoosn Abdall – a spot which attracted the munificent Emperors of Hindoostan. It is situated between two bare and lofty hills, whose brown and naked tops do not contribute much to its beauty; still it must be an enchanting place in the hot months. The garden-houses are now mouldering to decay, and weeds hide the flowers and roses; yet the peach and apricot trees glowed with blossom, vines clung to them, and the limpid water gushed in torrents from the rock. Some hundred springs rise in the limit of this small garden, and, after washing its beds, pay their tribute to a brook which passes on to the Indus. They form pools, which are stored with fish, that may be seen darting about in the clear water. The spring had commenced when we visited this delightful place. As we passed it, our view opened upon the valley of Drumtour, that leads to Cashmere; and the range of hills at Puklee, covered with snow, were to be traced in chain with more lofty mountains beyond them. The fertile plain of Chuch and Huzara also lay before us.

We came in sight of the Indus, at a distance of fifteen miles. It could be traced from its exit through the lower hills to the fort of Attock, by the vapour which hung over it like smoke. As the water of the Indus is much colder than the atmosphere, it may account for this phenomenon. We encamped at Huzroo [Hazro], which is a mart between Peshawur and Lahore. The people were now quite changed; they were Afghans, and spoke Pooshtoo [Pashto]. I was struck by their manly mien, and sat down with delight on a felt, along with an Afghan, who civilly invited me to converse with him. I did not regret to exchange the cringing servility of the Indians for the more free and independent manners of Cabool. An itinerant goldsmith, who had heard of our intended journey to Bokhara, came and chatted with us. He had travelled there, and even in Russia; and he showed us a copper copec which he had brought with him on his return. He spoke of the equity and justice of the people among whom we were to travel, which made this rambling jeweller a welcome visitor. He was a Hindoo.

On the morning of the 14th of March, we had the pleasure of encamping on the banks of the Indus, with the troops of Runjeet Sing, now on the frontier, under Sirdar Huree Sing. That chief came to meet us with all the forms of Eastern pomp, and conducted us to a comfortable suite of tents which he had prepared for us. On our march to the river, we passed the field of battle where the Afghans made their last stand [against the Sikhs], now some twenty years ago, on the eastern side of the Indus.

[The party then proceeded to the fortress of Attock and were eventually ferried across 'the grand boundary of India' on 17th March.]

The water was azure blue, and the current exceeded six miles an hour. We passed in four minutes. About 200 yards above Attock, and before the Indus is joined by the Cabool river, it gushes over a rapid with amazing fury. Its breadth does not here exceed 120 yards; the water is much ruffled, and dashes like the waves and spray of the ocean. It hisses and rolls with a loud noise, and exceeds the rate of ten miles in the hour. A boat cannot live in this tempestuous torrent; but after the Cabool river has joined it, the Indus passes in a tranquil stream, about 260 yards wide and 35 fathoms deep, under the walls of Attock. This fortress is a place of no strength: it has a population of about 2000 souls.

Before crossing the Indus, we observed a singular phenomenon at the fork of the Indus and Cabool river, where an *ignis fatuus* shows itself every evening. Two, three, and even four bright lights are visible at a time, and continue to shine throughout the night, ranging within a few yards of each other. The natives could not account for them, and their continuance during the rainy season is the most inexplicable part of the phenomenon, in their estimation. They tell you that the valiant Man Sing, a Rajpoot, who carried his war of revenge across the Indus, fought a battle in this spot; and that the lights now seen are the spirits of the departed. I should not have credited the constancy of this 'will-o'-the-wisp' had I not seen it. It may arise from the reflection of the water on the rock, smoothed by the current; but then it only shows itself on a particular spot, and the whole bank is smoothed. It may also be an exhalation of some gas from a fissure in the rock; but its position prevented our examining it.

We found the fishermen on the Indus and Cabool river washing the sand for gold. The operation is peformed with most profit after the swell has subsided. The sand is passed through a sieve, and the larger particles that remain are mixed with quicksilver, to which the metal adheres. Some of the minor rivers, such as the Swan and Hurroo, yield more gold than the Indus; and as their sources are not remote, it would show that the ores lie on the southern side of the Himalaya.

CHAPTER III

Peshawur

It required some arrangement to commence our advance into the country of the Afghans; for they and the Seiks entertain the most deep-rooted animosity towards each other. At Attock a friendly letter was sent to us by the chief of Peshawur, expressive of his good wishes. I therefore addressed that personage, Sooltan Mahommed Khan, informing him of our intentions and soliciting his protection. I likewise sent a letter of introduction from Runjeet to the chief of Acora; but so inconstant is power in these countries, that that person had been ejected during the few weeks we had been travelling from Lahore: but the usurper opened the communication, and kindly despatched a party to meet us. The subjects of Runjeet Sing escorted us to the frontier, which is three miles beyond the Indus; here we met the Afghans. Neither party would approach, and we drew up at a distance of about 300 yards of each other. The Seiks gave us their '*wagroojie futtih*', synonymous with our three cheers, and we advanced, and delivered ourselves to the Mahommedans; who said, '*Wuss-sulam alaikoom!* Peace be unto you!' We trod our way to Acora with our new people, the Khuttuks, a lawless race, and alighted at that village, which is nearly deserted, from the constant inroads of the Seiks.

The chief immediately waited upon us, and expressed his dissatisfaction at our having purchased some articles from the bazaar, since it was a reflection on his hospitality. I begged his pardon, and placed the mistake on my ignorance of Afghan customs, adding that I would not forget, as I advanced, the hospitality of the Khuttuks of Acora. The chief took his leave, charging us, before his departure, to consider ourselves as secure as eggs under a hen; a homely enough simile, the truth of which we had no reason to doubt. Yet it was at this place that Mr Moorcroft and his party encountered some serious difficulties, and were obliged to fight their way. We here received a

114

second and most friendly letter from the chief of Peshawur, which was truly satisfactory, since it had been written before he had got any of the letters of introduction which we forwarded. It intimated that a person was approaching to conduct us.

We had now quitted the territories of Hindoostan, and entered on a land where covetousness of a neighbour's goods is the ruling passion: we therefore marched with our baggage. Our few servants were also divided into regular watches for the night. We had two Afghans, two Indians, and two natives of Cashmere. A Cashmerian paired with an Indian, and the trustworthy with the most lazy, while we ourselves superintended the posting of the sentries. Our people laughed heartily at this military disposition, but it was ever after enforced in all our travels. We ourselves were now living as natives, and had ceased to repine at the hardness of the ground and the miserable hovels in which we sometimes halted. I had also disposed of my valuables in what then appeared to me a masterly manner: a letter of credit for five thousand rupees was fastened to my left arm, in the way that the Asiatics wear amulets. My polyglot passport was fixed to my right arm, and a bag of ducats was tied round my waist. I also distributed a part of my ready money to each of the servants, and so perfect was the check that had been established over them, that we never lost a single ducat in all our journey, and found most faithful servants in men who might have ruined and betrayed us. We trusted them, and they rewarded our confidence. One man, Ghoolam Hoosn, a native of Surat, followed me throughout the whole journey, cooked our food, and never uttered a complaint at the performance of such duties, foreign as they were to his engagements. He is now with me in England.

On our road to Acora, we passed a field of battle, at the small village of Sydoo where, it is said, 8000 Seiks had defended themselves against an enraged population of 150,000 Mahommedans. Bood Sing, their commander, threw up a small breastwork of loose stones, and extricated himself from his dilemma, so as to secure the praise even of his enemies. We now saw the place, and the bleaching bones of the horses which had fallen on the occasion. On the next march we passed the more celebrated field of Noushero [Nowshera], to which our attention had been directed by Runjeet Sing himself. Here he encountered the Afghans for the last time; but their chief, Azeem Khan, was separated from the greater part of his army by the river of Cabool. The Seiks defeated the divisions on the opposite side, mainly through the personal courage of Runjeet Sing, who carried a hillock with his guards, from which his other troops had three times retreated. Azeem Khan, of Cabool, fled without encountering the successful army, which had partly crossed the river to oppose him. It is believed that he feared the capture of his treasure, which would have fallen into Runjeet's power if he had advanced; but it is also said that he was terrified by the shouts of the Seiks on the night of their victory. He attributed their exclamations to the fresh arrival of troops: for they have a custom of shouting on such occasions.

As we traversed the plain to Peshawur, I felt elevated and happy. Thyme and violets perfumed the air, and the green sod and clover put us in mind of our native home. At Peerpaee, which is a march from Peshawur, we were joined by six horsemen, whom the chief sent to escort us. We saddled at sunrise, though it rained heavily, and accompanied the party to the city, trying sorely the patience of the horsemen by declining to halt half way, that they might give timely information of our approach. We pushed on till near the city, when their persuasion could be no longer resisted. 'The chief sent us to welcome you, and has ordered his son to meet you outside the city,' said their commander, 'and we are now within a few hundred yards of his house.'

We halted, and in a few minutes the eldest son of the chief made his appearance, attended by an elephant and a body of horse. He was a handsome boy, about twelve years old, and dressed in a blue tunic, with a Cashmere shawl as a turban. We dismounted on the high road and embraced; when the youth immediately conducted us to the presence of his father. Never were people received with more kindness: he met us in person at the doorway, and led us inside of an apartment, studded with mirror glass and daubed over with paint in exceedingly bad taste. His house, his country, his property, his all, were ours; he was the ally of the British government, and he had shown it by his kindness to Mr Moorcroft, which he considered as a treaty of friendship. We were not the persons who wished to infringe its articles. Sooltan Mahommed Khan is about thirty-five years old, rather tall in stature, and of dark complexion. He was dressed in a pelisse, trimmed with fur and the down of the peacock, which had a richer look than the furniture that surrounded him. We were glad to withdraw and change our wet clothes, and were conducted to the seraglio of Sooltan Mahommed Khan, which he had prepared, *I need not add, emptied*, for our reception. This was, indeed, a kind of welcome we had not anticipated.

An hour had not passed before we were visited by Peer Mohammed Khan, the younger brother of the chief, a jolly and agreeable person. The chief himself followed in the course of the evening, and a sumptuous dinner succeeded, of which we all partook. We ate with our hands, and soon ceased to wonder at a nobleman tearing a lamb in pieces and selecting the choice bits, which he held out for our acceptance. A long roll of leavened bread was spread in front of each of us as a plate and, as its size diminished as the meat disappeared, it did its part well. Pilaos and stews, sweets and sours, filled the trays, but the bonne bouche of the day was a lamb that had never tasted aught but milk. A bitter orange had been squeezed over it, and made it very savoury. Four trays of sweetmeats followed, with fruit, and the repast concluded with sherbet mixed with snow, the sight of which delighted us as much as our new friends. A watch of night was spent before we broke up, and after the chief had repeated in a whisper his devotion to our nation and anxiety for our welfare, he bade us good night. I had almost lost the use of my legs from the irksome position of constraint in which I had so long sat. If we had been prepared to like the manners of this people, there was much to confirm it this evening.

On the following day we were introduced to the remainder of the family. There are two brothers besides the chief, and a host of sons and relations. The most remarkable person of the family was a son of Futtih Khan, the Vizier of Shah Mahmood, who had been so basely and cruelly murdered. The lad is about fourteen years of age, and the solitary descendant of his ill-fated father. The sons of the Meer Waeez and Mookhtar-o-doula, who had dethroned Shah Shooja, were among the party, and the day passed most agreeably. The people were sociable and well-informed, free from prejudice on points of religion, and many of them were well versed in Asiatic history. They were always cheerful, and frequently noisy in their good-humour. During the conversation many of them rose up and prayed in the room when the stated hours arrived. As we got better acquainted in Peshawur, our circle of acquaintances was widely extended, and visitors would drop in at all hours, and more particularly if they found us alone. The Afghans never sit by themselves, and always made some apology if they found any of us solitary, though it would have been sometimes agreeable to continue so.

[In the afternoon the chief took his guests to see the sights of Peshawar. Burnes says nothing about the town itself, as it had already been exhaustively described by Mr Elphinstone in his 'valuable work', but he clearly enjoyed the expedition.]

I had accompanied the chief on a day most favourable to a stranger, the 'nouroz' or new year (the 21st of March), which is celebrated by the people. The greater part of the community were gathered in gardens, and paraded about with nosegays and bunches of peach-blossom. We entered the garden of Ali Murdan Khan and, seating ourselves on the top of the garden-house, looked down upon the assembled multitude. The trees were covered with blossom, and nothing could be more beautiful than the surrounding scene. The chief and his brothers took great pains to point out the neighbouring hills to me, explaining by whom they were inhabited, with every other particular which they thought might interest.

We soon got accustomed to our new mode of life and, as we made it a rule never on any occasion to write during the day, or in public, had leisure to receive every person who came to see us. In a short time we became acquainted with the whole society of Peshawur and, during the thirty days we remained there, had an uninterrupted series of visiting and feasting. Nothing, however, more contributed to our comfort and happiness than the kindness of our worthy host. Sooltan Mahommed Khan was not the illiterate Afghan whom I expected to find, but an educated and well-bred gentleman, whose open and affable manner made the most lasting impression. He is a person more remarkable for his urbanity than his wisdom, but he transacts all his own business; he is a brave soldier; his seraglio has about thirty inmates, and he has already had a family of sixty children.

[Burnes had the opportunity of seeing the chief play affectionately with his children when the whole family went out to a neighbouring garden on the Friday. The little boys, all under the age of five, sat expertly on horseback, 'for the Dooranees are taught to ride from infancy'.]

The chief's retinue consisted of his relations and servants: he had no guards, and at our first starting, was only accompanied by ourselves and two horsemen. There is a simplicity and freedom about these people greatly to be admired and, whatever the rule may be, I can at least vouch for petitioners having an ear given to their complaints. Every one seems on an equality with the chief, and the meanest servant addresses him without ceremony. He himself seems quite free from every sort of pride or affectation, and is only to be distinguished in the crowd by his dress, in which he is fond of richness and ornament.

In one of our rides about Peshawur with the chief we had a specimen of justice and Mahommedan retribution. As we passed the suburbs of the city we discovered a crowd of people and, on a nearer approach, saw the mangled bodies of a man and woman, the former not quite dead, lying on a dunghill. The crowd instantly surrounded the chief and our party, and one person stepped forward and represented, in a trembling attitude, to Sooltan Mahommed Khan that he had discovered his wife in an act of infidelity, and had put both parties to death. He held the bloody sword in his hands, and described how he had committed the deed. His wife was pregnant, and already the mother of three children. The chief asked a few questions, which did not occupy him three minutes: he then said in a loud voice, 'You have acted the part of a good Mahommedan, and performed a justifiable act.' He then moved on, and the crowd cried out 'Bravo!' ('Afreen!') The man was immediately set at liberty. We stood by the chief during the investigation and, when it finished, he turned to me and carefully explained the law. 'Guilt,' added he, 'committed on a Friday, is sure to be discovered,' for that happened to be the day on which it occurred. There is nothing new in these facts, but as an European I felt my blood run chill when I looked on the mangled bodies, and heard the husband justifying the murder of her who had borne him three children.

We were invited, shortly after our arrival at Peshawur, to pass a day with the chief's brother, Peer Mahommed Khan. He received us in a garden, under a bower of fruit trees, loaded with blossom. Carpets were spread, and before we sat down the boughs were shaken, which covered them with the variegated leaves of the apricot and peach. The fragrance and beauty were equally delightful. The children of the chief and his brothers were again present: they rioted among the confectionery, and four of them had a pitched battle with the blossom of the trees, which they threw at each other like snow. I do not remember to have seen any place more delightful than Peshawur at this season: the climate, garden and landscape delight the senses, and to all we had been so fortunate as to add the hospitality of the people.

I had brought no presents to conciliate these men, and I would therefore receive none at their hands, but on the present occasion, our host produced a small horse, of a hill breed, and insisted on my receiving it. 'Mr Moorcroft,' said he, 'accepted one of these same horses, which availed him in his difficulties, and I cannot therefore take a refusal, since you are entering such dangerous countries.' The horse was forcibly sent to my house. The sequel will show the strange Providence which is sometimes to be traced in the acts of man.

But our residence at the house of the chief was not without inconvenience, and it required some consideration to devise a plan for our extrication with credit. The chief of Peshawur was at enmity with his brother of Cabool, and wished to persuade us to pass through that city by stealth, and without seeing him. He offered, indeed, to send a Persian gentleman as our conductor beyond Afghanistan and, had I believed the arrangement practicable, I would have rejoiced. But it was obviously difficult to pass through the city of Cabool and the country of its chief without his knowledge, and a discovery of such an attempt might bring down upon us the wrath of a man from whom we had nothing to fear by openly avowing ourselves as British officers. I was resolved, therefore, to trust the chief of Cabool as I had trusted his brother of Peshawur, so soon as I could persuade Sooltan Mahommed Khan that our intercourse there should never diminish the regard which we felt for him personally.

In a few days he consented to our writing to Cabool and notifying our approach to Nuwab Jubbar Khan, the brother of the governor, whom I addressed under a new seal, cut after the manner of the country, and bearing the name of 'Sikunder Burnes'. Sooltan Mahommed Khan now confined himself to advice, and such good offices as would conduct us in safety beyond his dominions. He requested that we might still further change our dress, which we did, and left it as the best sign of our poverty. The outer garment which I wore cost me a rupee and a half, ready made, in the bazaar. We also resolved to conceal our character as Europeans from the common people, though we should frankly avow to every chief, and indeed every individual with whom we might come into contact, our true character. But our compliance with this counsel subjected us to the strongest importunities to avoid Toorkistan, and pass by the route of Candahar, into Persia. Nothing could save us from the *ferocious* and man-selling Uzbeks; the country, the people, everything was bad. They judged of the calamities of Moorcroft and his associates, and I listened in silence. The chief thought that he had so far worked upon us to abandon the design, that he prepared various letters for Candahar, and a particular introduction to his brother, who is chief of that place.

* * *

Among our visitors, none came more frequently than the sons of the chief and his brothers, and none were more welcome, for they displayed great intelligence and address. Nearly the whole of them were suffering from intermittent fever, that was soon cured by a few doses of quinine, of which we had a large supply. The knowledge exhibited by these little fellows induced me on one occasion to note their conversation. There were four of them present, and none had attained his twelfth year. I interrogated them, as they sat round me, on the good qualities of Cabool, giving to each two answers. They replied as follows: 1. The salubrity of the climate; 2. The flavour of the fruit; 3. The beauty of the people; 4. The handsome bazaar; 5. The citadel of the Balar Hissar; 6. The justice of the ruler; 7. The pomegranates without seed; and 8. Its incomparable '*ruwash*', or rhubarb. Four answers to its bad qualities gave the following information: 1. Food is expensive; 2. The houses cannot be kept in repair without constantly removing the snow from the roof; 3. The floods of the river dirty the streets; and 4. The immorality of the fair sex, which last is a proverb. It does not appear to me that boys in Europe show such precocity, and it is no doubt attributable to their earlier introduction into the society of grown up people. When a boy has arrived at his twelfth year, a separate establishment is maintained here on his account, and long before that time of life, he is prohibited from frequenting his mother's apartments but on certain occasions. Khoju Mahommed, the eldest son of the chief, came one day to invite us to dinner, and I expressed some surprise to hear that he had a house of his own. 'What!' replied the youth, 'would you have me imbibe the disposition of a woman, when I am the son of a Dooranee?'

As the time of our departure drew near, we had nothing but a continued succession of feasting. We dined with all the chiefs and many of their sons, with priests and Meerzas. Among the most pleasant of our parties was one given by Moollah Nujeeb, a worthy man, who had made an enterprising journey into the Kaffir country [the Swat valley, south-east of Chitral] at the suggestion of Mr Elphinstone, and for which he enjoys and merits a pension. He gave us good counsel and showed much interest in our behalf, but strongly dissuaded us from entertaining a holy person as our guide, on which I had resolved. The Uzbeks are described to be much under the influence of their priests and Syuds, and I thought that the company of one might avail us on an occasion of difficulty, since Moorcroft had entirely trusted to one of them, who is now in Peshawur. Moollah Nujeeb assured me, on the other hand, that such a person could never extricate us from any difficulties, and would publish our approach every where; and he further insinuated that many of the disasters which had befallen the unfortunate Moorcroft were to be attributed to one of these worthies. Such advice from one who was a priest himself deserved notice, and I afterwards ascertained the justness of the Moollah's views.

It was, however, necessary to conciliate the holy man to whom I have alluded, and I visited him. His name was Fuzil Huq, and he boasts a horde of disciples towards Bokhara, nearly as numerous as the inhabitants. Your safety, he said, will depend on your laying aside the name of European, at all events of Englishman; for the natives of those countries believe the English to be political intriguers, and to possess boundless wealth. Common sense and reflection suggested a similar line of conduct, but the performance was more difficult. The saint prepared his epistles, which he sent to us. They were addressed to the king of Bokhara and the chiefs on the Oxus, five in number, who owned him as their spiritual guide. We were described as 'poor blind travellers' who are entitled to protection from all members of the faithful. They abounded in extracts from the Koran, with many moral aphorisms enlisted for the occasion on our behalf. The saint, however, made a request that we should not produce these letters unless an absolute necessity compelled us; but I looked upon them as very valuable documents. I had many misgivings about him, for he is not without suspicion of having increased Moorcroft's troubles, and it is certain that the family of one of his disciples was enriched by the wealth of that ill-fated traveller. He, however, possesses documents which lead me to acquit him of every thing; yet I would rather avoid than court the man, and rather please than displease him.

Among other advice we were strongly recommended to desist from giving medicines to the people, for it had already rallied round the doctor some hundreds of patients, and would sound the tocsin of our approach as we advanced. I had thought that the medical character would have been our passport, and to adventurers I do not doubt its advantage; but our only object being to pass through in safety, it became a subject of great doubt if it should be maintained at all.

A month had now elapsed since we arrived at Peshawur and the rapid approach of the hot weather admonished us that we need not much longer fear the snows of Cabool and Hindoo Koosh. All was therefore bustle for our departure, and our movements were accelerated by the arrival of a letter from Cabool, which begged us to advance without delay. Yet it was no easy matter to bring the chief to pronounce our leave, which was fixed for the 19th of April, after much procrastination.

CHAPTER IV

Journey to Cabool

There are five different roads to Cabool, but we chose that which leads by the river, since the pass of Khyber is unsafe from the lawless habits of the people; and we therefore crossed the beautiful plain of Peshawur to Muchnee. At the city we had become intimate with one of the hill chiefs, who urged us to take the Khyber route, but no one trusts a Khyberee and it was not deemed prudent. We crossed the river of Cabool above Muchnee on a raft, which was supported on inflated skins and but a frail and unsafe mode of transport. The river is only 250 yards wide, but runs with such rapidity that we were carried more than a mile down before gaining the opposite bank. The horses and baggage ponies swam across. Muchnee is a straggling village, at the gorge of the valley where the Cabool river enters the plain.

On the 23rd of April we had adjusted all matters for our advance by conciliating the Momunds, a plundering tribe somewhat less ferocious than their neighbours of Khyber, through whose country we were to pass. They demanded half a rupee of every Mahommedan, and double the sum of a Hindoo, but much less satisfied them, though they quarrelled about its distribution. We commenced our march by scrambling over hills and rocks, and were soon satisfied of the influence of our friends as we met some individual passengers, escorted by mere children, whose tribe was a sufficient protection for them. After a fatiguing march over mountain passes we found ourselves on the Cabool river, which was to be crossed a second time. We had now a full insight into our mode of travelling, and the treatment which we were to expect. We never moved but in a body, and when we got to the banks of the river under a scorching sun, had no means of crossing it till our friends the Momunds could be again appeased. Towards afternoon our highlanders produced eight or ten skins, and we commenced crossing; but it was night before we had all passed, and we then set fire to the grass of the mountains to illuminate our neighbourhood and ensure safety to the frail raft. The passage of the river was tedious and difficult: in some places the rapidity of the stream, formed into eddies, wheeled us round, and we had the agreeable satisfaction of being told that, if we went some way down, there was a whirlpool and, if once enclosed in its circle, we might revolve in hunger and giddyness for a day. This inconvenience we all escaped, though some of the passengers were carried far down the river, and we ourselves had various revolutions in the smaller eddies. There was no village or people on either side of the river, and we spread our carpets on the ground and heartily enjoyed a cool night after the day's fatigue. The noise of the stream soon lulled most of us to sleep, and towards midnight nothing was to be heard but the voices of the mountaineers, who had perched themselves on a rock that projected over our camp, and watched till daylight. A truly cut-throat band they appeared, and it was amusing to observe the studied respect which all of us paid them.

After an exposure of about eight hours to a powerful sun, on the following morning we reached Duka by a rocky and difficult road and pushed on, in the afternoon, to Huzarnow, a journey of upwards of twenty miles. On reaching Duka, we had surmounted the chief part of our difficulties on the road to Cabool. The view from the top of a mountain pass, before we descended into the valley of the Cabool river, was very magnificent. We could see the town of Julalabad [Jalallabad], forty miles distant, and the river winding its way in a snaky course through the plain, and dividing it into innumerable fertile islands as it passed. The Sufued Koh, or white mountain, reared its crest on one side, and the towering hill of Noorgil or Kooner on the other. Here the Afghans believe the ark of Noah to have rested after the deluge, and this Mount Ararat of Afghanistan, from its great height, is certainly worthy of the distinction: it is covered with perpetual snow.

At Muchnee the hills are sandstone: on the tops of the passes there are veins of quartz. On the bed of the Cabool river the rocks are granite; and over the village of Duka the formation is mica, which occurs in vertical strata. A sweet aromatic smell was exhaled from the grass and plants. One shrub looked very like broom; another resembled the flower-de-luce, and supplies the people with mats to build their huts as well as sandals for their feet, to which they are fixed by a string of the same material. Our thirst and fatigue were much relieved by a plant of the sorrel kind, which we found most grateful, and gathered and ate as we climbed over the hills. The pasture is here favourable to cattle, and the mutton used in Peshawur owes its flavour to it.

Before leaving Duka we had a visit from the chief of the Momunds, Sadut Khan of Lalpoor, a handsome man of about thirty, with a good-humoured countenance. We sat under a mulberry tree on a cot or bed for half an hour; he pressed us much to cross the river and become his guests for a few days, when he would entertain and amuse us with his hawks, some of which were carried by his attendants. We declined his civilities on the excuse of our journey. I afterwards learned that this smiling Momund had raised himself to the chiefship of his clan by murdering two young nephews with their mother.

At Huzarnow we met a Khyberee with whom we had some acquaintance in the Punjab, where he had served as a *hirkaru*, or messenger, to Runjeet Sing. Immediately he heard of our arrival, he made his appearance, and catching me by the feet and then by the beard, intimated, in the little Persian which he could speak, that we were his guests and must occupy his house in the village, which we gladly accepted. He was a most uncouth looking being, with a low brow and sunken eyes. He had two sons, neither of whom he had seen for fourteen years, till within a few days of our arrival. He had, nevertheless, twice carried expresses to Cabool; and though he had passed his native village and home, he had never stopped to make an enquiry. He had now returned for good to his country.

After a fatiguing march of twelve hours on the saddle, three of which were spent in waiting for stragglers, we reached Julalabad on the morning of the 26th. Our route lay through a wide stony waste, a part of which is known by the name of the 'dusht' or plain of Butteecote, and famed for the pestilential wind or 'simoom' that prevails here in the hot season, though the mountains on both sides are covered with perpetual snow. The natives of this country describe the simoom as generally fatal. Travellers who have recovered say that it attacks them like dry wind, which makes them senseless. Horses and animals are subject to the simoom as well as man; and the flesh of those who fall victims to it is said to become so soft and putrid that the limbs separate from each other, and the hair may be pulled out with the least force.

We were not travelling in the season of hot and pestilential winds, but on this march we encountered one of these storms of wind and dust which are common in countries near the tropic. In the present instance, it was attended with rather a curious phenomenon: clouds of dust approached each other from *opposite* sides of the compass and, when they met, took quite a different direction. It is perhaps to be accounted for by the eddy of the wind in a low plain, about twelve or fifteen miles broad, with lofty mountains on either side. Julalabad, we found, had been deluged with rain, which we had entirely escaped.

In a hill north of the Cabool river and the village of Bussoul, we observed some extensive excavations in the rock, which are ascribed to the days of the Kaffirs, or infidels. These caves were hewn out in groups, the entrance to each being separate, and about the size of a common doorway. They may have formed so many villages, since it appears to have been common throughout Asia to dwell in such excavated places. Near Julalabad there are seven round towers, but they differ in construction from the 'topes' which I have described. They are said to be ancient and very large; copper coins are found near them. In the country of Lughman, between Julalabad and the mountains, the people point out the tomb of Metur Lam, or Lamech, the father of Noah.

We halted for a couple of days at Julalabad, which is one of the filthiest places I have seen in the East. It is a small town, with a bazaar of fifty shops and a population of about 2000 people; but its number increases tenfold in the cold season, as the people flock to it from the surrounding hills. The Cabool river passes a quarter of a mile north of the town, and is about 150 yards wide: it is not fordable. There are mountains of snow to the north and south of Julalabad that run parallel with each other. The southern range is called Sufued Koh, but more frequently Rajgul. To the north of Julalabad lies the famous Noorgil, before mentioned, about thirty miles distant, and to the north-west the lofty peaks of Hindoo Koosh begin to show themselves.

We left the river of Cabool and passed up a valley to Bala-bagh, and could now distinguish the rich gardens under the snowy hills, that produce the famous pomegranates without seed, which are exported to India. We halted in a vineyard. The vines of this country are not cut or pruned, but allowed to ascend the highest trees, and were growing at Bala-bagh on lilyoaks, about eighty feet from the ground. The grapes so produced are inferior to those reared on a framework. It rained at Bala-bagh, and our quarters were more romantic than comfortable; which led us at dusk to seek for shelter in the mosque. The people seemed too busy in the exercise of religious and worldly matters to mind us, and as yet we had not experienced the slightest incivility from any person in the country, though we strolled about every where. They do not appear to have the smallest prejudice against a Christian; and I had never heard from their lips the name of dog or infidel which figures so prominently in the works of many travellers. 'Every country has its customs' is a proverb among them, and the Afghan Mahommedans seem to pay a respect to Christians which they deny to their Hindoo fellow-citizens. Us they call 'people of the book', while they consider them benighted and without a prophet.

At Gundamuk [Gandomak] we reached the boundary of the hot and cold countries. It is said to snow on one side of the rivulet and to rain on the other. Vegetable life assumes a new form: the wheat, which was being cut at Julalabad, was only three inches above ground at Gundamuk. The distance does not exceed twenty-five miles. In the fields we discovered white daisies among the clover, and the mountains, which were but ten miles distant, were covered with forests of pine, that commenced about a thousand feet below the limit of the snow; we required additional clothing in the keen air. Travellers are subject to a variety of little troubles, which amuse or try the temper, according to the disposition of the moment. A cat possessed itself of my dinner this evening, as I was about to swallow it, yet I satisfied the cravings of a hungry appetite with bread and water which, I may add, was ate in a filthy stable; but we were fortunate in getting such accommodation. I beg to add my praise of the bread of this country, which they leaven, and bake much to the palate.

About three miles from Gundamuk we passed the garden of Neemla, celebrated for the field of battle in which Shah Shooja-ool-Mulk lost his crown, in the year 1809. It is a beautiful spot, but is ill-chosen for a battle, and the fortune of war was here strangely capricious. Shooja lost his throne and his vizier, sustaining a defeat from an army ten times inferior to his own. Never dreading such a result, he had brought his jewels and his wealth along with him, which he was happy to relinquish for his life. Futteh Khan, the vizier of Mahmood, who succeeded in gaining the day for his master, seated him on one of the state elephants, which had been prepared for the king, and took this mode to proclaim his victory. Shooja fled to the Khyber country, and has since failed in all his attempts to regain his kingdom.

We continued our march to Jugduluk and passed a Soorkh road, or red river, by a bridge, with a variety of other small streams which pour the melted snow of the Sufued Koh into that rivulet. The waters of all of them were reddish: hence the name. The country is barren and miserable. Jugduluk is a wretched place, with a few caves for a village. There is a proverb which describes its misery: 'When the wood of Jugduluk begins to burn, you melt gold' – for there is no wood at hand in the bleak hills. We halted under a grove of trees, which is memorable as the spot where Shah Zuman, one of the kings of Cabool, was blinded [by his brother and successor].

On our way we could distinguish that the road had once been made, and also the remains of the post-houses which had been constructed every five or six miles by the Mogul emperors, to keep up a communication between Delhi and Cabool. They may even be traced across the mountains to Balkh; for both Humaioon and Aurangzebe, in their youth, were governors of that country. What an opinion does this inspire of the grandeur of the Mogul empire! We have a system of communication between the most distant provinces as perfect as the posts of the caesars.

On our way to Cabool we met thousands of sheep tended by the wandering Ghiljees, a tribe of Afghans, who now that the snow was off the ground, were driving their flocks towards Hindoo Koosh, where they pass the summer. Nothing could be more pastoral. The grown up people followed the sheep as they browsed on the margin of the hills, and the boys and girls came up about a mile or two in rear, in charge of the young lambs. An old goat or sheep encouraged them to advance, and the young people assisted with switches of grass and such ejaculations as they could raise. Some of the children were so young that they could hardly walk, but the delight of the sport enticed them on. On the margin of the road we passed many encampments, where they were either moving or packing up. The Afghans have a low black, or rather brown, tent. The women did everything for their lazy husbands, loaded the camels and drove them on; they are indeed swarthy dames, not very remarkable for beauty, with all their Arcadian life. They are well clad, and shod with broad iron nails fixed to their soles. The children were uncommonly healthy and chubby. It is said that these wandering people do not marry till they reach their twentieth year.

After passing the Soorkh road, we reached Ispahan, a village that marks another of Shooja's defeats, but before he gained the throne. A story is told of the vizier Futteh Khan, who was afraid of being supplanted on this field of battle by the Dooranee nobleman who aspired to the office of vizier. This individual, whose name was Meer Alum, had on a former occasion insulted Futteh Khan, and even knocked out one of his front teeth. The injury had to all appearance been forgiven, for he had since married a sister of the vizier; but the alliance had only been formed that Futteh Khan might easier accomplish his base intentions. The night before the battle he seized upon his brother-in-law and put him to death. A heap of stones, here called a 'toda', marks the scene of the murder. The vizier's sister threw herself at her brother's feet, and asked why he had murdered her husband? 'What!' said he, 'have you more regard for your husband than your brother's honour? Look at my broken teeth, and know that the insult is now avenged. If you are in grief at the loss of a husband, I'll marry you to a mule-driver.' This incident is not a bad illustration of the boisterous manners and feelings of the Afghans. A saying among them tells one to fear the more, when an apparent reconciliation has taken place by an intermarriage.

By midnight on the 30th, we reached the pass of Luta-bund, from the top of which the city of Cabool first becomes visible, at a distance of twenty-five miles. The pass is about six miles long, and the road runs over loose round stones. We lay down at a spring called Koke Chushmu, or the Partridge Fountain, and slept without shelter through a bitterly cold night. Our conductor's hawks died from its effects, to his great grief. *Luta* means a shred or patch, and this pass is so called from most travellers leaving some shred of their clothes on the bushes in the pass. In the winter the snow blocks up this road.

We rose with the morning star and prosecuted our journey to Cabool, which we did not reach till the afternoon. The approach to this celebrated city is anything but imposing; nor was it till under the shade of its fine bazar that I believed myself in the capital of an empire. At Cabool we proceeded straight to the house of the Nawab Jubbar Khan, the brother of the governor, who gave us a cordial welcome and sent to the bazar for a dinner, which I enjoyed. Not so my unfortunate companion, whose health forsook him immediately after crossing the Indus; his strength was now completely under-mined. A doubt now arose as to the examination of our baggage at the custom-house, but I judged it more prudent to exhibit our poverty than allow the good people to form designs against our supposed wealth. We were not, however, prepared for the search, and my sextant and books, with the doctor's few bottles and boxes, were laid out in state for the inspection of the citizens. They did them no harm, but set us down without doubt as conjurors, after a display of such unintelligible apparatus.

Our worthy conductor, after he had safely delivered us into the hands of the Nawab, took his leave to enjoy his native city, which he had not seen for eight years. Mahommed Shureef was what might be termed a good fellow. Though but a young man, he had been a merchant and realised a fortune, which he now enjoyed in hunting and hawking, with 'a cup of good sack'. He was corpulent and dropsical but might be seen every morning with his hawks and pointer at his heels. He kept his revels more secretly. I never saw a boy more delighted than was this person as we entered Cabool: had it been Elysium he could not have said more in its praise. He had been a most companionable traveller, and added the address of a Persian to the warmth and good feeling of an Afghan. An incident occurred on our entering Cabool which would have delighted other men than him. A beggar had found out who he was, and within half a mile of the city gate began to call down every blessing on his head, and welcomed him by name to his home, in a strain of great adulation. 'Give the poor man some money,' said Mahommed Shureef to his servant, with a significant nod of the head; and it would have been a difficult matter to determine whether the merchant or the beggar seemed most delighted. Our conductor then bade us adieu, with a recommendation that we should trust any body but those who volunteered their services, as he did not give his countrymen credit for a high standard of morality. He exacted a promise that we would dine with him, and I thanked him for his advice and attentions.

CHAPTER V

Cabool

We had not been many hours in Cabool before we heard of the misfortunes of Mr Wolff, the missionary of the Jews, who was now detained at a neighbouring village. We lost no time in despatching assistance to him. He joined us the following day, and gave a long and singular account of his escape from death and slavery. This gentleman, it appears, had issued forth, like another Benjamin of Tudela, to inquire after the Israelites, and entered Tartary as a Jew, which is the best travelling character in a Mahommedan country. Mr Wolff, however, is a convert to Christianity, and he published his creed to the wreck of the Hebrew people. He also gave himself out as being in search of the lost tribes; yet he made but few inquiries among the Afghans of Cabool, though they declare themselves to be their descendants. The narration of Mr Wolff's adventures excited our sympathy and compassion: and, if we could not coincide in many of his speculations regarding the termination of the world, we made the reverend gentleman most welcome, and found him an addition to our society in Cabool. He had been in Bokhara, but had not ventured to preach in that centre of Islam. His after misfortunes had originated from his denominating himself a Hajee, which implies a *Mohammedan* pilgrim, and for which he had been plundered and beaten.

We had previously heard of the amiable character of our host, Nawab Jubbar Khan, and even found him, on personal acquaintance, to be quite a patriarch. He heals every difference among his many and turbulent brothers: himself the eldest of his family, he entertains no ambitious views, though he once held the government of Cashmere and other provinces of the Dooranee empire (Nawab is an Indian title). His brother, the present chief of Cabool, has requited many services by confiscating his estate; but he speaks not of his ingratitude. He tells you that God has bestowed on him abundance for his wants, and to reward those who serve him; that there are few pleasures equal to being able to give to those around, and to enjoy this world without being obliged to govern. I discovered, during my stay at Cabool, that the Nawab assumes no false character, but expresses himself, as he feels, with sincerity. Never was a man more modest, and more beloved. He will permit but a single attendant to follow him, and the people on the high and by ways stop to bless him; the politicians assail him at home to enter into intrigues, and he yet possesses the respect of the whole community and has, at the present moment, a greater moral influence than any of the Barukzye family in Afghanistan. His manners are remarkably mild and pleasing, and from his dress one would not imagine him to be an influential member of a warlike family. It is delightful to be in his society, to witness his acts, and hear his conversation. He is particularly partial to Europeans, and makes every one of them his guest who enters Cabool. All the French officers in passing to the Punjab lived with him, and still keep up a friendly intercourse. Such is the patriarch of Cabool; he is now about fifty years of age; and such the master of the house in which we were so fortunate as to dwell.

Our first object, after arrival, was to be introduced to the chief of Cabool, Sirdar Dost Mahommed Khan. The Nawab intimated our wishes, and we were very politely invited to dine with the governor on the evening of the 4th of May. Dr Gerard was unable to attend from sickness, but Mr Wolff and myself were conducted, in the evening, to the Bala Hissar, or Palace of the Kings, where the governor received us most courteously. He rose on our entrance, saluted in the Persian fashion, and then desired us to be seated on a velvet carpet near himself. He assured us that we were welcome to his country and, though he had seen few of us, he respected our nation and character. To this I replied as civilly as I could, praising the equity of his government, and the protection which he extended to the traveller and the merchant. When we sat down, we found our party to consist of six or eight native gentlemen, and three sons of the chief.

We occupied a small but neat apartment, which had no other furniture than the carpet. The conversation of the evening was varied, and embraced so many topics that I find it difficult to detail them, such was the knowledge, intelligence and curiosity that the chief displayed. He was anxious to know the state of Europe, the number of kings, the terms on which they lived with one another and, since it appeared that their territories were adjacent, how they existed without destroying each other. I named the different nations, sketched out their relative power, and informed him that our advancement in civilisation did no more exempt us from war and quarrels than his own country, that we viewed each other's acts with jealousy, and endeavoured to maintain a balance of power, to prevent one king from overturning another. Of this, however, there were, I added, various instances in European history, and the chief himself had heard of Napoleon. He next requested me to inform him of the revenues of England: how they were collected, how the laws were enacted, and what were the productions of the soil. He perfectly comprehended our constitution after a brief explanation, and said that there was nothing wonderful in our universal success, since the only revenue which we drew from the people was to defray the debts and expenses of the state. 'Your wealth, then,' added he, 'must come from India.' I assured him that the revenues of that country were spent in it; that the sole benefits derived from its possession consisted in its being an outlet to our commerce; and that the only wealth sent to the mother country amounted to a few hundred thousand pounds, in addition to the fortunes taken away by the servants of the government. I never met an Asiatic who credited this fact before. Dost Mahommed Khan observed, 'This satisfactorily accounts for the subjection of India. You have left much of its wealth to the native princes, you have not had to encounter their despair, and you are just in your courts.' He enquired into the state of the Mahommedan principalities in India, and the exact power of Runjeet Singh, for sparing whose country he gave us no credit. He wished to know if we had any designs upon Cabool.

[There seemed to be no end to the Khan's curiosity about the world, for he also quizzed Burnes on the method of recruiting to the army, on steam-engines and other items of European machinery, on western music, and foundling hospitals, and asked him what he

Dost Mahommed

knew about China. He finished by asking his guest which of the cities in 'Hindustan' he most admired, to which Burnes replied: Delhi.]

From these matters he turned to those which concerned myself; asked why I had left India, and the reasons for changing my dress. I informed him that I had a great desire to see foreign countries, and I now purposed travelling *towards* Europe by Bokhara, and that I had changed my dress to prevent my being pointed at in this land; but that I had no desire to conceal from him and the chiefs of every country which I entered, that I was an Englishman, and that my entire adoption of the habits of the people had added to my comfort. The chief replied in very kind terms, applauded the design, and the propriety of changing our dress.

Dost Mahommed then turned to Mr Wolff for an explanation of his history and, as he was aware of the gentleman's vocations, he had assembled among the party several Mahommedan doctors, who were prepared to dispute on points of religion. As is usual on such subjects, the one party failed to convince the other and, but for the admirable tact of the chief himself, the consequences might have been disagreeable. Before we withdrew, the chief made a very friendly tender to assist us in our journey, and offered us letters to the chiefs on the Oxus, and the King of Bokhara. He also requested that we should frequently visit him while in Cabool, as he liked to hear of other countries, and would always make us welcome. We left at midnight, quite charmed with our reception, and the accomplished address and manners of Dost Mahommed Khan.

I lost no time in making excursions near Cabool, and chose the earliest opportunity to visit the tomb of the Emperor Baber, which is about a mile from the city, and situated in the sweetest spot of the neighbourhood. The good Nawab was my conductor in the pilgrimage. A running and clear stream yet waters the fragrant flowers of this cemetery, which is the great holiday resort of the people of Cabool. In front of the grave there is a small but chaste mosque of marble, and an inscription upon it sets forth that it was built in year 1640 [Babur had died in 1530], by order of the Emperor Shah Jehan, after defeating Mahommed Nuzur Khan in Balkh and

Budukhshan [Badakhshan], 'that poor Mahommedans might here offer up their prayers'. It is pleasing to see the tomb of so great a man as Baber honoured by his posterity.

There is a noble prospect from the hill which overlooks Baber's tomb, and a summer-house has been erected upon it by Shah Zuman, from which it may be admired. The Nawab and myself climbed up to it, and seated ourselves. If my reader can imagine a plain, about twenty miles in circumference, laid out with gardens and fields in pleasing irregularity, intersected by three rivulets, which wind through it by a serpentine course, and wash innumerable little forts and villages, he will have before him one of the meadows of Cabool. To the north lie the hills of Pughman, covered half way down with snow, and separated from the eye by a sheet of the richest verdure. On the other side, the mountains, which are bleak and rocky, mark the hunting preserves of the kings; and the gardens of this city, so celebrated for its fruit, lie beneath, the water being conducted to them with great ingenuity. I do not wonder at the hearts of the people being captivated with the landscape, and of Baber's admiration, for in his words, ' its verdure and flowers render Cabool in spring, a heaven'.

Our intercourse with the people was on a much better footing in Cabool than in Peshawur, for we were no longer in the house of a chief, and not troubled by too many visitors. The Nawab occupied one side of a large mansion, and left the other part to us. He, however, rallied round him many good sort of people, with whom we became acquainted. He brought them over in person, and we passed to and fro between each other's apartments the whole day. The habits which we had adopted now gave us many advantages in our communications with the natives. We sat with them on the same carpet, ate with them, and freely mingled in their society. The Afghans are a sober, simple people. They always interrogated me closely regarding Europe, the nations of which they divide into twelve '*koollahs*' or crowns, literally hats. It was delightful to see the curiosity of even the oldest men. The greatest evil of

Over: The bazar at Cabool

139

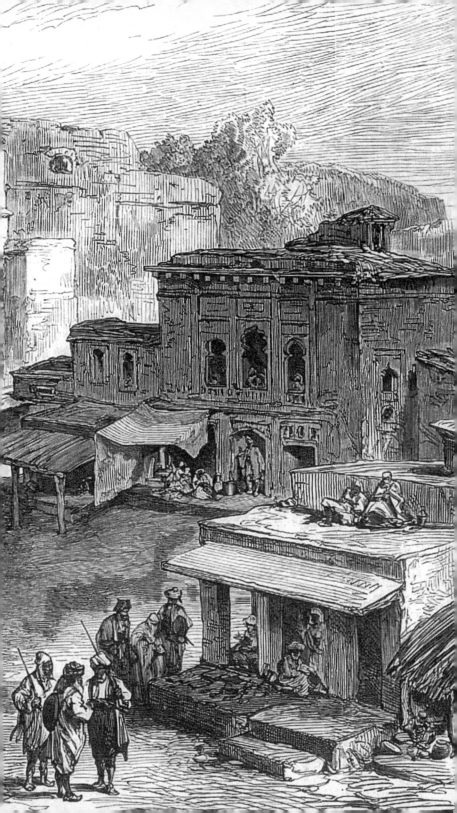

Mahommedanism consists in keeping those who profess it within a certain circle of civilisation. Their manners never appear to alter. They have learning, but it is of another age, and any thing like philosophy is unknown in their history. The language of the Afghans is Persian, but it is not the smooth and elegant tongue of Iran. Pooshtoo [Pashtu] is the dialect of the common people, but some of the higher classes cannot even speak it.

The Afghans are a nation of children; in their quarrels they fight and become friends without any ceremony. They cannot conceal their feelings from one another, and a person with any discrimination may at all times pierce their designs. If they themselves are to be believed, their ruling vice is envy, which besets even the nearest and dearest relations. No people are more incapable of managing intrigue. I was particularly struck with their idleness; they seem to sit listlessly for the whole day, staring at each other. How they live it would be difficult to discover, yet they dress well, and are healthy and happy. I imbibed a very favourable impression of their national character.

[Burnes clearly loved Afghanistan and its people, and he made many friends in Kabul. Perhaps as a Scot he felt a kinship with its hardy mountain dwellers, and with the rugged magnificence of its scenery – especially after the stifling plains of India. But this is a startlingly rose-tinted assessment of the national character. Afghans could be exceedingly cruel and vengeful, and were quite capable of hiding their real feelings under a duplicitous mask of friendship – as becomes clear in the course of his own narrative.]

Cabool is a most bustling and populous city. Such is the noise in the afternoon, that in the streets one cannot make an attendant hear. The great bazar, or *Chouchut*, is an elegant arcade, nearly 600 feet long and about 30 broad: it is divided into four equal parts. Its roof is painted, and over the shops are the houses of some of the citizens. The plan is judicious, but it has been left unfinished, and the fountains and cisterns, that formed part of it, lie neglected. Still there are few such bazars in the East, and one wonders at the silks, cloths and goods, which are arrayed under its piazzas. In the evening it presents a very interesting sight: each shop is lighted up by a lamp suspended in front, which gives the city an appearance of being illuminated. The number of shops for the sale of dried fruits is remarkable, and their arrangement tasteful. In May one may purchase the grapes, pears, apples, quinces and even the melons of the by-gone season, then ten months old. Every trade has its separate bazar, and all of them seem busy. Around the bakers' shops, crowds of people may be seen, waiting for their bread. I observed that they baked it by plastering it to the sides of the oven. Cabool is famed for its *kabobs*, or cooked meats, which are in great request: few cook at home. '*Rhuwash*' was the dainty of the May season in Cabool. It is merely blanched rhubarb, which is reared under a careful protection from the sun, and grows up rankly under the hills in the neighbourhood. Its flavour is delicious. '*Shabash rhuwash!*' ('Bravo rhuwash!') is the cry in the streets, and every one buys it.

There are no wheeled carriages in Cabool: the streets are not very narrow; they are kept in a good state during dry weather, and are intersected by small covered aqueducts of clean water, which is a great convenience to the people. We passed along them without observation, and even without an attendant. To me, the appearance of the people was more novel than the bazars. They sauntered about, dressed in sheep-skin cloaks, and seemed huge from the quantity of clothes they wore. All the children have chubby red cheeks, which I at first took for an artificial colour, till I found it to be the gay bloom of youth. The older people seem to lose it. Cabool is a compactly built city, but its houses have no pretension to elegance. They are constructed of sun-dried bricks and wood, and few of them are more than two stories high. It is thickly peopled, and has a population of about sixty thousand souls. The river of Cabool passes through the city, and tradition says that it has three times carried it away, or inundated it. In rain, there is not a dirtier place than Cabool.

*   *   *

In the number of our visitors was an Armenian, of the name of Simon Murgurditch, commonly called Sooliman, who gave us a sad account of the dispersion of his tribe. There are but twenty-one persons now remaining, from a colony of some hundreds introduced by Nadir and Ahmed Shah from Joolfa and Meshed in Persia [in the 18th century]. By inscriptions in their burying-ground, it would appear that Armenian merchants settled in Cabool even before that period. During the Dooranee monarchy, they held offices under the government, and were respected till the time of Timour Shah's death [in 1793]. In the disputes about the succession, they have gradually withdrawn their families to other countries; and the present chief of Cabool, with the best intentions, has utterly ruined the Armenian colony, by prohibiting them from preparing wine and spirits, by which they gained their livelihood. He has also forbidden dice, with every description of incontinence, and likewise threatened to grill some of the bakers in their ovens for light weights.

After a life by no means temperate, this chief has renounced wine, and commands, under the severest penalties, that his subjects should be equally abstemious. The Armenians and Jews of Cabool have, therefore, fled to other lands, as they had no means of support but in distilling spirits and wine. There are but three Jewish families in Cabool, the wreck of a hundred which it could last year boast. If Dost Mahommed Khan can succeed in suppressing drunkenness by the sacrifice of a few foreign inhabitants, he is not to be blamed; since forty bottles of wine or ten of brandy, might be purchased from them for a single rupee. As the chief in person shows so good an example to his people, we shall not criticise his motives, nor comment on the inconsistency of a reformed drunkard. Cabool seems to have been always famed for its revels.

The Armenians clung to us as if we had been an addition to their colony, and we breakfasted with Simon Mugurditch and his family, where we met all the members of it. The little children came running out to meet us, kissed our hands, and then placed their foreheads upon them. They are a very handsome people. We saw their church – a small building, which could never have contained a hundred people. Our host Simon gave us a very comfortable entertainment, and laid it out on a cloth covered with sentences of the Koran. 'It was an Afghan cloth,' said he, 'and Christians are not injured by these sentences, nor do they eat a less hearty meal.' The Armenians have adopted all the customs and manners of Mahommedans, and take off both shoes and turbans on entering their church. They are a harmless inoffensive people, but fond of money.

Since our departure, we had been travelling in a perpetual spring. The trees were blossoming as we left Lahore in February, and we found them full-blown in March at Peshawur. We had now the same joyous state of the season in Cabool, and arrived at an opportune time to see it. This state of the spring will give a good idea of the relative height of the different places, and of the progress of their seasons. Cabool is more than 6000 feet above the level of the sea. I passed some delightful days in its beautiful gardens. One evening I visited a very fine one, in company with the Nawab, about six miles from the city. They are tastefully laid out and well kept; the fruit trees are planted at regular distances; most of the gardens rise with the acclivity of the ground in plateaus, or shelves, over one another. The ground was covered with the fallen blossoms, which had drifted into the corners, like so much snow. The Nawab and myself seated ourselves under a pear tree of Samarcand, the most celebrated kind in the country, and admired the prospect. Great was the variety and number of fruit trees. There were peaches, plums, apricots, pears, apples, quinces, cherries, walnuts, mulberries, pomegranates and vines, all growing in one garden.

There were also nightingales, blackbirds, thrushes and doves, to raise their notes, and chattering magpies on almost every tree, which were not without their attraction, as reminding me of England. I was highly pleased with the nightingale and, on our return, the Nawab sent me one in a cage, which sang throughout the night. It is called the 'Boolbool i huzar dastan', or the nightingale of a thousand tales; and it really seemed to imitate the song of every bird. The cage was surrounded by a cloth, and it became so noisy a companion that I was obliged to send it away before I could sleep. This bird is a native of Budukhshan. The finest garden about Cabool is that called the king's garden, laid out by Timour Shah, which lies north of the town, and is about half a mile square. The road which leads to it is about three miles long, and formed the royal race-ground. There is a spacious octagon summer-house in the centre, with walks that run up from each of its sides, shaded with fruit trees, having a very pretty effect. The people are passionately fond of sauntering in these gardens, and may be seen flocking to them every evening.

The climate of Cabool is most genial. At mid-day the sun is hotter than in England; but the nights and evenings are cool, and in August only do the people find it necessary to sleep on their balconies. There is no rainy season, but constant showers fall as in England. The snow lasts for five months in winter. During May the thermometer stood at 64 degrees in the hottest time of the day, and there was generally a wind from the north, cooled by the snow that covers the mountains. It must usually blow from that quarter, since all the trees of Cabool bend to the south. Cabool is particularly celebrated for its fruit, which is exported in great abundance to India. Its vines are so plentiful that the grapes are given, for three months of the year, to cattle. A pound of grapes sells for a halfpenny. There are no date trees in Cabool, though they are to be found both east and west of it – at Candahar and Peshawur. Peshawur is celebrated for its pears, Ghuzni for its plums (which are sold in India under the name of the plum of Bokhara), Candahar for its figs, and Cabool for its mulberries; but almost every description, particularly stone fruit, thrives in Cabool. Fruit is more plentiful than bread, and is considered one of the necessaries of human life.

Among the public buildings in Cabool, the Bala Hissar or citadel claims the first importance, but not from its strength. Cabool is enclosed to the south and west by high rocky hills, and at the eastern extremity of these the Bala Hissar is situated, which commands the city. It stands on a neck of land, and may have an elevation of about 150 feet from the meadows of the surrounding country. There is another fort under it, also called the Bala Hissar, which is occupied by the governor and his guards. The citadel is uninhabited by the present chief, but his brother built a palace in it called the 'Koollah-i-Feringee', or the Europeans' Hat, which is the highest building. Dost Mahommed Khan captured the Bala Hissar by blowing up one of its towers: it is a poor, irregular and dilapidated fortification, and could never withstand a siege. The upper fort is small, but that below will contain about five thousand people. The king's palace stands in it. The Bala Hissar was built by different princes of the house of Timour [i.e. Tamerlane], from Baber downwards. Aurangzebe prepared extensive vaults under it to deposit his treasure, which may yet be seen. While it formed the palace of the kings of Cabool, it was also the prison of the younger branches of the royal family, where they were confined for life. They tell a story that, when set free from it, after murdering their keeper, they looked with astonishment at seeing water flow – so close had been their confinement in this walled abode. It is difficult to say whether these unfortunate men were not happier than in their present state, which is that of abject poverty. Many of the sons of Timour Shah came in absolute hunger to solicit alms from us. I advised them to make a petition to the chief for some permanent relief, but they said that they had no mercy to expect from the Barukzye family, now in power, who thirsted after their blood.

[Timur Shah was the son of the great Durrani leader Ahmad Khan Abdali who had died in 1772 after forging a vast Afghan empire. When Timur died in 1793 the struggle for the succession among his sons Zaman, Shuja and Mahmud (which dragged on for years, with each of them reigning for a while and then being supplanted by one of the others) weakened the empire and allowed the Barukzye family, who were also Durranis but from a different clan, to increase their power – especially in the person of Mahmud's vizier, Fathi Khan, who effectively ran the country. So envious was Mahmud's eldest son, Kamran, that he had Fathi Khan seized and blinded, and later persuaded his father to have him cut to pieces. But the atrocity was soon avenged by Fathi's younger brother, Dost Mahommed, who succeeded in driving out Mahmud and Kamran, and assumed the leadership himself. However the Afghanistan he now ruled was very much reduced in size. Balkh had been seized by the Emir of Bokhara, the trans-Indus districts were occupied by the Sikhs, and the outlying provinces of Sind and Baluchistan had declared independence. In effect, Dost Mahommed ruled only the districts of Ghazni, Kabul and Jalalabad, for Kamran and his faction still held Herat.]

Near the Bala Hissar, and separated from it and every part of the city, the Persians, or Kuzzilbashes as they are called, reside. They are Toorks, and principally of the tribe of Juwansheer, who were fixed in this country by Nadir Shah [in the early 18th century]. Under the kings of Cabool they served as body-guards, and were a powerful engine of the state. They yet retain their language, and are attached to the present chief, whose mother is of their tribe. I had an opportunity of seeing these people to advantage, being invited to a party given by our conductor from Peshawur, the jolly Naib Mahommed Shureef. I met the whole of the principal men, and their chief Sheereen Khan. The entertainment was more Persian than Afghan. Among them, I could discover a new people and a new mode of thinking, for they have retained some of the wit that marks their countrymen. [In fact part of the evening's entertainment consisted in a loquacious and daring Mirza mimicking the speech and habits of the neighbouring nationalities: the Afghans were not allowed into paradise because of their horrid and unintelligible language and had to be packed off to hell, the 'uncouth' Uzbeks, the 'whining, cheating and deceitful' Kashmiris, and the cheating customs officials of Herat were all consigned to a similar fate – amid general hilarity.]

During our stay the 'Eed' [Eid] occurred, which is the festival kept in commemoration of Abraham's intention to sacrifice his son Isaac. It was observed with every demonstration of respect: the shops were shut, and the chief proceeded to prayer at an appointed place, with a great concourse of persons. In the afternoon, every one was to be seen flocking to the gardens; nor could I resist the impulse, and followed the crowd. In Cabool you no sooner leave the bazar, than you find yourself on the banks of the river, which are beautifully shaded by trees of mulberry, willow and poplar. Almost all the roads round the city lead by the verge of aqueducts or running water. They are crossed by bridges, and the large river has three or four of these edifices, though they cannot boast of architectural beauty.

The finest gardens of Cabool lie north of the city; and they, again, are far surpassed by those beyond, in the district of Istalif, under the first snow-clad mountains, towards Hindoo Koosh. Their site is to be seen from Cabool. I was conducted to the tomb of Timour Shah, which stands outside the city, and is a brick building of an octagon shape, rising to the height of 50 feet. The interior of it is about 40

148

feet square, and the architecture resembles that of Delhi. The building is unfinished. A lamp was formerly lighted on this sepulchre, but the sense of this king's favours, like that of many others, has faded. Timour Shah made Cabool his capital, and here is his tomb. His father [Ahmad Khan Abdali] is interred at Candahar, which is the native country of the Dooranees.

I moved about every where during the day, and had the pleasure of many sociable evenings with our host the Nawab whom, I found, like many of his countrymen, in search of the philosopher's stone. Such an opportunity as our arrival seemed to promise him a rich harvest. I soon undeceived him, and laughed at the crucibles and recipes which he produced. I explained to him that chemistry had succeeded alchymy, as astronomy had followed astrology; but as I had to detail the exact nature of these sciences, my asseverations of being no alchymist had little effect. He therefore applied himself to the doctor, from whom he requested recipes for the manufacture of calomel and quinine, plasters and liniments – which it was no easy matter to furnish. He could not credit that the arts of giving and manufacturing medicines were distinct, and set us down as very ignorant or very obstinate. He would not receive the prepared medicines, as they would be of no use to him after we had left. We found this feeling generally prevalent – and woe be to the doctor in these parts who gives medicines which he cannot make. We kept the Nawab in good humour, though we would not believe that he could convert iron into silver.

I informed him that I belonged to a sect called Freemasons, and gave some account of the craft. It was an institution, I said, where, though we did not change the baser metals into gold, we sought to transform the baser and blacker passions of man into philanthropy and charity. He particularly requested that he might be admitted into the fraternity without delay. But as the number of brethren must be equal to that of the Pleiades, I put it off to a convenient opportunity. He confidently believed that he had at last got scent of magic in its purest dye, and had it been in my power, I would have willingly initiated him. He made me promise to send some flower-seeds of our country, which he wished to see in Cabool, and I faithfully forwarded them. I cut the plates out of Mr Elphinstone's

History of Cabool, and gave them to the Nawab at a large party. Not only is the costume exact, but in some of the figures, to their great delight, they discovered likenesses. Pictures are forbidden among the Soonee [Sunni] Mahommedans, but in the present instance they proved very acceptable. Among the Nawab's friends we met a man 114 years old, who had served with Nadir Shah [the last of the Persian Shahs to rule Afghanistan]. He had been upwards of eighty years in Cabool, and seen the Dooranee dynasty founded and pass away. This venerable person walked up the stairs to our rooms.

As the chief desired, I passed another evening with him, and the doctor, being convalescent, accompanied me. Mr Wolff had proceeded on his journey to India. Dost Mahommed Khan pleased us as much as ever. He kept us till long past midnight, and gave us a full insight into the political affairs of his country, and the unfortunate differences that exist between him and his brothers. He expressed hopes of being able to restore the monarchy, evinced a cordial hatred towards Runjeet Sing, and seemed anxious to know if the British Government would accept his services as an auxiliary to root him out; but I replied that he was our friend. He then promised me the command of his army, if I would remain with him; an offer which he afterwards repeated. 'Twelve thousand horse and twenty guns shall be at your disposal.' When he found that I could not accept the honour, he requested me to send some friend to be his generalissimo. On this occasion, we had some highly interesting conversation regarding the Kaffirs, who live in the hills north of Peshawur and Cabool, and are supposed to descend from Alexander. The Chief, on the former occasion, had produced a young Kaffir boy, one of his slaves, about ten years old, who had been captured for about two years. His complexion, hair and features were quite European; his eyes were of a bluish colour. We made him repeat various words of his language, some of which were Indian. The Kaffirs live in a most barbarous state, eating bears and monkeys. There is a tribe of them called 'Neemchu Moosulman' or half-Mahommedans, who occupy the frontier villages between them and the Afghans, and transact the little trade that is carried on between them. It is curious to find a people so entirely distinct from the other inhabitants but, unfortunately, every thing that regards them rests in obscurity. [Burnes thought they were probably the aboriginal inhabitants of Afghanistan, rather than the descendants of Alexander's army.]

We had passed nearly three weeks in Cabool, which appeared as a few days. It was now necessary to prepare for our journey, which did not seem an easy matter. No caravan was yet ready, and it was even doubtful if the roads were passable, as snow had fallen during the month. It occurred to me that our best plan would be to hire a Cafila-bashee, a conductor of one of the great caravans, as our own servant; and we might thus proceed at once, without any delay attendant upon a caravan and, I hoped, with equal safety. The Nawab did not altogether relish the plan, nor our precipitate departure. He would have willingly kept us for months.

We however entertained one Hyat, a hale old man, who had grown grey in crossing the Hindoo Koosh. When the Nawab found our determination to depart, he urged his relative the Ameen-ool-Moolk, a nobleman of the late Shah Mahmood, who carries on commercial transactions with Bokhara and Russia, to despatch one of his trusty persons with us. It was therefore determined that a brother of his nazir, or steward, named Doulut, a respectable Afghan, also styled the Nazir, should proceed with us. He had business in Bokhara and was even going on to Russia: our movements expedited his departure. Every thing looked well, and we were furnished, by the Nawab's kindness, with letters to the Afghans in Bokhara. The most influential of these was Budr-oo-deen. His agent in Cabool, who brought me the letters, was resolved on being rewarded for doing so by an enjoyment of our society. His name was Khodadad and he was a moollah. He stopped and dined with us on boiled fowl and rice; but he declared that, whatever might be our wisdom as a nation, we had no correct ideas of good living. He did not like our English fare which was cooked with water, he said, and only fit for an invalid. Khodadad was a very intelligent man, who had travelled in India and Tartary, and was well read in Asiatic lore. He had also studied Euclid, whom his countrymen, he said, nicknamed 'Uql doozd' or wisdom-stealer, from the confusion he had produced in men's heads.

The chief also prepared his letters, but there is little communication between the Afghans and Uzbeks, and we found them of no service; that for the King of Bokhara was lost or stolen. One of Dost Mahommed Khan's court however, the governor of Bameean, Hajee Kauker, furnished us with letters which were of real use, as will afterwards appear. This man, though serving under the chief of Cabool, is more friendly to his brother of Peshawur, by whom we were introduced to him. I held my intercourse with him secret, and he tendered the services of fifty horsemen, which it was prudent to decline.

Before our departure from Cabool, I made the acquaintance of many of the Hindoo or Shikarpooree merchants. The whole trade of Central Asia is in the hands of these people, who have houses of agency from Astracan and Meshed to Calcutta. They are a plodding race, who take no share in any business but their own, and secure protection from the government by lending it money. They have a peculiar cast of countenance, with a very high nose: they dress very dirtily. Few of them are permitted to wear turbans. They never bring their families from their country, which is Upper Sinde, and are constantly passing to and from it, which keeps up a national spirit among them. In Cabool there are eight great houses of agency belonging to these people, who are quite separate from the other Hindoo inhabitants. Of them, there are about three hundred families. I met one of these Shikarpooree merchants on the island of Kisham, in the Gulf of Persia; and were Hindoos tolerated in that country I feel satisfied they would spread all over Persia, and even Turkey.

With such an extensive agency distributed in the parts of Asia which we were now about to traverse, it was not, as may be supposed, a very difficult task to adjust our money matters, and arrange for our receiving a supply of that necessary article, even at the distance which we should shortly find ourselves from India. Our expenses were small, and golden ducats were carefully sewed up in our belts and turbans; though, as we had to leave these at the door of every house, I did not always approve of such stowage. I had a letter of credit in my possession for the sum of five thousand rupees, payable from the public treasuries of Lodiana or Delhi, and the Cabool merchants did not hesitate to accept it. They expressed their readiness either to discharge it on the spot with gold, or give bills on Russia at St Macaire (Nijni Novgorod), Astracan or Bokhara, which I had no reason to question; I took orders on the latter city. The merchants enjoined the strictest secrecy, and their anxiety was not surpassed by that of our own to appear poor; for the possession of so much gold would have ill tallied with the coarse and tattered garments which we now wore. But what a gratifying proof have we here of the high character of our nation, to find the bills of those who almost appeared as beggars cashed, without hesitation, in a foreign and far distant capital! Above all, how much is our wonder excited to find the ramifications of commerce extending uninterruptedly over such vast and remote regions, differing as they do from each other in language, religion, manners and laws!

CHAPTER VI

Journey over the Hindoo Koosh, or Snowy Mountains

If we had quitted Peshawur with the good wishes of the chief, we were now accompanied by those of his brother, the Nawab. On the 18th of May, which happened on a Friday, we quitted Cabool after noontide prayers, according to the usual custom of travellers, that we might not offend the prejudices of the people, who also consider that hour auspicious. We thought we had parted from the good Nawab at the door of his house, when he gave us his blessing; but before leaving the city, he once more joined us, and rode out for two or three miles, when this worthy man left us, much to our regret. He seemed to live for every one but himself. He entertained us with great hospitality during our stay; and had, day by day, urged us to take any other road than that of Toorkistan, prognosticating every evil to us. He now took leave of us with much feeling; nor was it possible to suppress a tear as we said adieu. Though his brother the chief had not caressed us as he of Peshawur, he had yet shown great politeness and attention, of which we expressed ourselves most sensible before taking our departure.

We halted for the night at a small village called Killa-i-Kazee and, at the first outset, experienced the influence and utility of our Cafila-bashee. He cleared out a house for us, by bribing a moollah to leave it, and we found the quarters very snug, for it was piercingly cold. Prudence dictated our proceeding very quietly in this part of our journey, and we were now designated 'Meerza' or secretary, a common appellation in these countries, which we ever after retained. The doctor allowed his title to slumber; but it was soon apparent that we should have been helpless without our conductor, for on the following morning a fellow, possessing some little authority, seized my horse's bridle, and demanded a sight of the contents of my saddle-bags. I was proceeding with all promptness to display my poverty, when a word from the Cafila-bashee terminated the investigation. We were not now recognised as Europeans by any one, which certainly gave a pleasing liberty to our actions.

We left the road which leads to Candahar on our left, and proceeded up the valley of the Cabool river to its source at Sirchushma. Before entering the valley of the river, we left the famous Ghuzni to the south: it is only sixty miles from Cabool. This ancient capital is now a dependency on that city, and a place of small note: it contains the tomb of the great Mahmood, its founder [the Turko-Afghan warrior-king of the 11th century, whose empire stretched from the Caspian to the Indus, and who made frequent raids deep into India to bring back plunder to his capital Ghazni]. Baber expresses his surprise that so great a monarch should have ever made Ghuzni his capital, but the natives will tell you that the cold renders it inaccessible for some months in the year, which gave him greater confidence while desolating Hindoostan and the land of the infidels.

We wound up the valley, which became gradually narrower, till we reached a level tract on the mountains – the pass of Oonna – the ascent to which is guarded by three small forts. Before reaching the summit we first encountered the snow, with which I was too happy to claim acquaintance after a separation of a dozen winters; though there were no companions with whom I could renew the frolics of youth. It snowed as we crossed the pass, which is about 11,000 feet high, and at length we found ourselves, with pleasure, at a small village, free from the chilling wind which blew all day. We had already made considerable progress in our mountain journey: the rivers now ran in opposite directions; and our advance had brought us into the cold country of the Huzaras [Hazaras], where the peasants were only ploughing and sowing, while we had seen the harvest home at Peshawur and the grain in ear at Cabool.

We continued our mountain journey by the base of the lofty and ever-snow-clad mountain of Koh-i-Baba, which is a remarkable ridge, having three peaks that rise to the height of about 18,000 feet. On the evening of the 21st of May we reached the bottom of the pass of

Hajeeguk, half dead with fatigue and nearly blind from the reflection of the snow. For about ten miles we had travelled in the bed of a rivulet that was knee deep, fed by melting snow, which we crossed more than twenty times. We then entered the region of the snow, which still lay deep on the ground: by noon it became so soft that our horses sunk into it, threw their burdens and riders, and in several places were with the utmost difficulty extricated. That part of the ground which was free from snow had become saturated with the melted water, and a quagmire, so that we alternately waded through mud and snow. The heat was oppressive – I imagine from reflection, I had almost lost the use of my eyes, and the skin peeled from my nose before we reached a little fort under the pass, at which we alighted in the evening with a Huzara family.

We had here an opportunity of seeing the Huzaras in their native state among the mountains, and were received by an old lady in a miserable flat-roofed house, partly below ground, with two or three openings in the roof as windows. She was taking care of her grand-child, and bade us welcome by the lordly name of 'Agha'. I called her 'Mother'. We were taken for Persians and, since the Huzaras are of the same creed as that nation [i.e. Shia Muslims], were honoured guests. The Huzaras are a simple-hearted people and differ much from the Afghan tribes. In physiognomy they more resemble Chinese, with their square faces and small eyes. They are Tartars by descent, and one of their tribes is now called Tatar Huzara. The women have great influence and go unveiled: they are handsome and not very chaste, which has perhaps given rise to the scandal among their Soonee neighbours, who detest them as heretics. Were their country not strong they would soon be extirpated, for they have enemies in every direction. The good matron, who gave us an asylum from the snow and frost, tendered also her advice for my eyes, which she said had been *burned* by the snow. She recommended the use of antimony, which I applied with the pencil, much to the improvement of my appearance, as she informed me; but I can more surely add, to my relief and comfort when I again encountered the snow.

After a night's rest, and the friendly advice of the Huzara matron, we commenced the ascent of the pass of Hajeeguk, which was about

1000 feet above us, and 12,400 feet from the sea. We took our departure early in the morning of the 22nd of May; the frozen snow bore our horses, and we reached the summit before the sun's influence had softened it. The thermometer fell 4 degrees below the freezing point; the cold was very oppressive, though we were clad in skins with the fur inside. I often blessed the good Nawab of Cabool, who had forced a pelisse of otter skin upon me, that proved most useful. The passage was not achieved without adventure, for there was no road to guide us through the snow, and the surveyor Mahommed Ali, along with his horse, went rolling down a declivity for about thirty yards. This exhibition in front served to guide the rear to a better path, but it was impossible to resist laughing at the Jack and Jill expedition of the poor surveyor and his horse. We were now about to commence the ascent of the pass of Kaloo, which is still 1000 feet higher than that of Hajeeguk, but our progress was again arrested by snow. We doubled it, by passing round its shoulder, and took a side path through a valley, watered by a tributary of the Oxus, which led us to Bameean [Bamyan]. Nothing could be more grand than the scenery which we met in this valley. Frightful precipices hung over us, and many a fragment beneath informed us of their instability. For a mile it was impossible to proceed on horseback and we advanced on foot, with a gulf beneath us.

Bameean is celebrated for its colossal idols and innumerable excavations, which are to be seen in all parts of the valley. The hills at Bameean are formed of indurated clay and pebbles, which renders their excavation a matter of little difficulty, but the great extent to which it has been carried excites attention. Caves are dug on both sides of the valley, but the greater number lie on the northern face, where we found the great idols: altogether they form an immense city. [Burnes mentions a local legend that a mother once lost her child in the cave network and only found him again twelve years later!] Bameean is subject to Cabool: it would appear to be a place of high antiquity and is, perhaps, the city which Alexander founded at the base of Paropamisus, before entering Bactria. The country, indeed, from Cabool to Balkh, is yet styled 'Bakhtur Zumeen' or Bakhtur country. [Few Europeans had been to Bamyan at this time and Burnes gives detailed descriptions of the statues, and even a sketch. Fortunately they were much photographed in more recent times, before being blown up by the Taliban in March 2001.]

After a day's delay at Bameean we set out for Syghan, a distance of thirty miles. At the pass of Akrobat, which we passed half way, we left the dominions of modern Cabool. We were conducted to the pass by twenty horsemen, which a letter of introduction to the governor of Bameean from Hajee Khan of Cabool had procured as a protection from the Dih Zungee Huzaras, who plunder these roads. The escort was mounted on fine Toorkman horses, and accompanied by some native greyhounds – and a fleet sort of dog with long shaggy hair on the legs and body. The party took their leave on the pass, where we bade farewell to them and the kingdom of Cabool.

At Syghan we found ourselves in the territory of Mahommed Ali Beg, an Uzbek, who is alternately subject to Cabool and Koondooz [Kunduz] as the chiefs of these states respectively rise in power. He satisfies the chief of Cabool with a few horses, and his Koondooz lord with a few men, captured in forays by his sons and officers, who are occasionally sent out for the purpose. Such is the difference between the taste of his northern and southern neighbours. The captives are Huzaras, on whom the Uzbeks nominally wage war for their Shiah creed, that they may be converted to Soonees and good Mahommedans. A friend lately remonstrated with this chief for his gross infringement of the laws of the Prophet, in the practice of man-stealing. He admitted the crime, but as God did not forbid him in his sleep and his conscience was easy, he said that he did not see why he should desist from so profitable a traffic. He is no-wise famed for justice, or protection of the traveller: a caravan of Jews passed his town last year, en route to Bokhara; he detained some of their women, and defended the outrage by replying to every remonstrance that their progeny would become Mahommedan, and justify the act. Our Cafila-bashee waited on this person to report our arrival, and told him, it seems, that we were poor Armenians. A nankeen pelisse, with eight or nine rupees (the usual tax on a caravan) satisfied this man-selling Uzbek, and we passed a com-fortable night in a very nicely carpeted 'mihman khana' [guest house] at the verge of the village, the chief himself sending us a leg of venison as we were known to his friends in Cabool.

We were already in a different country; the mosques were spread with felts, which indicated greater attention to matters of religion, and they were also much better buildings. We were instructed not to sleep with our feet towards Mecca, which would be evincing our contempt for that holy place, and I ever after observed the bearings of the compass indoors, as attentively as I had hitherto done outside. I also cut the central portion of the hair of my mustachios, since the neglect of such a custom would point me out as a Shiah, and consequently an infidel. We made all these arrangements in Syghan, which is a pretty place, with fine gardens, though situated in a dreary valley, destitute of all vegetation beyond its immediate precincts. When we left it next morning, a man came about five hundred yards from the village to give us the 'fatha' or blessing, as is usual in this country; and we departed, and stroked down our beards with gravity at the honour.

Seeing this rigid adherence to the laws of Mahommed and the constant recurrence to the practice of the Koran in every act of life, I was not disposed to augur favourably for our comfort, or the reliance which we could place upon the people with whom we were now to mingle. I thought of the expeditions of Prince Beckevitch, and our own unfortunate predecessors, poor Moorcroft and his party. The fate of the Russian Count and his little army is well known: they were betrayed and barbarously massacred. [Peter the Great had sent the small expedition to Khiva in 1717. The Khan had greeted them in friendly fashion, tricked them into dispersing their force of 4,000 men into small groups, and then had them slaughtered.] The lot of Moorcroft was equally melancholy, since he and his associates perished of fever – and not without suspicion of some more violent death. I shall have occasion to speak of them hereafter. It may be imagined that our feelings at this moment were not of an agreeable nature, but fuller experience dissipated many of our fears. The notions even of our conductor were singular. Shortly after leaving Cabool, I took up a stone by the roadside, to examine its formation, and the Cafila-bashee, who observed me, asked with anxiety, 'Have you found it?' – 'What?' – 'Gold.' I threw away the stone and became more cautious in my future observations.

[The party continued through the pass of Dundan Shikun (the 'Tooth-breaker') and into a valley so narrow that they were unable to take bearings from the stars at night. However there was a long and beautiful apricot orchard near the village of Kamurd.] At Kamurd we passed the seat of another petty chief, Ruhmut oollah Khan, a Tajik deeply addicted to wine. He had been without a supply for ten days and he produced a flagon, with the earnest request that the Cafila-bashee would replenish it at Khooloom [Kholm] and send it to him by the first opportunity. A coarse loongee, coupled with a promise of the wine, satisfied this chief; for he also claims a tax on the traveller, though he is but a tributary of Koondooz. His power is limited, and it is curious to observe how he keeps on terms with his master, Mahommed Moorad Beg. Unable to make 'chupaos' or forays and capture human beings like his neighbour of Syghan, he last year deliberately seized the whole of the inhabitants of one of his villages and despatched them, men, women and children, as slaves, to Koondooz. He was rewarded by three additional villages for his allegiance and services; yet we here hired a son of this man to escort us on our travels, and it was well we did so.

*   *   *

On the 26th of May we crossed the last pass of the Indian Causasus – the Kara Koottul or Black Pass – but had yet a journey of ninety-five miles before we cleared the mountains. We descended at the village of Dooab into the bed of the river of Khooloom and followed it to that place among terrific precipices, which at night obscured all the stars but those of the zenith. On this pass we had an adventure which illustrates the manners of the people among whom we were travelling, and might have proved serious. Our Cafila-bashee had intimated to us that we had reached a dangerous neighbourhood, and consequently hired an escort, headed by the son of Ruhmut oollah Khan. In ascending the pass, we met a large caravan of horses en route to Cabool and, on reaching the top, descried a party of robbers advancing over a ridge of hills, and from the direction of Hindoo Koosh. The cry of 'Allaman, Allaman!' which here means robber, soon spread, and we drew up with our escort to meet, and if possible, fight the party.

The robbers observed our motions, and were now joined by some other men, who had lain in ambush, which increased their party to about thirty. Each of us sent on two horsemen, who drew up at a distance of an hundred yards, and parleyed. The robbers were Tartar Huzaras, commanded by a notorious freebooter named Dilawur, who had come in search of the horse caravan. On discovering that it had passed, and that we were in such good company as the son of the chief of Kamurd, they gave up all intentions of attack, and we pushed on without delay. Immediately we had cleared the pass, they occupied it, but the whole of their booty consisted of two laden camels of the caravan, which had loitered behind. These they seized in our view, as well as their drivers, who would now become slaves for life. Had we not hired our escort we should have perhaps shared a similar fate, and found ourselves next day tending herds and flocks among the mountains. The party was well mounted, and composed of desperate men: disappointed of their prey, they attacked the village of Dooab at night, where we first intended to halt. We had luckily pushed on three miles farther, and bivouacked in the bed of a torrent in safety. The incidents of our escape furnished some room for reflection, and we had to thank the Cafila-bashee for his prudence, which had cleared us of the danger. The old gentleman stroked down his beard, blessed the lucky day, and thanked God for preserving his good name and person from such scoundrels.

The life which we now passed was far more agreeable than a detail of its circumstances would lead one to believe, with our dangers and fatigues. We mounted at daylight and generally travelled without intermission till two or three in the afternoon. Our day's progress averaged about twenty miles, but the people have no standard of measure, for they always reckon by the day's journey. We often breakfasted on the saddle, on dry bread and cheese, slept always on the ground and in the open air, and after the day's march, sat down cross-legged till night and sleep overtook us. We continued our descent by Khoorrum and Sarbagh to Heibuk, which is but a march within the mountains, and gradually exchanged our elevated barren rocks for more hospitable lands. Our road led us through tremendous defiles, which rose over us to a height of from two to three thousand feet, and overhung the pathway, while eagles and hawks wheeled in giddy circles over us: among them we distinguished the black eagle, which is a noble bird.

We now found vast flocks browsing on the aromatic pastures, and passed extensive orchards of fruit trees. Herds of deer might be seen bounding on the summits of the rocks, and in the valleys the soil was every where turned up by wild hogs, which are here found in great numbers. The people also became more numerous as we approached the plains of Tartary, and at Heibuk we had to encounter another Uzbek chief named Baba Beg, a petty tyrant of some notoriety. As we approached his town, a traveller informed us that the chief was anticipating the arrival of the Firingees (Europeans), whose approach had been announced for some time past. This person is a son of Khilich Ali Beg, who once ruled in Khooloom with great moderation; but the child has not imitated the example of his parent. He poisoned a brother at a feast, and seized upon his father's wealth before his life was extinct. He had greatly augmented the difficulties of Mr Moorcroft's party, and was known to be by no means favourable to Europeans. His subjects had driven him from his native town of Khooloom for his tyranny, and he now only possessed the district of Heibuk. We saw his castle about four in the afternoon, and approached with reluctance; but our arrangements were conducted with address, and here also we escaped in safety.

On arrival, our small caravan alighted outside Heibuk, and we lay down on the ground as fatigued travellers, covering ourselves with a coarse horse-blanket until it was night. In the evening the chief came in person to visit our Cabool friend the Nazir, to whom he offered every service; nor did he appear to be at all aware of our presence. Baba Beg, on this occasion, made an offer to send the party, under an escort of his own, direct to Balkh, avoiding Khooloom – an arrangement which I heard with pleasure and, as it will soon appear, that might have saved us a world of anxiety. Our fellow-travellers, however, declined the proffered kindness and vaunted so much of their influence at Khooloom, that we had no dread in approaching a place where we were ultimately ensnared.

We set out in the morning before the sun had risen, and congratulated ourselves at having passed with such success a man who would have certainly injured us. Heibuk is a thriving village, with a castle of sun-dried brick built on a commanding hillock. For the first time among the mountains, the valley opens and presents a sheet of gardens and most luxuriant verdure. The climate also undergoes a great change, and we find the fig tree, which does not grow in Cabool, or higher up the mountains. The elevation of Heibuk is about 4000 feet. We had expected to be rid of those troublesome companions of a tropical climate, snakes and scorpions; but here they were more numerous than in India. The construction of the houses at Heibuk arrested our attention: they have domes instead of terraces, with a hole in the roof as a chimney; so that a village has the appearance of a cluster of large brown beehives. The people, who were now as different as their houses, wore conical skull-caps instead of turbans, and almost every one we met appeared in long brown boots. The ladies seemed to select the gayest colours for their dresses, and I could now distinguish some very handsome faces, for the Mahommedan ladies do not pay scrupulous attention to being veiled in the villages. They were much fairer than their husbands, with nothing ungainly in their appearance, though they were Tartars. I could now, indeed, understand the praises of the Orientals as to the beauty of these Toorkee girls.

On the 30th of May we made our last march among the mountains, and debouched into the plains of Tartary at Khooloom, or Tash Koorghan, where we had a noble view of the country north of us, sloping down to the Oxus. Khooloom contains about ten thousand inhabitants, and is the frontier town of Moorad Beg of Koondooz, a powerful chief, who has reduced all the countries north of Hindoo Koosh to his yoke. We alighted at one of the carvanserais, where we were scarcely noticed. We here rested after our arduous and fatiguing journey over rocks and mountains, and were, indeed, refreshed by the change. Since leaving Cabool we had slept in our clothes, where we could seldom if ever change them. We had halted among mud, waded through rivers, tumbled among snow, and for the last few days been sunned by heat. These are but the petty inconveniences of a traveller, which sink into insignificance when compared with the pleasure of seeing new men and countries, strange manners and customs, and being able to temper the prejudices of one's country by observing those of other nations.

CHAPTER VII

Serious Difficulties – a Journey to Koondooz

We had entered Khooloom with an intention of setting out next day on our journey to Balkh, placing implicit reliance on the assertion of our friends that we had nothing to apprehend in doing so. Judge then, of our surprise, when we learned that the officers of the custom-house had despatched a messenger to the chief of Koondooz, to report our arrival and request his instructions as to our disposal. We were, meanwhile, desired to await the answer. Our companion, the Nazir, was much chagrined at the detention; but it was now useless to upbraid him for having ever brought us to Khooloom. He assured us that it was a mere temporary inconvenience, and likewise despatched a letter to the minister at Koondooz, requesting that we might not be detained, since his business in Russia could not be transacted without us. The minister was a friend of the Nazir's family, but I could not but regret that I had ever allowed myself to be seduced by the advice of any one. At midnight on the 1st of June we received a summons to repair to Koondooz with all despatch; while the minister, in reply to our conductor's letter, begged he would not allow himself to be detained on our account, but proceed on his journey to Bokhara! Our surprise may be better imagined than described.

It was now too late to make our escape, for we were watched in the caravanserai, and the officers would not even allow my horse to be taken into the town and shod. I urged an immediate departure for Koondooz, leaving Dr Gerard, and all the party except two, at Khooloom. I was now resolved on personating the character of an Armenian, and believed that despatch would avail me and allay suspicion. I had letters from the saint at Peshawur, which would bear me out, as I thought, in the new character; but my fellow-travellers assured me that the very possession of such documents would prove our real condition, and I destroyed them all, as well as the letters of the Cabool chief. I discovered that the Nazir had no relish for a journey to Koondooz, and seemed disposed to stay behind, almost frantic with despair; but shame is a great promoter of exertion, and I begged he would accompany me, to which he agreed.

The better to understand the critical situation in which we were now placed, I shall give a brief sketch of the disasters which befell Mr Moorcroft in this part of the country in the year 1824, from the very personage who now summoned us to Koondooz. On that traveller crossing the mountains, he proceeded to wait on the chief and, having made him some presents suitable to his rank, returned to Khooloom. He had no sooner arrived there, than he received a message from the chief saying that some of his soldiers had been wounded, and requesting that he would hasten his return, and bring along with him his medical instruments and Mr Guthrie, an Indo-Briton who had accompanied Mr Moorcroft as a surgeon. He set out for Koondooz without suspicion but found, on his arrival there, that his surgical services were not wanted and it was merely a plan to ensnare him. After a month's delay, he only succeeded in liberating himself by complying with the most extravagant demands of Moorad Beg. By one means or another, he possessed himself of cash to the value of 23,000 rupees, before Mr Moorcroft was permitted to depart; and it would have been well had the matter here terminated – but the cupidity of the chief had been excited. The party prepared to quit Khooloom for Bokhara but, on the very eve of departure, were surrounded by 400 horsemen and again summoned to Koondooz. It was not now concealed that the chief was resolved on seizing the whole of the property, and putting the party to death.

[Only the intervention of an influential holy man saved them, and they did manage to get to Bokhara. But on their return journey, the following year, they all died in the region of Balkh, possibly of fever, though that seemed slightly suspicious. Moorcroft was the first to go: he made a detour to a village which was reputed to have good horses, and never returned. By the time his companions found him, his body was already decomposing. They brought the remains back to the outskirts of Balkh and buried them in a makeshift grave. Guthrie was apparently next, then their men all succumbed one after another, leaving the young Trebeck to die alone. Rumours began to fly around that they had been poisoned on the orders of Murad Beg, who was known to be planning to waylay them when they passed through his territory.]

On the evening of the 2nd of June I set out on my journey to Koondooz, which lies higher up the valley of the Oxus, having previously prevailed on the custom-house officer, who was a Hindoo, to accompany me. I did not leave Khooloom under very encouraging circumstances, having just discovered that a Hindoo of Peshawur had *kindly* apprised the authorities of many of our acts, circumstances and condition since leaving Hindoostan; adding, indeed, many exaggerations to the narration, in which we were set forth as wealthy individuals, whose bills had even affected the money market. When beyond the town, we found our caravan to consist of eight or ten tea merchants, of Budukhshan and Yarkund [Badakhshan and Yarkand], who had disposed of their property and were returning to their country. In our own party there was the Nazir, Cafila-bashee and myself, with the Hindoo, whose name was Chumundass. I discovered that this latter person had a pretty correct knowledge of our affairs, but I did not assist to fill up the thread of his discourse, and boldly denominated myself a Hindoostan Armenian. The name of Englishman, which had carried us through safely in all other places, was here replete with danger, since it not only conveyed notions of great wealth, but a belief that that can be renewed from the inferior metals. I had, however, discovered that the Hindoo was a good man, for his easy manner in searching our baggage at the caravanserai, after our first arrival, left a favourable impression on my mind; and he himself declared to the Nazir that it was no fault of his that we were dragged to Koondooz, since he was but a custom-house officer and obliged to report our arrival. He and I soon fell into conversation, and I found him to be a native of Mooltan, who had long resided in these countries.

[Having so recently visited Multan, during his voyage up the Indus,

Burnes quickly made friends with the Indian, and they were able to converse fairly safely in an Indian language. After a tiring seventy mile journey they eventually arrived at Kunduz. The Nazir's friend, the minister, received them graciously and put them up in his guest-house. While Burnes kept up the part of a humble Armenian traveller, the Nazir was only too pleased to put on airs and act as the master of the party.]

During the day I had seen a good deal of the people, for there were many visitors and, though most of them courted the great man, a few found their way to me in the corner. Nothing is done in this country without tea, which is handed round at all times and hours, and gives a social character to conversation, which is very agreeable. The Uzbeks drink their tea with salt instead of sugar, and sometimes mix it with fat; it is then called 'keimuk chah'. After each person has had one or two large cups, a smaller one is handed round, made in the usual manner, without milk. The leaves of the pot are then divided among the party, and chewed like tobacco. Many of the strangers evinced an interest in the affairs of Cabool; some spoke of Runjeet Sing, and a few of the English in India. Most of them were merchants, who trade between this and China. They spoke much of that singular nation, and praised the equity and justice that characterised their commercial transactions. These merchants were Tajiks, and natives of Budukhshan, a country on which we now bordered.

Early on the morning of the 5th we set out on our journey to Moorad Beg. We found him at the village of Khanu-abad, which is about fifteen miles distant, and found ourselves at the gate of a small but neatly fortified dwelling, in which the chief was now holding his court. A Hindoo belonging to the minister went inside to announce our arrival and, in the meantime, I rehearsed my tale and drew on a pair of boots, as well for the uniformity as to hide my provokingly white ankles. My face had long been burned into an Asiatic hue, and from it I feared no detection. We were summoned, after about an hour's delay, and passed into the first gateway. We here found an area in which stood the attendants and horses of the chief. Six or eight 'yessawuls' or doorkeepers then announced our approach, as we entered the inner building. Moorad Beg was seated on a tiger skin, and stretched out his legs covered with huge boots, in contempt of all Eastern rules of decorum. The chief was a man of tall stature, with harsh Tartar features; his eyes were small to deformity, his forehead broad and frowning, and he wanted the beard which adorns the countenance in most Oriental nations. He proceeded to converse with the Nazir, and put several questions regarding Cabool; and then on his own affairs, during which he spoke of our poverty and situation.

Then came the Hindoo of the custom-house with my tale. 'Your slave,' said he, 'has examined the baggage of the two Armenians, and found them to be poor travellers. It is in every person's mouth that they are Europeans (Firingees), and it would have placed me under your displeasure had I let them depart; I have therefore brought one of them to know your orders.' The moment was critical, and the chief gave me a look, and said in Turkish – 'Are you certain he is an Armenian?' A second assurance carried conviction, and he issued an order for our safe conduct beyond the frontier. I stood by, and saw his secretary prepare and seal the paper, and I could have embraced him when he pronounced it finished.

It was now necessary to retreat with caution, and evince as little of the joy we felt as possible. The chief had not considered me even worthy of a question, and my garb – torn and threadbare – could give him no clue to my condition. His attendants and chiefs, however, asked me many questions, and his son sent for me to know the tenets of the Armenians: if they said prayers, believed in Mahommed, and would eat with the 'Faithful'. I replied that we were 'people of the book', and had our prophets; but to the home question of our credence in Mahommed, I said that the New Testament had been written before that personage (on whom be peace) had appeared on earth. The lad turned to the Hindoos who were present and said, 'Why, this poor man is better than you.'

We were soon outside the fortifications and across the bridge, but the heat of the sun was oppressive and we alighted at a garden to pass a few hours. The Hindoos got us refreshment, and, yet enacting the part of a poor man, I had a portion of the Nazir's pillao sent to me, and ate heartily by myself. In the afternoon we returned to

Koondooz, and the good Hindoo of the custom-house told me by the way that the Uzbeks were bad people, and did not deserve truth. 'Whoever you be, therefore, you are now safe.' [Although nothing was said, Burnes realised that most of the Hindus had seen through his disguise, being accustomed to seeing Englishmen in India, and he was grateful for their discretion and loyalty.]

At Koondooz we alighted in our old quarters, at the house of the minister. The town is situated in a valley, surrounded on all sides by hills, except the north where the Oxus flows at a distance of about forty miles. The climate is so insalubrious that there is a proverb among the people: 'If you wish to die, go to Koondooz.' The greater part of the valley is so marshy, that the roads are constructed on piles of wood, and run through the rankest weeds. It has at one time been a large town, but its population does not now exceed 1500 souls, and no person makes it a residence who can live in any other place – though it be yet the market town of the neighbourhood. The chief never visits it but in winter. We could not quit Koondooz without the formal sanction of the minister, and waited for his pleasure till three in the afternoon. [When they left, they rode non-stop to Khooloom – a gruelling seventy miles, which took them twenty hours – and Burnes was again thankful for the gift of the sturdy horse which had been pressed on him by his host in Peshawar.]

It was with heartfelt satisfaction that I again found myself with Dr Gerard and our own party, and witnessed the universal joy. Khooloom is a much more pleasant place than Koondooz, and has many beautiful gardens, and fine fruit; but it was not prudent to incur further risks, with such an example as that of poor Moorcroft before us, and we prepared for a start on the following morning. We showed the order of Moorad Beg to the Wallee [Wali], or governor, and he appointed the prescribed escort to attend us. During night, I transferred a portion of my gold to the Hindoo of the custom-house, for his eminent services, and, to elude discovery, paid it through the hands of the Nazir; but my astonishment may be conceived when I discovered in the morning that, out of twenty gold pieces, he had pocketed fifteen, and put off the Hindoo with five! It was no time for explanation, and after ascertaining the correctness of the fact, I paid it a second time, and left Khooloom in the company of our avaricious Nazir. This *honest* person made us stop by the way, to give him an opportunity of reading a chapter of the Koran, with which he always travelled. Dr Gerard and myself preceded our people, who followed with a caravan, and reached Muzar in the afternoon of the 8th, a distance of thirty miles beyond Khooloom.

The country between these places is barren and dreary, and the road leads over a low pass, called Abdoo, which is the resort of robbers from every quarter, since the whole of the neighbouring chiefs plunder on it. Our escort of Uzbeks reconnoitred the pass, from which Muzar is visible about fifteen miles off, and then left us to journey by ourselves. These men were speaking of the spoil which they themselves had captured a few days before, and I cannot say that I regretted their departure. On our route we saw a very magnificent mirage on our right hand – a snaky line of vapour, as large as the Oxus itself, and which had all the appearance of that river. It mocked our parched tongues, for we had expended the contents of the leathern bottles which we always carried, long before we reached the village.

Muzar is the place where Mr Trebeck, the last of Moorcroft's unfortunate party, expired. One of our companions, a Hajee, attended him on his death-bed, and conducted us to the spot in which he is laid, which is in a small burying-ground westward of the town, under a mulberry tree that was now shedding its fruit upon the grave. This young man has left a most favourable impression of his good qualities throughout the country which we passed, and I could not but feel for his melancholy fate. After burying his two European fellow-travellers, he sank, at an early age, after four months' suffering, without a friend, without assistance, and without consolation. [Some, at least, of Moorcroft's maps and manuscripts were later recovered, and his significant contribution to geographical studies of the region was duly recognised.]

On the morning of the 9th of June we entered the ancient city of Balkh, which is in the dominions of the King of Bokhara, and wound among its extensive ruins for nearly three miles before reaching a caravanserai in the inhabited corner of this once proud 'Mother of Cities'. On the way we were met by two police officers, Toorkmuns, who searched us for our money, that they might tax it. I told them at once that we had twenty gold *tillas* each, and they demanded one in twenty, according to their law, since we were not Mahommedans. We complied, and took a sealed receipt, but they returned in the evening and demanded as much more, since we avowed ourselves as Europeans, and were not subject to a Mahommedan ruler. I discovered that their position was legal, and paid the sum; but I had a greater store of gold than that about my own person. The people gave us no molestation, and our baggage and books were freely submitted to the eye and astonishment of the police.

One of the most satisfactory feelings which we experienced on our arrival at Balkh, was the sure relief from the hands of our enemy at Koondooz and, I may now add, from the tricks of our conductor the Nazir; for he had lately adopted so unworthy a line of conduct that we resolved no longer to place reliance upon him. As we were now in the territories of a king, we could tell him our opinions; though it had, perhaps, been more prudent to keep them to ourselves. If experience had proved the Nazir unworthy of our confidence, Hyat, the Cafila-bashee, had fully established himself in our good graces by his sensible and faithful conduct. He deprecated the meanness of the Nazir, and evinced more detestation of it than ourselves. Hyat was a man of no small penetration, and I was a little staggered at a conversation which passed between us as we approached Balkh, when discussing the motives which had led to our undertaking such a journey. I stated that Bokhara lay on the road to Europe: but Hyat rejoined that the Firingees sought for information on all countries, and that the untimely death of Mr Moorcroft had withheld any correct knowledge of Toorkistan; and we had, probably, been depatched in a quiet way to procure it, as much of that gentleman's misfortunes were to be referred to the mode in which he had travelled. I smiled at the shrewd guess of the man, gave an ironical shout of 'Barikilla!' (Bravo!), and praised his sagacity: but Hyat and I had become good friends, and we had not only nothing to fear, but much to hope, from his kind offices.

CHAPTER VIII

Balkh – and Continuation of the Journey to Bokhara

We continued at Balkh for three days to examine the remains of this once proud city. Its ruins extend for a circuit of about twenty miles, but present no symptoms of magnificence. They consist of fallen mosques and decayed tombs, which have been built of sun-dried brick; nor are any of these ruins of an age prior to Mahommedanism, though Balkh boasts an antiquity beyond most other cities in the globe. By the Asiatics it is named 'Mother of Cities', and said to have been built by Kyamoors, the founder of the Persian monarchy. After the conquest of Alexander the Great it flourished under the name of Bactria, with a dynasty of Grecian kings. In the third century of the Christian era, 'Artaxerxes had his authority solemnly acknowledged in a great assembly held at Balkh, in Khorasan.' [Gibbon] It continued subject to the Persian empire, and the residence of the Archimagus, or head of the Magi, till the followers of Zoroaster were overthrown by the inroads of the caliphs. Its inhabitants were butchered in cold blood by Jenghis Khan; and under the house of Timour it became a province of the Mogul empire. It formed the government of Aurungzebe in his youth, and was at last invaded by the great Nadir. On the establishment of the Duranee monarchy, after his death, it fell into the hands of the Afghans, and within the last eight years has been seized by the King of Bokhara, whose deputy now governs it.

Its present population does not amount to 2000 souls, who are chiefly natives of Cabool, and the remnant of the Kara noukur, a description of militia established here by the Afghans. There are also a few Arabs. The Koondooz chief has marched off a great portion of its population, and constantly threatens the city, which has driven the inhabitants to the neighbouring villages. There are three large colleges, of a handsome structure, now in a state of decay, with their cells empty. The citadel, or Ark, on the northern side, has been more solidly constructed, yet it is a place of no strength. There is a stone of white marble in it, which is yet pointed out as the throne of Kai Kaoos, or Cyrus. There are many inequalities in the surrounding fields which may arise from ruins and rubbish. The city itself, like Babylon, has become a perfect mine for bricks for the surrounding country. Most of the old gardens are now neglected and overgrown with weeds, the aqueducts are dried up, but there are clumps of trees in many directions. The fruit of Balkh is most luscious, particularly the apricots which are nearly as large as apples. The climate of Balkh is very insalubrious, but not disagreeable. Its unhealthiness is ascribed to the water, which is so mixed up with earth and clay as to look like a puddle after rain. All old cities and ruins are, perhaps, more or less unhealthy. It is not probable, however, that so many kings and princes would have patronised a site which was always unfavourable to the health of man, and Balkh itself is not situated in a country naturally marshy, but on a gentle slope which sinks towards the Oxus, about 1800 feet above the level of the sea.

On the 12th of June the caravan arrived from Khooloom with our people, and we prepared to accompany it in its onward journey to Bokhara. For three days we had been living with our friend the Cafila-bashee, who managed to get rice and meat for us from the bazaar, but we made a bungling matter of our cookery. This was but a minor inconvenience, and not without a hope of remedy. It was now necessary, however, to give our Cafila-bashee leave to return to Cabool, since an Afghan would be of little use among Uzbeks. I was indeed sorry to part with Hyat, as his temper and disposition were admirably fitted for managing the people, and he had friends every where who esteemed and respected him. I feared we should miss the man who used to get us food and lodging, when procurable, and tell lies by wholesale regarding our character when necessary. We made him presents in return for his good offices – their value far surpassed his expectations – so that he was more than happy. I gave him a note of hand expressive of our sense of his services; and he ran about in every direction to assist us when setting out, took the Cafila-bashee of the new caravan aside, and pointed out to him how much it would be his interest to serve us. He waited till the caravan departed, and seeing us in our panniers (the new mode of travelling on camels), he bade us farewell, consigned us to God, and left us to plod our way. [Later, in Bokhara, they received a package from the honest Hyat, containing a knife which he discovered they had left behind.]

The caravan assembled outside the city, and near to another melancholy spot: the grave of poor Moorcroft, which we were conducted to see. Mr Guthrie lies by his side. It was a bright moonlight night, but we had some difficulty in finding the spot. At last, under a mud wall which had been purposely thrown over, our eyes were directed to it. The bigoted people of Balkh refused permission to the travellers being interred in their burial-ground, and only sanctioned it near the city upon condition of its being concealed, lest any Mahommedan mistake it for a tomb of one of the true believers and offer up a blessing as he passed it. It was impossible to view such a scene at the dead of night without many melancholy reflections. A whole party buried within twelve miles of each other, held out small encouragement to us, who were pursuing the same track, and led on by nearly similar motives. It was fortunate that the living experienced no such contempt as the dead, for we received no slight from any one, though our creed and our nation were not concealed.

We left Balkh at midnight, with a small caravan of twenty camels, and now exchanged our horses for these useful animals. Two panniers, called '*kujawa*', are thrown across each camel: the Doctor weighed against an Afghan, and I was balanced by my Hindoostanee servant. At first this sort of conveyance was most inconvenient, for the panniers were but four feet long and two and a half wide, and it required some suppleness and ingenuity to stow away a body of five feet nine inches in such a space, tumbled in like a bale of goods. Custom soon reconciled us to the jolting of the camels and the smallness of the conveyance, and it was a great counterbalance to discover that we could read and even note without observation.

On the 14th of June we entered the desert, and travelled all night on our way to the Oxus. We left the great high road from Balkh to

Kilef, the usual ferry, from a fear of robbers, and journeyed westward. At daylight we halted, and had an insight of what we were to expect in the deserts of Tartary. The mountains of Hindoo Koosh had entirely disappeared below the horizon, and a wide plain like an ocean of sand surrounded us on all sides. Here and there were a few round huts or, as they are called, '*khirghas*', the abode of the erratic Toorkmuns. The inhabitants were few in number; at first sight they present a fierce and terrible aspect to a stranger. We alighted near one of their settlements, and they strutted about, dressed in huge black sheepskin caps, but did not molest us. We pitched our camp in their desert, and found a scanty supply of water that had trickled down thus far from the canals of Balkh. We had now no tent, nor shelter of any kind, but a coarse single blanket which we used to stretch across two sets of panniers. Even this flimsy covering sheltered us from the sun's rays; and at night we had it removed and slept in the open air. Our food now consisted of bread and tea, for the Toorkmuns often object to dispose of their sheep, since it injures their estate. Europeans, who are so much accustomed to animal food, are sensible of the change to a diet of bread, but we found it tolerably nutritive, and had much refreshment from tea, which we drank with it at all hours.

It appeared that we had not altogether escaped the tracks of plunderers by our diversion from the main road, and we therefore hired a guard of Toorkmuns to escort us to the Oxus, now only a march distant. We saddled at sunset and after a journey of fifteen hours, and a distance of thirty miles, found ourselves on the banks of that great river, which I gazed on with feelings of great delight. It now ran before us in all the grandeur of solitude, as a reward for the toil and anxiety which we had experienced in approaching it. It might not have been prudent to commit ourselves to a guard of Toorkmuns in such a desert, but they conducted us in safety and made few or no inquiries about us. They spoke nothing but Turkish. They rode good horses and were armed with a sword and long spear. They beguiled the time by singing together, in a language that is harsh but sonorous. They never use more than a single rein, which sets off their horses to advantage.

We halted on the banks of the river, near the small village of Khoju Salu. The vicinity of the Oxus is intersected by aqueducts for nearly two miles, but by no means industriously cultivated. It was a better sign of a more tranquil country to see each peasant's house standing at a distance from that of his neighbour, and in the midst of his own fields. We were detained for two days on the banks of the river, till it came to our turn of the ferry boat, which transferred our caravan, on the 17th, to the northern bank, or the country of Mawurool nuhr, a part of Tartary (or Tatary), but, more correctly speaking, Toorkistan. This river is called Jihoon and Amoo [Amu-darya] by the Asiatics.

After our passage of the Oxus, we commenced our journey towards Bokhara, and halted at Shorkudduk, where there were no inhabitants and about fifteen or twenty brackish wells. The water was clear, but bitter and ill-tasting. Our manner of journeying now became more agreeable. We started about five or six p.m. and travelled till eight or nine next morning. The stages exceeded twenty-five miles; but camels cannot march for a continuance beyond that distance, on account of heat. At night they move steadily forward at the rate of two miles an hour, and are urged on by a pair of tinkling bells hung from the breast or ears of the favourite, that precedes each '*kittar*' or string. The sound is enlivening and cheerful, and when their jingle ceases by a halt of the caravan, the silence which succeeds, in an uninhabited waste, is truly striking.

In the society of a caravan there is much good fellowship, and many valuable lessons for a selfish man. It levels all distinctions between master and servant and, where both share every thing, it is impossible to be singular. Our servants now ate from the same dishes as ourselves. An Asiatic will never take a piece of bread without offering a portion of it to those near him. The Indian Mahommedans were surprised at their brethren in the faith, who gave us a share of their food, and freely partook of our own. One of the tea merchants of the caravan paid us frequent visits at our halting-ground, and we soon became intimate with him. He was a Khwaju, as the followers of the first caliphs are called, and was both a priest and a merchant. He appeared pleased with our society, and we drank tea together on the banks of the Oxus. We told him our true story.

Our next march, to a place called Kirkinjuk, brought us to a settlement of the Toorkmuns, and the country changed from hillocks to mounds of bare sand. The well water was now double the depth, or about thirty-six feet from the surface. The flocks of the Toorkmuns cropped the scanty grass around us, and horses, camels and sheep roamed about loose, as in a state of nature. A shepherd who tended these flocks lingered long near our encampment. He was an unfortunate Persian who had been captured about eight years before, near Meshed, along with 300 other persons, and now sighed for his liberty. His name had been Mahommed; it was changed to Doulut, or the Rich – a singular cognomen for a poor wretch who tended sheep in a desert under a scorching sun. The poor man prowled all day about our caravan, and expressed many a wish to accompany it. He had, however, been purchased for thirty pieces of gold, and if had no riches of his own, he yet formed a part of those of his owner.

In the afternoon of the 20th, as we approached the town of Kurshee [Karshi or Qarshi], we descried at sunset, far to the eastward of us, a stupendous range of mountains covered with snow. As this was in the middle of summer, their elevation must be greater than is assigned to any range north of Hindoo Koosh. They were at a distance of perhaps 150 miles, and we could distinguish them but faintly on the following morning, and never saw them again. At daylight we came to the oasis of Kurshee, a cheering scene after having marched from the Oxus, a distance of eighty-five miles, without seeing a tree. On nearing this town, we entered a flat and champaign country, which was entirely desolate, till within the limits of the river: tortoises, lizards and ants appeared to be its only inhabitants. As a welcome to this first Tartar town, one of our friends in the caravan sent us, as a delicacy, two bowls of 'keimuk chah' or tea, on which the fat floated so profusely that I took it for soup; but it was really tea, mixed with salt and fat, and is the morning beverage of the Uzbeks. Custom never reconciled me to this tea, but our Afghan fellow-travellers spoke of it in loud strains of praise; nor did the manner in which our gift speedily disappeared, when handed over to them, at all belie their taste.

[At Karshi the whole party – and most of the caravan – were

struck down by fever. For three or four days they lay under some trees in the blazing heat with their teeth chattering, and quenched their thirst with 'sherbet of cherries, cooled by ice'. At this inopportune moment they heard rumours that the king of Bokhara, hearing of their approach, had given orders that they were on no account to be allowed into the city. Indeed, it was said, he objected to their travels in his territory altogether, and his officials were about to seize them. This seemed quite possible to Burnes, as their baggage had already been aggressively searched three times in as many days, so he knew he must act swiftly. He managed to compose a suitably diplomatic letter to the vizier (or minister), full of the customary flattering phrases and mentioning that while they had been well received by many other princes, their delight would now be crowned by a visit to the renowned city of Bokhara, that veritable citadel of Islam. A servant was speedily despatched with this missive, which evidently did the trick, for permission was given for them to enter the holy city.]

At Kurshee we were joined by some other travellers, among whom was a moollah from Bokhara, who introduced himself to me: the people of this country possess great affability of manner, and make agreeable companions. The priest and I rode together on our last march to the city, being the only persons on horseback. He gave me an account of the college to which he belonged in Bokhara, and requested me to visit it, which I did not fail to do. My other friend, the Khwaju, at length changed conveyances with the priest, and entertained me for half the night, by repeating and explaining odes and lines of poetry, more to my amusement than edification, for they were all about nightingales and love. It is curious to find so much said on this passion, in a country where there is really so little of it. They marry without seeing each other, or knowing further than that they are of different sexes; nor is this all, for a merchant in a foreign land marries for the time he is to continue in it, and dismisses the lady when he returns to his native country – when both of them seek for other alliances.

Our journey from the Oxus to Bokhara had been of a most fatiguing and trying nature. In Cabool we had been chilled by cold, and were now almost burned up with heat. Our mode of travelling, too, had been extremely irksome, for camels only advance at half the pace of a horse, and we spent double the time on the march, which increased the fatigue. The only horse which accompanied us was so completely knocked up that he fell down in several places before entering Bokhara. We also travelled at night, and the rest which one gets on a camel is broken and disturbed. Our water had often been bad, and our food chiefly consisted of hard biscuit. All these inconveniences were, however, drawing to a close, and before we had reached the gates of Bokhara, they had given rise to reflections of a more pleasing nature.

At the outset of our journey we used to look forward with some anxiety to the treatment we might experience in that city, and, indeed, in many of the then remote places which we had already passed. As we advanced, these apprehensions had subsided, and we now looked back with surprise at the vast expanse of country which we had traversed in safety. Bokhara, which had once sounded as so distant from us, was now at hand, and the success which had hitherto attended our endeavours gave us every hope of bringing the journey to a happy termination. With these feelings we found ourselves at the gates of this eastern capital, an hour after sunrise on the 27th of June, but there was nothing striking in the approach to Bokhara. Though the country is rich, it is flat, and the trees hide the walls and mosques till close upon it. We entered with the caravan, and alighted in a retired quarter of the city, where our messenger had hired a house.

CHAPTER IX

Bokhara

Our first care on entering Bokhara was to change our garb and conform to the usages prescribed by the laws of the country. Our turbans were exchanged for shabby sheep-skin caps, with the fur inside, and our '*kummurbunds*' were thrown aside for a rude piece of rope or tape. The outer garment of the country was discontinued, as well as our stockings, since these are the emblems of distinction in the holy city of Bokhara between an infidel and a true believer. We knew also that none but a Mahommedan might ride within the walls of the city, and had an inward feeling which told us to be satisfied if we were permitted, at such trifling sacrifices, to continue our abode in the capital. A couplet which describes Samarcand as the paradise of the world, also names Bokhara as the strength of religion and of Islam; and, impious and powerless as we were, we could have no desire to try experiments among those who seemed, outwardly at least, such bigots. The dress which I have described is nowhere enjoined by the Koran; nor did it obtain in these countries for two centuries after the prophet, when the prejudice of some of the caliphs discovered that the 'Faithful' should be distinguished from those who were not Mohammedans.

On entering the city, the authorities did not even search us, but in the afternoon an officer summoned us to the presence of the minister. My fellow-traveller was still labouring under fever and could not accompany me; I therefore proceeded alone to the ark or palace, where the minister lived along with the king. I was lost in amazement at the novel scene before me, since we had to walk for about two miles through the streets of Bokhara, before reaching the citadel. I was immediately introduced to the minister or, as he is styled, the Koosh Begee, or Lord of all the Begs, an elderly man of great influence, who was sitting in a small room that had a private courtyard in front of it. He desired me to be seated outside on the pavement, yet evinced both a kind and considerate manner, which set my mind at ease. I presented a silver watch and a Cashmere dress, which I had brought for the purpose, but he declined to receive any thing, saying that he was but the slave of the king.

He then interrogated me for about two hours as to my own affairs, and the objects which had brought me to a country so remote as Bokhara. I told our usual tale of being in progress *towards* our native country, and produced my passport from the Governor-General of India, which the minister read with peculiar attention. I then added that Bokhara was a country of such celebrity among Eastern nations, that I had been chiefly induced to visit Toorkistan for the purpose of seeing it. 'But what is your profession?' said the minister. I replied that I was an officer of the Indian Army. 'But tell me,' said he, 'something about your knowledge,' and he here made various observations on the customs and politics of Europe, but particularly of Russia, on which he was well informed. In reply to some inquiries regarding our baggage, I considered it prudent to acquaint him that I had a sextant, since I concluded that we should be searched, and it was better to make a merit of necessity. I informed him, therefore, that I liked to observe the stars and the other heavenly bodies, since it was a most attractive study. On hearing this the Vizier's attention was roused and he begged, with some earnestness, and in a subdued tone of voice, that I would inform him of a favourable conjunction of the planets and the price of grain which it indicated in the ensuing year. I told him that our astronomical knowledge did not lead to such information; at which he expressed himself disappointed. On the whole, however, he appeared to be satisfied as to our character, and assured me of his protection. While in Bokhara, he said that he must prohibit our using pen and ink, since it might lead to our conduct being misrepresented to the king, and prove injurious. He also stated that the route to the Caspian Sea, by way of Khiva, had been closed for the last year, and that if we intended to enter Russia we must either pursue the northern route from Bokhara, or cross the Toork-mun desert, below Orgunje [Urgench, near Khiva], to Astrabad on the Caspian.

182

[So pleased was the Vizier with his foreign visitor, that Burnes was summoned to see him two days later so that he could display him to his friends and colleagues. On this occasion Burnes presented the minister with a new and very beautifully made patent compass and explained how it could be used to locate the position of Mecca, and therefore to correct the orientation of the Grand Mosque which was currently being built in Bokhara.]

The Koosh Begee packed up the compass with all the haste and anxiety of a child, and said that he would take it direct to his majesty, and describe the wonderful ingenuity of our nation. Thus fell one of my compasses. It was a fine instrument by Schmalcalder, but I had a duplicate, and I think it will be admitted that it was not sacrificed without an ample return. Had we been in Bokhara in disguise, and personating an assumed character, our feelings would have been very different from what they now were. Like owls, we should only have appeared at night; but after this incident we stalked abroad in the noontide sun and visited all parts of the city.

My usual resort in the evening was the Registan of Bokhara, which is the name given to a spacious area in the city, near the palace, which opens upon it. On two other sides there are massive buildings, colleges of the learned, and on the fourth side is a fountain, filled with water and shaded by lofty trees, where idlers and news-mongers assemble round the wares of Asia and Europe, which are here exposed for sale. A stranger has only to seat himself on a bench of the Registan, to know the Uzbeks and the people of Bokhara. He may here converse with the natives of Persia, Turkey, Russia, Tartary, China, India and Cabool. He will meet with Toorkmuns, Calmuks and Cossacks from the surrounding deserts, as well as the natives of more favoured lands.

The Uzbek of Bokhara is hardly to be recognised as a Toork or Tartar from his intermixture of Persian blood. Those from the neighbouring country of Kokand are less changed, and the natives of Orgunje, the ancient Kharasm [Chorasmia], have yet a harshness of feature peculiar to themselves. They may be distinguished from all the others by dark sheep-skin caps, called '*tilpak*', about a foot high. A red beard, grey eyes, and fair skin will now and then arrest the notice of a stranger, and his attention will have been fixed on a poor Russian, who has lost his country and his liberty, and drags out a miserable life of slavery. A native of China may be seen here and there in the same forlorn predicament, shorn of his long cue of hair, with his crown under a turban, since both he and the Russian act the part of Mahommedans. Then follows a Hindoo, in a garb foreign to himself and his country. A small square cap, and a string instead of a girdle, distinguishes him from the Mahommedans and, as the Moslem tells you, prevents their profaning the prescribed salutations of his language by using them to an idolater. The Jew is as marked a being as the Hindoo: he wears a somewhat different dress and a conical cap. No mark, however, is so distinguishing as the well known features of the Hebrew people. In Bokhara they are a race remarkably handsome, and I saw more than one Rebecca in my peregrinations. [Jewish women were not obliged to be veiled.] Their features are set off by ringlets of beautiful hair hanging over their cheeks and necks. There are about 4000 Jews in Bokhara, emigrants from Meshed in Persia, who are chiefly employed in dyeing cloth. They receive the same treatment as the Hindoos. A stray Armenian, in a still different dress, represents this wandering nation. With these exceptions, the stranger beholds in the bazars a portly, fair and well dressed mass of people, the Mahommedans of Toorkistan.

A large white turban and a '*chogha*', or pelisse, of some dark colour, over three or four others of the same description, is the general costume, but the Registan leads to the palace, and the Uzbeks delight to appear before their king in a mottled garment of silk, called '*udrus*', made of the brightest colours and which would be intolerable to any but an Uzbek.

[Udrus, or adras, is in fact a fabric made with a silk warp and cotton weft, though some of these Central Asian garments were made of pure silk. The 'mottled' effect is achieved by the complicated ikat technique of dyeing, where the design is coloured on to the warp threads by repeated tie-dyeing, before they are carefully arranged on the loom. The warp shifts slightly during the weaving process, giving feathered edges to the geometrical shapes of the design. The weft threads are generally of a plain colour, although in 'double-ikat' they are also tie-dyed. The dyes used in the 1830s were probably still made from natural ingredients, giving relatively soft shades, but the Central Asians love bright colours and were delighted to incorporate shocking pink and acid green when chemical dyes were introduced later in the 19th century. Burnes would no doubt have found them unbearably gaudy.]

Some of the higher persons are clothed in brocade, and one may distinguish the gradations of the chiefs, since those in favour ride into the citadel, and others dismount at the gate. Almost every individual who visits the king is attended by his slave; this class of people are for the most part Persians, or their descendants, and have a peculiar [i.e. characteristic] appearance. It is said, indeed, that three fourths of the people of Bokhara are of slave extraction; for of the captives brought from Persia into Toorkistan few are permitted to return and, by all accounts, there are many who have no inclination to do so. A great portion of the people of Bokhara appear on horseback; but whether mounted or on foot they are dressed in boots, and the pedestrians strut on high and small heels, in which it was difficult for me to walk or even stand. They are about an inch and a half high, and the pinnacle is not one third of that in diameter. This is the national dress of the Uzbeks. I must not forget the ladies in my enumeration of the inhabitants. They generally appear on horseback, riding as the men; a few walk, and all are veiled with a black hair-cloth. No-one must speak to them, and if any of the king's harem pass, you are admonished to look in another direction, and get a blow on the head if you neglect the advice.

My reader may now, perhaps, form some idea of the appearance of the inhabitants of Bokhara. From morn to night the crowd which assembles raises a humming noise, and one is stunned at the moving mass of human beings. In the middle of the area the fruits of the season are sold under the shade of a square piece of mat, supported by a single pole. One wonders at the never-ending employment of the fruiterers, in dealing out their grapes, melons, apricots, apples, peaches, pears and plums, to a continued succession of purchasers.

It is with difficulty that a passage can be forced through the streets, and it is only done at the momentary risk of being rode over by some one on a horse or donkey. These latter animals are exceedingly fine and amble along at a quick pace with their riders and burdens. Carts of a light construction are also driving up and down, since the streets are not too narrow to admit of wheeled carriages.

In every part of the bazar there are people making tea, which is done in large European urns, instead of teapots, and kept hot by a metal tube. The love of the Bokharees for tea is, I believe, without parallel, for they drink it at all times and places, and in half a dozen ways: with and without sugar, with and without milk, with grease, with salt, &c. Next to the vendors of this hot beverage one may purchase 'rahut i jan' or the delight of life – grape jelly or syrup, mixed up with chopped ice. This abundance of ice is one of the greatest luxuries in Bokhara, and it may be had till the cold weather makes it unnecessary. It is a refreshing sight to see the huge masses of it, with the thermometer at 90 degrees, coloured, scraped, and piled into heaps like snow. It would be endless to describe the whole body of traders; suffice it to say that almost every thing may be purchased in the Registan: the jewellery and cutlery of Europe, the tea of China, the sugar of India, the spices of Manilla &c. &c. One may also add to his lore both Toorkee and Persian at the book-stalls, where the learned, or would-be so, pore over the tattered pages.

As one withdraws in the evening from this bustling crowd to the more retired parts of the city, he winds his way through arched bazars, now empty, and passes mosques, surmounted by handsome cupolas, and adorned by all the simple ornaments which are admitted by Mahommedans. After the bazar hours these are crowded for evening prayers. With the twilight this busy scene closes, the king's drum beats, it is re-echoed by others in every part of the city and, at a certain hour, no one is permitted to move out without a lantern. From these arrangements the police of the city is excellent, and large bales of cloth are left on the stalls at night with perfect safety. All is silence until morning, when the bustle again commences in the Registan. The day is ushered in with the same guzzling and tea-drinking, and hundreds of boys and donkeys laden with milk hasten to the busy throng.

Soon after our arrival, I paid a visit to our late travelling companions, the tea-merchants, who had taken up their abode in a caravanserai, and were busy in unpacking, praising, and selling their tea. They sent to the bazar for ice and apricots, which we sat down and enjoyed together. One of the purchasers took me for a tea-merchant, from the society I was in, and asked for my investment. His request afforded the merchants and myself some amusement; but they did not undeceive the person as to my mercantile character, and we continued to converse together. In return we had visits from these merchants, and many other persons, who came to gratify curiosity at our expense. We were not permitted to write, and it was an agreeable manner of passing time, since they were very communicative. The Uzbeks are a simple people, with whom one gets most readily acquainted, though they speak in a curious tone of voice, as if they depised or were angry with you. Many of our visitors betrayed suspicions of our character, but still evinced no unwillingness to converse on all points, from the politics of their king to the state of their markets. Simple people! They believe a spy must measure their forts and walls; they have no idea of the value of conversation.

I took an early opportunity of seeing the slave-market of Bokhara, which is held every Saturday morning. The Uzbeks manage all their affairs by means of slaves, who are chiefly brought from Persia by the Toorkmuns. Here these poor wretches are exposed for sale, and occupy thirty or forty stalls where they are examined like cattle, only with this difference, that they are able to give an account of themselves *viva voce*. On the morning I visited the bazar there were only six unfortunate beings, and I witnessed the manner in which they are disposed of. They are first interrogated regarding their parentage and capture, and if they are Mahommedans – that is Soonees. The question is put in that form, for the Uzbeks do not consider a Shiah to be a true believer; with them, as with the primitive Christians, a sectary is more odious than an unbeliever. After the intended purchaser is satisfied of the slave being an infidel (kaffir), he examines his body, particularly noting if it be free from leprosy, so common in Toorkistan, and then proceeds to bargain for the price.

Three of the Persian boys were for sale at thirty tillas of gold apiece (200 rupees), and it was surprising to see how contented the poor fellows sat under their lot. There was one unfortunate girl, who had been long in service and was now exposed for sale by her master because of his poverty. I felt certain that many a tear had been shed in the court where I surveyed the scene, but I was assured from every quarter that slaves are kindly treated; and the circumstance of so many of them continuing in the country after they have been manumitted, seems to establish this fact.

From the slave-market I passed on to the great bazar, and the very first sight which fell under my notice was the offenders against Mahommedanism of the preceding Friday. They consisted of four individuals who had been caught asleep at prayer time, and a youth who had been smoking in public. They were all tied to each other, and the person who had been found using tobacco led the way, holding the hookah in his hand. The officer of police followed with a thick thong and chastised them as he went, calling aloud 'Ye followers of Islam, behold the punishment of those who violate the law!' Never, however, was there such a series of contradiction and absurdity as in the practice and theory of religion in Bokhara. You may openly purchase tobacco, and all the most approved apparatus for inhaling it, yet if seen smoking in public you are straightway dragged before the Cazee, punished by stripes, or paraded on a donkey with a blackened face, as a warning to others. If a person is caught flying pigeons on a Friday, he is sent forth with the dead bird round his neck, yet there are bands of the most abominable wretches who frequent the streets at evening, for purposes as contrary to the Koran as to nature.

The Hindoos of Bokhara courted our society, for that people seem to look upon the English as their natural superiors. They visited us in every country through which we passed, and would never speak any other language but Hindoostanee, which was a bond of union between us and them. In this country they appeared to enjoy a sufficient degree of toleration to enable them to live happily. There are about 300 Hindoos in Bokhara, living in a caravanserai of their own. They are chiefly natives of Shikarpoor in Sinde. The Uzbeks and, indeed, all the Mahommedans, find themselves vanquished by the industry of these people, who will stake the largest sums of money for the smallest gain.

The house in which we lived was exceedingly small, and overlooked on every side, but we could not regret it, since it presented an opportunity of seeing a Toorkee beauty, a handsome young lady, who promenaded one of the surrounding balconies, and *wished to think* she was not seen. A pretended flight was not even neglected by this fair one, whose curiosity often prompted her to steal a glance at the Firingees. Since we had a fair exchange, she was any thing but an intruder, though unfortunately too distant for us to indulge 'in the sweet music of speech'. The ladies of Bokhara stain their teeth quite black; they braid their hair, and allow it to hang in tresses down their shoulders. Their dress differs little from the men: they wear the same pelisses, only that the two sleeves, instead of being used as such, are tucked together and tied behind. In the house even they dress in huge Hessian boots made of velvet and highly ornamented. On the head they wear large white turbans, but a veil covers the face, and many a lovely countenance blooms unseen. The exhibition of beauty, in which so much of a woman's time is spent in more favoured countries, is here unknown. A man may shoot his neighbour if he sees him on a balcony at any but a stated hour. Assassination follows suspicion; for the laws of the Koran, regarding the sex, are most strictly enforced. But jealousy is not the worst vice of the Uzbeks.

I did not omit to pay my respects to the minister while I rambled about the city, and Dr Gerard, in the course of ten days, was sufficiently recovered to accompany me. The Vizier was equally inquisitive with the Nawab at Cabool regarding the preparation of medicines and plasters, of which he wished the doctor to inform him. We had, however, got into a more civilised region on our approach to Europe, since the Vizier had received quinine and other medicines from Constantinople. We sat with the minister while he was transacting business, and saw him levying duties on the merchants, who are most liberally treated in this country. The webs of cloth are produced, and every fortieth piece is taken in place of duties; which gives the merchant his profit without distressing him for ready money. With every disposition to judge favourably of the Asiatics – and my opinions regarding them improved as I knew them better – I have not found them free from falsehood. I fear, therefore, that many a false oath is taken among them.

The Vizier, on this occasion, conversed at great length on subjects of commerce relating to Bokhara and Britain, and expressed much anxiety to increase the communication between the countries, requesting that I myself would return as a trading ambassador to Bokhara, and not forget to bring a good pair of spectacles that he might read his Koran with greater ease. Our intercourse was now established on a footing which promised well: I took occasion therefore to express a wish to the Vizier of paying our duty to the king. I had touched on a delicate point; for it appeared that the minister had feared our being charged with some proposals to his majesty, which we concealed from himself. 'I am as good as the Ameer,' said he (so the king is called), 'and if you have no matters of business to transact with the king, what have travellers to do with courts?' I told him of our curiosity on these points, but he did not choose that we should have the honour, and that was sufficient for abandoning the suit.

I was, nevertheless, resolved to have a sight of royalty, and at midday on the following Friday repaired to the great mosque, a building of Timourlane, and saw his majesty and his court passing from prayers. The king appeared to be under thirty years of age, and had not a prepossessing countenance: his eyes are small, his visage gaunt and pale. He was plainly dressed in a silken robe of 'udrus' with a white turban. He sometimes wears an aigrette of feathers ornamented with diamonds. The Koran was carried in front of him, and he was preceded and followed by two golden mace bearers, who exclaimed in Turkish, 'Pray to God that the Commander of the Faithful may act justly!' His suite did not exceed a hundred people; most of them were dressed in robes of Russian brocade and wore gold ornamented swords – I should call them knives – the mark of distinction in this country. The character of this king, Buhadoor [Bahadur] Khan, stands high among his countrymen: at his elevation to the throne he gave away all his own wealth. He is strict in his religious observances, but less bigoted than his father Meer Hyder. The revenues of the country are said to be spent in maintaining moollahs and mosques; but this young king is ambitious and warlike, and I believe it to be more probable that he uses his treasures to maintain his troops and increase his power.

The life of the king of Bokhara is less enviable than that of most private men. The water which he drinks is brought in skins from the river, under the charge and seal of two officers. It is opened by the Vizier, first tasted by his people and then by himself, when it is once more sealed and despatched to the king. The daily meals of his majesty undergo a like scrutiny: the minister eats, he gives to those around him, they wait the lapse of an hour to judge of their effect, when they are locked up in a box and despatched. His majesty has one key and his minister another. Fruit, sweetmeats, and every eatable undergo the same examination; and we shall hardly suppose that the good king of the Uzbeks ever enjoys a hot meal or a fresh cooked dinner. Poison is common; and the rise of his majesty to the throne on which he now sits is not without strong suspicions of a free distribution of such draughts.

I expressed a wish soon after reaching Bokhara to see some of the unfortunate Russians who have been sold into this country. One evening a stout and manly-looking person fell at my feet and kissed them. He was a Russsian of the name of Gregory Pulakoff, who had been kidnapped when asleep at a Russian outpost, about twenty-five years ago. He was the son of a soldier, and now followed the trade of a carpenter. I made him sit down with us, and give an account of his woes and condition: it was our dinner-time, and the poor carpenter helped us to eat our pilao. Though but ten years of age when captured, he yet retained his native language, and the most ardent wish to return to his country. He paid seven tillas a year to his master, who allowed him to practise his trade and keep all he might earn beyond that sum. He had a wife and child, also slaves. 'I am well treated by master,' said he. 'I go where I choose, I associate with the people and play the part of a Mahommedan; I appear happy, but my heart burns for my native land, where I would serve in the most despotic army with gladness. Could I but see it again, I would willingly die. I tell you my feelings, but I smother them from the Uzbeks. I am yet a Christian (here the poor fellow crossed himself after the manner of the Greek church), and I live among a people who detest, with the utmost cordiality, every individual of that creed. It is only for my own peace that I call myself a Mahommedan.' He enquired with much earnestness if there were any hopes of him and his comrades being released; but I could give him no further solace than the floating rumours which I had heard of the Emperor's intention to suppress the traffic by an army.

CHAPTER X

Bokhara

Tradition assigns the foundation of the city of Bokhara to the age of Sikunder Zoolkurnuen, or Alexander the Great, and the geography of the country favours the belief of its having been a city in the earliest ages. A fertile soil, watered by a rivulet, and surrounded by a desert, was like a haven to the mariner. Bokhara lies embosomed among gardens and trees, and cannot be seen from a distance: it is a delightful place and has a salubrious climate. The circumference of Bokhara exceeds eight English miles, its shape is triangular and it is surrounded by a wall of earth about twenty feet high, which is pierced by twelve gates. Few great buildings are to be seen from the exterior, but when the traveller enters, he winds his way among lofty and arched bazars of brick, and sees each trade in its separate quarter of the city. Every where he meets with ponderous and massy buildings, colleges, mosques and lofty minarets.

Twenty caravanserais contain the merchants of different nations, and about one hundred ponds and fountains, constructed of squared stone, furnish its numerous population with water. The city is intersected by canals shaded by mulberry trees, which bring water from the river of Samarcand. However, Bokhara is very indifferently supplied with water; the river is about six miles distant and the canal is only opened once in fifteen days. In summer the inhabitants are sometimes deprived of good water for months, and when we were in Bokhara the canals had been dry for sixty days. The snow had not melted in the highlands of Samarcand, and the scanty supply of the river had been wasted before reaching Bokhara. The water is bad, and said to be the cause of Guinea worm, a disease frightfully prevalent in Bokhara, which the natives will tell you originates from the water; and they add that these worms are the same that infested the body of the prophet Job!

Bokhara has a population of 150,000 souls: there is scarcely a garden or burying ground within the city walls. With the exception of its public buildings, most of its houses are small and of a single storey; yet there are many superior dwellings in this city. We saw some of them neatly painted with stuccoed walls; others have Gothic arches, set off with gilding and lapis lazuli, and the apartments were both elegant and comfortable. The common houses are built of sun-dried bricks on a framework of wood, and are all flat-roofed. The greatest of the public buildings is a mosque which occupies a square of 300 feet, and has a dome that rises to about a third of that height. It is covered with enamelled tiles of an azure blue colour, and has a costly appearance. It is a place of some antiquity, since its cupola, which was once shaken by an earthquake, was repaired by the renowned Timour. Attached to this mosque is a lofty minaret, built of bricks which have been distributed in most ingenious patterns. Criminals are thrown from this tower; and no one but the chief priest may ever ascend it (and that only on Friday, to summon the people to prayers), lest he might overlook the women's apartments of the houses in the city. The handsomest building of Bokhara is a college of the King Abdoolla. The sentences of the Koran, written over a lofty arch under which is the entrance, exceed the size of two feet, and are delineated on the same beautiful enamel. Most of the domes of the city are thus adorned, and their tops are covered by nests of the 'luglug' – a kind of stork – and a bird of passage which frequents this country and is considered lucky by the people.

I now availed myself of the acquaintance which I had made with the Moollah on my road from Kurshee, to visit his college, which was one of the principal buildings of that description in Bokhara: the 'Madrussa [Madresseh] I Cazee Kulan'. I received the fullest information regarding these institutions from my host and his acquaintance, who produced his tea-pot and gossiped for a length of time. There are about 366 colleges at Bokhara, great and small, a third of which are large buildings that contain upwards of seventy or eighty students. Many have but twenty, some only ten. The colleges are built in the style of caravanserais; a square building is surrounded by a number of small cells. The colleges are well endowed; the whole of the bazars and baths of the city, as well as most of the surrounding fields, have been purchased by different pious individuals for that purpose. In the colleges, people may be found from all the neighbouring countries except Persia, and the students are both young and aged. After seven or eight years of study, they return to their country with an addition to their knowledge and reputation, but some continue for life at Bokhara. The students are entirely occupied with theology, which has superseded all other points: they are quite ignorant even of the historical annals of their country.

After we had been about fifteen days in Bokhara, the Vizier sent for us about midday and kept us till evening: he happened to have some leisure time, and took this means to employ it. We found him in the company of a great many Uzbeks, and it came out that the subjects on which he was to interrogate us were not terrestrial. He wished to know if we believed in God, and our general notions upon religion. I told him that we believed the Deity to be without equal; that he had sent prophets on earth; and that there was a day of judgment, a hell and a heaven. He then entered upon the more tender point of the Son of God, and the prophetic character of Mahommed; but, though he could approve of Christian opinions on neither of these subjects, he took no offence, as I named their prophet with every respect. 'Do you worship idols?' continued the Vizier, to which I gave a strong and negative reply that seemed to excite his wonder. He looked to some of the party, and one of them said that we were practising deceit, for it would be found that we had both idols and crosses round our necks. I immediately laid open my breast, and convinced the party of their error, and the Vizier observed with a smile, 'They are not bad people.' The servants were preparing the afternoon tea, when the Vizier took a cup and said, 'You must drink with us for you are "people of the book", better than the Russians, and seem to have pretty correct notions of truth!' We bowed at the distinction, and were ever after honoured with tea on our visits to the minister.

[The Koosh Begee went on to quiz Burnes on the attitude of the English to Armenians, Jews, and the Hindu and Moslem populations of India, and then slipped in a trick question.]

The cunning catechist now asked me if we ate pork; but here it was

195

absolutely necessary to give a qualified answer; so I said we did, but that the poor people mostly used it. 'What is its taste?' said he. I saw the cross question. 'I have *heard* it is like beef.' He enquired if I had tried horse-flesh since my arrival in Bokhara: I said that I had, and had found it good and palatable. He then asked if we had visited the famous shrine of Bhawa Deen near Bokhara and, on my expressing a wish to see it, he desired a man to accompany us, and requested that we would go quietly. The old gentleman called for a musket, which he put into my hands, and requested me to perform the platoon exercise, which I did. He observed that it differed from the drill of the Russians, of which he knew a little, and began to march, with much grimace, across the room. As we stood and enjoyed the scene, the Koosh Begee, who was a tall broad-shouldered Uzbek, looked at us and exclaimed, 'All you Firingees are under-sized people; you could not fight an Uzbek, and you move like sticks.'

The Vizier then communicated to us that a caravan was preparing for the Caspian Sea, as also for Russia, and that he would take steps to secure our protection if we proceeded; all of which, as well as the kindness and great toleration of the man (for an Uzbek) were most gratifying. We did not leave the minister till it was dark; and he requested the doctor to visit one of his children, whose disease had baffled physic. He found it rickety, and in a very precarious state. The Vizier heard afterwards of its probable end without emotion, saying that he had thirteen sons, and many more daughters.

We took an early opportunity of visiting the shrine near Bokhara, which lies some few miles on the road to Samarcand. I thought little of any tomb while journeying in such a direction, but I did not deem it prudent to sue for permission to visit that celebrated city with our doubtful character. It is only 120 miles from Bokhara, and at Kershee we had been within two marches of it. We were now obliged to rest satisfied with an account of a capital, the existence of which may be traced to the time of Alexander. It was the metropolis of Timour, and the princes of his house passed their winters at it. 'In the whole habitable world,' says Baber, 'there are few cities so pleasantly situated as Samarcand.' The city has now declined from its grandeur to a provincial town of 8000, or at most 10,000 inhabitants, and gardens and fields occupy the place of its streets and mosques, but it is still regarded with high veneration by the people.

The prohibition to mount a horse did not extend beyond the limits of Bokhara, and our servants had the satisfaction of riding our ponies to the gate, as we walked by their side. When outside the city, we soon reached the tomb of Bhawa Deen Nukhsbund, one of the greatest saints of Asia, who flourished in the time of Timour. A second pilgrimage to his tomb is said to be equal to visiting Mecca itself. We entered the sacred spot with no other ceremonies than leaving our slippers outside. We were also taken to visit the holy man who had charge of it, and who gave us cinnamon tea and wished to kill a sheep for our entertainment. He, however had so many diseases, real or imaginary, that after a detention of two hours we were glad to get away.

About twenty-five miles north-west of Bokhara, and on the verge of the desert, there lie the ruins of an ancient city called Khojuoban, and which is assigned by tradition to the age of the caliph Omar. Mahommedans seldom go beyond the era of their Prophet, and this proves nothing. Many coins are found in this neighbourhood, and I am fortunate in possessing several beautiful specimens, which turn out to be genuine relics of the monarchs of Bactria. They are of silver, and nearly as large as a half-crown piece. A head is stamped on one side, and a figure is seated on the reverse. The execution is very superior, and the expression of features and spirit of the whole do credit even to the age of Greece, to which it may be said they belong. They brought numerous antiques from the same place, representing the figures of men and animals cut out on cornelians and other stones. Some of these bore a writing that differs from any which I have seen before, and resembled Hindee.

A month had nearly elapsed since our arrival in Bokhara, and it was necessary to think of moving onwards; but the route that we should follow became a subject of serious consideration, from the troubled state of the country. The object which we had in view was to reach the Caspian, and the higher up we should land on its shores the better, but there were difficulties on every side. No caravan had passed from Khiva to the Caspian for a year, owing to a blood feud with the Khirgizzes of the steppe. A Bokhara caravan lay at Khiva, and one from Astracan at Mangusluk on the Caspian: neither party could advance till some adjustment was made; which was more hoped for than expected. How much our good fortune predominated, in not accompanying the Khiva caravan, will hereafter appear. [Months later, while in Khorasan, Burnes met up with a party of pilgrims from Bokhara who told him that the Russian caravan had been attacked and plundered by Kirghiz bandits near Khiva.] The direct road, by the territories of Khiva to Astrabad in Persia, was also closed to us, for the Khan of Khiva had taken the field to oppose the Persians, and lay encamped in the desert south of his capital, whither he ordered all the caravans to be conducted. The route by Merve and Meshed was open and more safe, but it appeared advisable for us to pursue the second of these routes, since we should see a portion of the territories of Khiva, then effect our passage to the frontiers of Persia, and ultimately reach the Caspian Sea by the desert of the Toorkmuns. All our friends, Hindoo, Armenian and Afghan, dissuaded us from encountering the Khan of Khiva, who was described as inimical to Europeans; but since we resolved to run every risk, and follow the route which would lead us upon him, I waited on our patron, the Vizier, and made him acquainted with these intentions. He urged our proceeding by a caravan of two hundred camels that was just starting for Russia, and which would lead us to Troitskai in that country, but this did not suit our plans, as the route had been travelled by the Russian mission, and we had no wish to enter Asiatic Russia, but to reach the Caspian. The Vizier said that he would make inquiries regarding the departure of the caravan, and as we desired to follow the route that would lead us to the frontiers of Persia, he would afford us his assistance as far as it lay in his power. The caravan only awaited his commands to set out on its journey.

On the 21st of July we made our farewell visit to the Vizier of Bokhara, and our audience of leave places the character of this good man even in a more favourable light than all his previous kindness. The Koosh Begee is a man of sixty, his eyes sparkle, though his beard is silvered by age. His countenance beams with intelligence, but it is marked with cunning, which is said to be the most striking feature in his character. He showed much curiosity regarding our language, and made me write the English numbers from one to a thousand in the Persian character, as well as a few words which expressed the common necessaries of life. He spent about an hour in this lesson, and regretted that he had no better opportunity of acquiring our language. He then begged that we would return to Bokhara as 'trading ambassadors', to establish a better understanding and a more extended commerce with the country.

He now summoned the Cafila-bashee of the caravan, and a chief of the Toorkmuns, who was to accompany it as a safeguard against his tribe. He wrote down their names, families, habitations and, looking at them, said, 'I consign these Europeans to you. If any accident befall them, your wives and families are in my power, and I will root them from the face of the earth. Never return to Bokhara, but with a letter containing an assurance, under their seal, that you have served them well.' Turning to us, he continued, 'You must not produce the "firman" of the king, which I now give you, till you find it necessary. Travel without show, and make no acquaintances; for you are to pass through a dangerous country. When you finish your journey, pray for me, as I am an old man and your well-wisher.'

I had not reached home before I was again sent for, and found the Vizier sitting with five or six well-dressed people, who had been evidently talking about us. 'Sikunder' (as I was always addressed), said the Koosh Begee, 'I have sent for you to ask if anyone has molested you in this city, or taken money from you in my name, and if you leave us contented.' I replied that we had been treated as honoured guests, that our baggage had not even been opened, nor our property taxed, and that I should ever remember, with the deepest sense of gratitude, the many kindnesses that had been shown to us in the holy Bokhara. The reply closed all our communications with the Vizier; and the detail will speak for itself. I quitted the worthy man with a full heart and with sincere wishes, which I still feel, for the prosperity of this country.

In the afternoon the camels were laden and ready to take their departure. The last person we saw in our house was the landlord, who came running in the bustle of preparation to bid us farewell. He brought me a handsome and highly wrought skull-cap as a present: nor did I consider it necessary to tell him that a few months more would change my costume, and render his present useless. I gave him a pair of scissors in return, and we parted with the greatest demonstrations of friendship. The camels preceded us and we ourselves, accompanied by an Uzbek acquaintance, took our last walk through the streets of Bokhara. I cannot say that I felt much regret at clearing the gates of the city, since we should now be more free from suspicion, and able both to ride and write. We had, indeed, managed to use the pen at night with leaden eyes, but even then, we did it with fear. We joined the caravan about half a mile beyond the city gate, where we bivouacked for the night in a field.

CHAPTER XI

Detention in the Kingdom of Bokhara

Three short marches brought us to the home of the Cafila-bashee of our caravan: a small village of twenty houses, called Meerabad, forty miles from Bokhara in the district of Karakool [Karakul]. What was our disappointment to discover, on the eve of prosecuting our journey, that the whole of the merchants declined to advance, and had taken alarm at the proceedings of the Khan of Khiva. That personage, in examining the bales of a caravan from Persia, discovered some earth from the holy Kerbela, which had been packed up with the goods, according to custom, as a spell on their safe transit. [Karbala, in present-day Iraq, is revered by Shia Muslims as the place where their Imam Hussain, grandson of the Prophet, met his death.] But the precaution, so much at variance with orthodox Mahommedanism, had a very contrary effect. The greater portion of the goods was plundered, and since many of our merchants were Persians, at least Shiahs, they resolved to run no risks, and wait either for the withdrawal of the army, or an assurance of protection to their property, under the seal of the Khan. The last alternative seemed the most judicious mode of terminating all anxiety, and it was discussed in full assemblage.

The merchants formed a congress at the hut in which we were living, for the Vizier had kindly made mention of us to all of them. After some pressing and refusing, one individual was singled out as the scribe of a letter to the officer of the Khan of Khiva. [The petition, couched in polite but plain phrases, asked the Khan to confirm that he would impose only the customary taxes on their caravan, and would not despoil their goods. Burnes was impressed that even the flowery Persians could, when push came to shove, come so quickly to the point. A Turkman was despatched with the missive and promised to be back in a week.] After the messenger had been depatched, the whole of the principal merchants of the caravan returned to Bokhara, and we were left in an obscure village of Tartary, to consider whether we should continue in our present abode or return to the capital. We resolved to pursue the first course, and made up our minds to our unlucky detention.

In our journey from Bokhara we had some opportunities of adding to our knowledge of the country. Four or five miles from the city we entered on a tract which was at once the extreme of richness and desolation. To the right, the land was irrigated by the aqueducts of the Kohik, and to our left the dust and sand blew over a region of dreary solitude. After travelling for a distance of twenty miles in a WSW direction, we found ourselves on the banks of the river of Samarcand, which the poets have styled 'Zarufshan', or gold-scattering; but we must attribute its name to the incomparable blessings bestowed upon its banks, rather than the precious ores which it deposits. This river did not exceed the breadth of fifty yards, and was not fordable. It had much the appearance of a canal for, a little further down, its waters are hemmed in by a dam, and distributed with care among the neighbouring fields. The stripe of cultivated land on either bank did not exceed a mile in breadth and was often less; for the desert pressed closely in upon the river. The number of inhabited places was yet great, and each different settlement was surrounded by a wall of sun-dried bricks, as in Cabool; but the houses were neither so neat nor so strong as in that country. At this season (July), every cultivated spot groaned under the gigantic melons of Bokhara, many of which were also being transported in caravans of camels to the city.

The direct course which we were pursuing to the Oxus led us away from the Kohik, but after crossing a belt of sand-hills, about three miles wide, we again descended upon it. Its bed was entirely dry, since the dam of Karakool which we had passed, prevents the egress of its scanty waters at this season. We found that this river, instead of flowing into the Oxus, forms a rather extensive lake, called 'Dengiz' ('sea' in Turkish) by the Uzbeks, and close to which we were now encamped. We were now living among the Toorkmuns, who occupy the country between the Oxus and Bokhara. They only differ from the great family to which they belong in residing in permanent houses, and being peaceable subjects of the King of Bokhara. About forty different '*robats*' or clusters of their habitations lay in sight of ours, and we passed nearly a month in their neighbourhood and society without receiving insult or injury or aught, I believe, but their good wishes. In our unprotected state, this was highly creditable to the natives of Toorkistan.

Ernuzzer, the Toorkmun chief to whom we had been introduced at Bokhara, was both an useful and amusing companion. He was a tall bony man, about fifty, with a manly countenance, improved by a handsome beard that was whitening by years. In early life, he had followed the customs of his tribe and proceeded on 'allaman' (plundering) excursions to the countries of the Huzara and Kuzzil-bash [Persians]; and some fearful wounds on his head showed the dangerous nature of that service. Ernuzzer had now relinquished the occupations of his youth and the propensities of his race, but though he had transferred his family to Merve, as civilised and reformed Toorkmuns, his aspect and his speech were still those of a warrior.

One of the most remarkable of our Toorkmun visitors was a man of mature age and blunt address. His name was Soobhan Verdi Ghilich: which, being interpreted, means '*the sword given by God*', and no visitor was more welcome than Verdi, who described in animated strains his attacks on the Kuzzil-bash. The Toorkmun shook with delight as I made him detail the mode of capturing them, and sighed that his age now prevented him from making war on such infidels. Verdi now possessed flocks of sheep and camels, and since his years did not permit of his continuing forays, he despatched his sons on that service. He would tell me that his camels and his sheep were worth so many slaves, and that he had purchased this horse for three men and a boy, and that one for two girls: for such is the mode of valuing their property. These are desperate men, and it is a fortunate circumstance that they are divided among one another, or greater might be the evils which they inflict on their fellow men. This great family of the human race roams from the shores of the Caspian to Balkh, changing their place of abode as inclination prompts them.

The tribe we were now living with is known by the name of Ersaree;

and for the first time in a Mahommedan country, we saw the ladies unveiled: but this is a prevalent custom throughout the Toorkmun tribes. In no part of the world have I seen a more rude and healthy race of damsels in form or feature, though they are the country-women of the delicate Roxana, the bewitching queen of Alexander, whom he married in Transoxiana.

Though the village in which we were now residing could not boast of more than twenty houses, there were yet eight Persian slaves; and these unfortunate men appear to be distributed in like proportion throughout the country. They are employed as cultivators and were at this time engaged in gathering in the crop, though the thermometer was 96 degrees within doors. Three or four of them were in the habit of visiting us, and I took letters from some of them to their friends in Persia, which were afterwards delivered. Many slaves save a sufficiency to redeem themselves: for a Persian is a sharper being than an Uzbek, and does not fail to profit by his opportunities. At Meerabad two or three slaves had gathered sums that would liberate them; but though they fully intended to avail themselves of an opportunity to return to Persia, I never heard these people, in my different communications with them, complain of the treatment which they experienced in Toorkistan. It is true that some of their masters object to their saying their prayers and observing the holidays prescribed by the Koran, since such sanctity would deprive them of a portion of their labour, but they are never beaten, and are clothed and fed as it they belonged to the family. It has been observed that Mahommedan slavery differs widely from that of the negroes, nor is the remark untrue; but the capture of the inhabitants of Persia, and their forcible exile among strangers, is as odious a violation of human rights and liberties as the African slave-trade.

The condition of our own little party perhaps afforded as much ground for curiosity and reflection as the strange people among whom we were living. At dusk in the evening we would draw forth our mats and spread them out, and huddle together, master and servant, to cook and eat within the limited circle. In a remote country, and in an obscure village of Tartary, we slept in the open air, lived without an escort, and passed weeks without molestation. Before

204

one has encountered such scenes, the vague and indefinite ideas formed of them give rise to many strange thoughts; but when among them they appeared as nothing. In every place we visited we had been in the power of the people, and one cross-brained fool, of which every country has many, might have destroyed at once all our best laid plans and schemes. We mixed with the people, and our continued collision placed us in constant danger, but yet we had happily escaped it all. A chain of circumstances, fortuitous indeed, and for which we could not but feel sensibly grateful, with the tranquil state of the countries through which we passed, had been the great cause of our good fortune; for confidence and prudence, though they be the foremost requisites of a traveller, avail not in a country that is torn by factions and rebellion.

Our party had considerably diminished since I last described it on the Indus; one of the Indians had retraced his steps from Cabool, and the chilling blasts of Hindoo Koosh had frightened the doctor's servant, who was a native of Cashmere. Otherwise we had to bear the most ample testimony to the patience and perseverance of those we had chosen. Of these the most remarkable was Mohun Lal, the Hindoo lad from Delhi, who exhibited a buoyancy of spirit and interest in the undertaking most rare in an Indian. At my request he kept a minute journal of events; and I venture to believe, if hereafter published, that it will arrest and deserve attention. [It was indeed published, in 1846, with the title *Travels in the Panjab, Afghanistan & Turkistan: to Balk, Bokhara and Herat.*] On his route to Bokhara his tale had run, that he was proceeding to his friends in that country and, as we had passed that city, he was now joining his relatives at Herat! The native surveyor, poor Mahommed Ali, whose loss I have since had to deplore, generally travelled as a pilgrim proceeding to Mecca, holding little or no open communication with us.

[To relieve the tedium of their protracted stay at Meerabad, Burnes re-read Arrian and Curtius and poked about in the nearby ruins of Bykund, using as his guide a manuscript history of the area which he had bought in Bokhara. He later gave this document, called the 'Nursukhee', to the Oriental Translation Committee in London.]

About midnight on the 10th of August, when we had almost despaired of the return of our messenger to the Orgunje camp, we were roused from sleep by the shout of 'Ullaho Acbar' from five or six Toorkmuns. They accompanied their countryman with the joyful information that the chief of Organje would not offer any obstacles to the advance of our caravan. He gave us a frightful account of the desert south of the Oxus, and the great difficulty of finding the road, which was now hidden by clouds of sand that were disturbed by the wind. We took his advice and hired two extra camels, which were to be the bearers of six skins of water, the supply which was deemed necessary to store before we took leave of the Oxus.

Our stay near Karakool had now been prolonged to the middle of August, and were I not more anxious to enter on other matters, I might give some account of this region of lamb-skins, supplying as it does, the whole of Tartary, China, Persia and Turkey. The caravan soon collected once more at our quarters, and on the morning of the 16th of August there appeared about eighty camels to prosecute the journey to the Oxus, all of them laden with the precious skins of the little distict of Karakool, where we had passed nearly a month among Toorkmuns and shepherds who talked of nothing but fleeces and markets. Among the arrivals from Bokhara, we were agreeably surprised and delighted to find a small packet to my address, the contents of which consisted of three newspapers and a most kind letter from my friend M. Allard at Lahore. The packet had been three months in coming and afforded us indescribable pleasure, after our long ignorance of what was passing in the world. We had not seen a newspaper since crossing the Indus in the middle of March, and were now indebted to a foreigner for those which we had received. In one of the papers it was curious enough to observe a long paragraph regarding the unfortunate Mr Moorcroft, who preceded us in these countries. We learned from it that the world was deeply interested in the lands where we now sojourned, and that the Geographical Society of London had resolved on rescuing the papers of the traveller from oblivion. With these circumstances before us, and even in the absence of any communications from our own countrymen, we had a pleasing reflection that we should not be forgotten in our wanderings.

CHAPTER XII

Journey in the Desert
of the Toorkmuns

At midday on the 16th of August we commenced our march on the Oxus, which was about twenty-seven miles distant. After journeying for ten miles we halted in the evening at a small village, and set out at midnight for the river, under a bright moon. For a great part of the night our route led us among vast fields of soft sand, formed into ridges which exactly resembled, in colour and appearance, those on the verge of the ocean. The belt of these sand-hills, which lie between Bokhara and the Oxus, varies in breadth from twelve to fifteen miles. They were utterly destitute of vegetation. There was a remarkable uniformity in their formation; the whole of them preserved the shape and form of a horse-shoe, the outer rim presenting itself to the north, the direction from which the winds of this country blow. On this side the mounds sloped, while the interior of the figure was invariably precipitous; but the loose sand will ever take its position from the prevailing winds. None of the hills exceeded the height of fifteen or twenty feet, and they all rested on a hard base. About an hour after the sun had risen we exchanged this dreary route for verdant fields, irrigated by the Oxus, and after winding them for about four miles, encamped on the verge of the river, where we hid ourselves from the sun's rays under the panniers of our camels.

We had come down upon the Oxus at Betik, which is opposite to Charjooee [Charjui], and one of the greatest ferries between Persia and Toorkistan. There was, therefore, every facility for crossing, and the beasts and baggage were thrown into boats and soon transported to the opposite bank. The farmer of the customs killed his sheep, and invited most of the merchants to partake of his fare. He enquired very particularly regarding us, and requested a sight of our passport. He then waited on us in person with a couple of melons and some cakes, which we sat down and enjoyed along with him and his party on the banks of the river, and I believe mutually amused each other.

As we were preparing to embark, I had an example of the meanness of native traders. Our boat had no horses to drag it across, and it was proposed that we should hire them; to which I gave a ready assent, saying that we should be happy to contribute our share of the expense. The reply was unsatisfactory, since they wished we should bear it all; but this was peremptorily refused, and we embarked without the horses. We crossed the Oxus in safety, and I did not regret the opportunity that had presented itself to show our fellow-voyagers that we were as poor in our purses as in our dress and condition.

We found the stream of the Oxus with a breadth of 650 yards, and in some places 25 and 29 feet deep, so that it was both narrower and deeper than at the point at which we had before crossed it. Some fish of an enormous size, weighing from five to six hundred pounds, are procured in this river, a kind of dog-fish, which are used as food by the Uzbeks. Across the Oxus we found ourselves about six miles distant from the town of Charjooee, which was in sight. For the first time, this noble river was turned to the purposes of navigation, since there is a commercial communication kept up, by means of it, between that place and Orgunje. In the morning we moved up to Charjooee, which in all our maps is erroneously set down on the northern bank of the Oxus. The place is governed by a Kalmuk, and is pleasantly situated on the verge of culture and desolation, with a pretty fort that crowns a hillock and overlooks the town. It is said to have resisted the arms of Timour, but its present condition would not impress any one with any great notions of its strength, or that conqueror's power.

The people of Charjooee do not exceed 4000 or 5000 souls; but a greater portion of its population wander up and down the Oxus during the hot months. We halted here for four days, since it was the last inhabited spot of civilisation between Bokhara and Persia. The market day, or bazar, occurred during our stay, and I proceeded along with Ernuzzar, the Toorkmun, to see the assemblage – in which I passed quite unnoticed. I sauntered through the bazar, much more amused with the people than the wares they were selling, which were in every respect poor. There were knives, saddles and bridles, cloth, and horsecloths, of native manufacture; but the only articles of European fabric were a few beads, and chintz skullcaps, which latter were purchased very readily. There were also lanterns, ewers, and copper pots in considerable number; the vendors of many of these retailed their goods *on horseback*, and all the purchasers were mounted. No person ever attends the bazar in Toorkistan but on horseback; and on the present occasion there was not a female to be seen, veiled or unveiled. Most of the people were Toorkmuns of the Oxus, dressed in high sheepskin hats, like the natives of Orgunje.

There were about two or three thousand people in the bazar, but there was very little bustle and confusion, though there was much both of buying and selling. The custom of having market days is uncommon in India and Cabool, but of universal use in Toorkistan: it perhaps gives a stimulus to trade and is most convenient, since all the people of the country for miles around assemble for the occasion. Every person seems to think it incumbent upon him to be present. The different articles are arranged in separate parts of the bazar, with as much regularity as in Bokhara itself. The streets are so narrow that the bazar is generally held at one end of the country towns, and such was the case at Charjooee; so that fruit, grain, or any thing which requires to be displayed, is spread out on the ground. The bazar lasts from eleven to four o'clock, which is the hottest time of the day.

The wants of all had been supplied during our stay at Charjooee, every one was ready to move, and every skin, pot and pitcher was filled to the brim from the canals of the Oxus. At noon on the 22nd we commenced our march, and before we had travelled a distance of two miles, entered upon the great desert which separates the kingdoms of Iran and Tooran [Turan or Turania, an old name for the region north of Persia and next to the Caspian Sea, including what is now Turkmenistan]. The mode of travelling in Toorkistan is to start at midday and march till sunset and, after a couple of hours' rest and

the indispensable cup of tea, to resume the task and advance to the
stage, which is usually reached at daylight. We made the usual
evening halt, and then travelled till sunrise, when we reached
Karoul, a well of brackish water, thirty feet under ground, lined
with branches of trees, at which we halted – a distance of twenty-two
miles from Charjooee. The whole tract presented to our view was a
dreary waste of sand-hills, but by no means so destitute of vegetation
and underwood as on the northern bank of the Oxus. In the hollows
and on the brow of the sand-hills, we found a shrub like tamarisk,
also a kind of grass and two thorny shrubs, neither of them the
common camel-thorn, but on which the camels delighted to browse.

In the middle of our march through the desert, we met seven
unfortunate Persians who had been captured by the Toorkmuns,
and were now on their road to Bokhara, where they would be sold.
Five of them were chained together, and trod their way through the
deep sand. There was a general shout of compassion as the caravan
passed these miserable beings, and the sympathy did not fail to
affect the poor creatures themselves. They cried, and gave a longing
look, as the last camel of the caravan passed to their dear native
country. The camel on which I rode happened to be in the rear, and
I stayed to hear their tale of woe. They had been seized by the
Toorkmuns at Ghaeen, near Meshed, a few weeks before, when the
culture of their fields had led them beyond the threshold of their
homes. They were weary and thirsty, and I gave them all I could – a
single melon; a civility, little as it was, which was received with
gratitude. The Toorkmuns evince but little compassion for their
Persian slaves: and what other treatment is to be expected from men
who pass their lives in selling human beings? They give them but a
scanty supply of food and water, that they may waste their strength
and prevent their escape; but beyond this the Toorkmun inflicts no
other ills. The tales which have been circulated of their cutting the
sinew of the heel, and of their passing a cord round the collar-bone,
are at variance with the truth, since these blemishes would diminish
the value of the slave.

As we reached our halting-ground in the morning, we had an
opportunity of observing the number and composition of our caravan.

There were upwards of eighty camels and about 150 persons, who accompanied their merchandise to the markets of Persia. Some travelled in panniers placed on camels, others rode, many on donkeys, but every person had some kind of conveyance. The scene was altogether curious and novel. Among the party were eight or ten Persians who had passed many years of slavery in Toorkistan, and after purchasing their liberty were now returning by stealth to their homes. Some of them had been no less than three times captured, and as often had they redeemed themselves, for the Uzbeks are readily imposed upon and cheated by their slaves, who amass money in their service. I conversed with several of them, and it was equally painful to hear their past sufferings and present anxiety. Their influential countrymen in the caravan had put several of them in charge of a portion of their merchandise, that they might be the less noticed, and considered rather as traders than emancipated slaves, for a Persian merchant in a caravan is generally safe. In spite of all this arrangement, some hard-hearted wretches had told tales on the banks of the Oxus; one individual had been forced to return to Bokhara, and some of the others had crossed with difficulty.

In marching from Karoul, we quitted the high road of the caravans, which leads to Merve, and proceeded westward into the desert, by a way that is altogether unfrequented. We had no option in the selection of such a route, since the officer who commands the Orgunje army sent a messenger to direct our march upon his camp. We were thus thrown into the jaws of the lion, but were helpless; and the merchants appeared to regret it more than ourselves. After the usual halt, we reached the well of Balghooee, twenty-four miles distant, on the morning of the 23rd. It was a small and single well, about four feet in diameter, and the Toorkmuns only discovered it after a zigzag search of some hours. We soon emptied it (for the water was good), and had to wait a night till it again filled.

We had before heard of the deserts south of the Oxus, and had now the means of forming a judgment from personal observation. We saw the skeletons of camels and horses which had perished from thirst bleaching in the sun. The nature of the roads or pathways admits of their easy obliteration and, if the beaten track be once forsaken, the traveller and his jaded animal generally perish. A circumstance of this very nature occurred but a few days previous to our leaving Charjooee. A party of three persons travelling from the Orgunje camp lost the road, and their supply of water failed them. Two of their horses sank under the parching thirst, and the unfortunate men opened the vein of their surviving camel, sucked its blood, and reached Charjooee from the nourishment which they thus derived. The camel died. These are facts of frequent occurrence.

After a day's detention to rest the camels, we marched at sunrise and continued our progress, with a short halt, till the same time next day. We journeyed thirty-five miles, and alighted at a fetid well called Seerab; and from well to well we had no water. We appeared to have lost the great sand-hills in our advance westward. The desert, though it had the same features as before, now presented an undulating and uneven country of sand, partially covered with shrubs. Our Toorkmun Sirdar made his appearance shortly after our arrival, to claim his cup of tea; I always felt the happier in the company of this man, for I looked upon him as the only bond between us and the barbarians we had to encounter. Ernuzzer did not deceive us, and the tea and sugar which he consumed were but a small tax for his services.

A caravan is a complete republic, but I do not believe that most republics are so orderly. Of our eighty camels every three or four belonged to different individuals, and there were four Cafila-bashees. Still there was no disputing about the arrangement or order of the march, and it is a point of honour that the one shall at all times wait for the other. If a single camel throws its load, the whole line halts till it is replaced, and one feels pleased at such universal sympathy. These feelings make it agreeable to travel in a caravan, for the detentions are much fewer than would be readily imagined. The more I mingled with Asiatics in their own sphere, and judged them by their own standard, the more favourable impressions I imbibed regarding them. One does not see in civilised Europe that generous feeling which induces the natives of Asia, great and small, to share with each other every mouthful that they possess. The khan fares as simply as the peasant, and never offers to raise a morsel to his lips till he has shared it with those near him. I myself frequently have been partaker of this bounty from rich and poor, for nothing is enjoyed without society.

Our next march brought us at midnight to Ooch-ghooee, or the Three Wells, which we had great difficulty in finding. We wandered to the right and left, and the Toorkmuns dismounted in the dark and felt for the pathway with their hands among the sand. We had almost despaired of recovering it, and were preparing for our bivouac, when the bark of a dog, and a distant answer to our repeated calls, dispelled our anxiety, and we were soon encamped at the well. We here found a few wandering Toorkmuns, the first we had seen since leaving the Oxus. The water was bitter, but these shepherds seem indifferent to its quality. The Toorkmuns rallied round us next morning and we had the freest intercourse with them, for they were quite ignorant of our character, and the presence of one of their own tribe, our Toorkmun Ernuzzer, proved a sufficient attraction to these 'children of the desert'. They spoke of the piercing cold of winter in this country, and assured us that the snow sometimes lay a foot deep. We ourselves had experienced a depression of ten degrees in the temperature since leaving the Oxus.

We were now informed that we were approaching the camp of the Khan of Orgunje which, it appears, was on the banks of the Moorghab [Murghab] or Merve river, considerably below the place of that name, and about thirty miles distant from us. We set out at noon, and by the time the sun had set, found ourselves among the ruins of forts and villages, now deserted, which rose in castellated groups over an extensive plain. We had been gradually emerging from the sand-hills, and these marks of human industry were the ancient remnants of civilisation of the famous kingdom of Merve, or, as our historians have erroneously called it, Meroo. [Modern maps call it 'Mary'.] Before we had approached them, we had not wanted signs of our being delivered from the ocean of sand, since several flocks of birds had passed over us. As the mariner is assured by such indications that he nears land, we had the satisfaction of knowing that we were approaching the water, after a journey of 150 miles through a sterile waste, where we had suffered considerable inconvenience from the want of it. We were not yet within the pale of habitations, but after a cool and pleasant march over a perfectly flat and hard plain, every where interspersed with forts and ruins, we found ourselves about nine in the following morning at a large Toorkmun camp (or, as it is called, an Oba) near the banks of the Moorghab. The name of the place was Khwaju Abdoolla, and the whole colony sallied forth to meet the caravan. We took up a position on a hillock about two or three hundred yards distant, and the merchants instructed us to huddle together among ourselves, and appear lowly and humble. We did so, and the Toorkmuns of the encampment soon crowded around us, begging for tobacco, for which they brought loads of the most luscious melons, that we cut up and enjoyed in the company of camel drivers and slaves.

It was now discovered that the Orgunje camp lay on the other side of the river, which was not fordable but in certain places. The merchants decided that they themselves, with all the Cafila-bashees, should forthwith proceed in person to the spot, and use their utmost to conciliate the officer in charge, for the Khan had returned within these few days to Khiva. Their great object seemed to be to effect a discharge of the duties in the spot where they were now encamped, since no one wished to trust their property within reach of an Orgunje detachment. If the party prayed for success, I can add that we were equally fervent, and the deputation accordingly set out with the good wishes of every one. We were left among the 'oi polloi' of the caravan, and when night came, stretched our felts under a clear and cloudless sky, and slept without fear or anxiety from our man-selling neighbours; for a Toorkmun, though he can engage in a foray, and execute it with unexampled address, cannot commit a theft in a quiet way, which is not congenial to his nature.

The Toorkmun camp at which we halted presented to us a scene of great novelty. It consisted of about 150 conical movable huts, called '*khirgahs*', which were perched on a rising ground. There was no order in the distribution, and they stood like so many gigantic beehives, and we might also take the children as the bees, for they were very numerous. I wondered at the collection of so many rising plunderers. Seeing the Toorkmuns in a body, it may be certainly distinguished that they have something Tatar in their appearance: their eyes are small and the eyelids appear swollen. They are a handsome race of people. All of them were dressed in the *'tilpak'*, a square or conical black cap of sheepskin, about a foot high, which is far more becoming than a turban, and gives to a party of Toorkmuns the appearance of a soldier-like and disciplined body. The Toorkmuns are very fond of bright-coloured clothes, and choose the lightest shades of red, green and yellow as the patterns of their flowing *'chupkuns'*, or pelisses. In my notice of the Toorkmuns I must not now forget the ladies, whose head-dress would do honour to the galaxy of an English ball-room. It consists of a lofty white turban, shaped like a military chako, but higher, over which a red or white scarf is thrown, that falls down to the waist. Some of these Toorkmun females were fair and handsome, adorning themselves with a variety of ornaments that were attached to their hair, which hangs in tresses over their shoulders. Their head-dress is perhaps a little large, but they themselves are generally on a large scale, and as they never veil, it becomes them. The other part of their costume consists of a long gown that reaches to the ankle, and hides both it and the waist – the very standard points of beauty in our country.

The party which had proceeded to the Orgunje camp returned next morning with the deputy of the Yooz-bashee, or the Commander of a Hundred, and his very appearance made the hearts of the merchants thrill with fear. No taxes had been collected before this, and every thing was uncertain. The deputy was an elderly man, with a large *tilpak* stuck on his head like a regimental cap. He was accompanied by a party of desert Toorkmuns, among whom was a chief or *'aksukal'*, (literally a white beard) of the great tribe of Saruk. The merchants seated the deputation in the place of honour, addressed the deputy as if he had been the Yooz-bashee himself, refreshed him with tea and tobacco (for they now smoked in public), and presented him with silks, cloths, raisins, and sugar, and then proceeded to display their merchandise. Every person made an offering, and we sent two handfuls of raisins and a bit of sugar as our homage. We sat at a short distance in our panniers and witnessed the whole scene. The Yooz-bashee now spoke out to all the members of the caravan, and in the most candid manner said that he had been directed to levy the lawful tax of one in forty, but that he would dispense with opening the bales. Truth, said he, had better be told, for if I have reason to doubt any of you, I will examine them and you will then experience the wrath of the Khan of Orgunje, my lord and master. This speech was listened to with terror; some, I believe, actually said that they had more goods than they really possessed; and as far as I could judge, no one deviated from the truth.

While the merchants were disputing about tillas, and flattering the Yooz-bashee, we had taken up a quiet position, and even pretended to be wrapped in sleep. I never was more awake in my life, and was near enough to hear and see every thing. Several questions were put regarding us, and the principal merchants spoke with earnestness and kindness. We had never instructed them, but they now chose to denominate us Hindoos from Cabool, who were proceeding on a pilgrimage to the flames of Bakoo [Baku, in Azerbaijan], on the Caspian. We had been successively Englishmen, Afghans, Uzbeks, Armenians and Jews, and they now denominated us Hindoos. These people are very simple, nor do they ever interrogate closely.

Shortly after the subject of our character and objects had been discussed, the Toorkmun Aksukal rose from the party and most unwelcomely seated himself by us. He spoke a little Persian, and said, 'You are from Cabool?' to which I gave a nod of assent. The doctor stretched himself back in his pannier, and our visitor addressed himself to an Afghan, one of our people, of which I was glad, since it would keep up the illusion. It is said that the natives of Orgunje are, of all the tribes in Toorkistan, most hostile to Europeans, as well from their vicinity to Russia, as their knowledge that the Persians, who threaten their country, are assisted by them. They of course know nothing of the different nations of Europe, and look upon all Europeans as their enemies. I was not sorry when the Toorkmun chief selected another group. The whole scene appeared to me a perfect riddle, for we ourselves had mixed with the Toorkmuns of our party as Europeans, and our real character was known to every individual of the caravan. Fear may have prevented some of them from making a full disclosure, but it was very creditable.

Evening advanced, and our transactions with the Orgunje Yooz-bashee drew to a close. The Commander of a Hundred carried off two hundred golden tillas, and all the merchants accompanied him to his horse, and saw him beyond the limits of the camp. Such is the dread of authority, and the power of the meanest man who wears it. In the dusk the merchants came to visit us, and related the affairs of the day over a cup of tea. We had to thank an Uzbek, named Ullahdad, and Abdool, a Persian; but we had to make some acknowledgment to all, for we had now become intimate with every body. Whenever the horsemen of the caravan passed us on the road, they would shout out, 'Ah, Meerza! How are you?' with all the consecutive compliments of their language. Little did many of them know that the name of 'Meerza Sikunder', or the secretary Alexander, which they had given me, was so well merited; since I took every opportunity, that I secretly could, to use the pen and ink, and give a secretary's account of all their proceedings. On this day I felt pleased with mankind, for we were now free to prosecute our journey.

CHAPTER XIII

Continuation of the Journey in the Toorkmun Desert

On the morning of the 29th of August we moved at dawn, with buoyant spirits, and followed the course of the Moorghab, or river of Merve, for twelve miles before we could cross it. We found it about eighty yards wide and five feet deep, running within steep clayey banks at the rate of five miles an hour. We crossed by an indifferent ford, over a clay bottom with many holes. There was no village, but the place is called Uleesha. This river rises on the mountains of Huzara, and was long believed to fall into the Oxus or Caspian. Both opinions are erroneous, since it forms a lake, or loses itself in one, about fifty miles N.W. of Merve. The river was formerly dammed above that town, which turned the principal part of its waters to Merve, and raised that city to the state of richness and opulence which it once enjoyed. The dam was thrown down about forty-five years ago by Shah Moorad, a king of Bokhara, and the river now only irrigates the country in its immediate vicinity.

The transition which we had experienced, from a sandy desert to the verge of a running stream, was most gratifying: every one seemed delighted, and even the animals appeared to feel the change. We were now in the vicinity of Merve, and several members of the caravan, on their approach to the river, declared that they had a view of the elevated mound of its ruined castle. I sought in vain; but the other spectators were looking for their native city and wished, perhaps, to persuade themselves that they beheld it. I listened to the tales of valour which these people related to me of one Bairam Khan and a chosen body of seven hundred, that long resisted the arms of the Uzbeks of Bokhara, till Shah Moorad finally subdued them by a stratagem in war, and forcibly transferred the whole population to his capital.

Some circumstances here came to our knowledge that called for prudence and caution, and which appeared to excite the justest alarm. As our party had arrived at the Orgunje camp, they found the chief in the act of despatching a body of 350 Toorkmuns on a foray to the frontiers of Persia. The Yooz-bashee in their presence charged the robbers to be of good cheer, and remember the good work on which they were to be engaged, and the golden tillas to be reaped in the land of the Kuzzilbash. 'Go,' exclaimed he, 'and bring the Prince Royal of Persia, Abbas Meerza himself, to the feet of the Khan Huzrut.' The Allamans mounted in a moment, and one of the merchants, who seemed to have his senses about him, begged that the formidable band would spare our caravan. The Yooz-bashee gave instructions to that effect; but they now shook their heads, and seemed but little disposed to put the honesty of such men to a trial. The doctor and myself, I believe, were the only members of the caravan who would have liked to have a peep at the ferocious Allamans, but I daresay it was fortunate that our curiosity was not gratified. Since such a horde of plunderers was abroad, it was decided that we should march upon Shurukhs [Sarakhs], a large Toorkmun settlement, and there await the result of their expedition, which was expected to return on the tenth day.

In the catalogue of human miseries there are few more severely felt, and the consequences of which are more destructive of domestic happiness, than the cruel system of man-stealing. Great as are the miseries produced by this, the hordes who engage in it appear to derive none of the luxuries or enjoyment of human life from such an occupation, and live in rags and penury, seemingly without advantage from their devastation. The terror which the Toorkmuns inspire among the people of the neighbouring countries is fearful. 'A Toorkmun,' they will tell you, 'is dog, and will only be kept quiet with a bit of bread, like a dog: give it, then, is the doctrine of the traveller, and pass on unmolested.' They have likewise the character of being perfidious and treacherous, nor is it altogether unmerited. The Persians have endeavoured, but without success, to put a stop to these reckless inroads of the Toorkmun, but he himself lives in a desert where he is safe, and is encouraged by the ready sale which he finds for his captives in the favoured countries that lie beyond his own desolate region. In their expeditions into Persia, some Toorkmuns are occasionally captured, and an exorbitant ransom has been placed upon their heads; but yet they have been redeemed by their kinsmen.

As we approached Shurukhs we could distinguish a gradual rise in the country. We had been treading in our last marches on the very ground which had been disturbed by the hoofs of the Toorkmuns who were advancing on Persia. It was with no small delight that we at last lost our traces of the formidable band, which we could discover had branched off the high road towards Meshed. Had we encountered them, a second negotiation would have been necessary, and the demands of the robbers might not have been easily satisfied. Allamans seldom attack a caravan, but still there are authenticated instances of their having murdered a whole party on the very road we were travelling. We reached Shurukhs at sunrise on the 2nd, after having performed a journey of seventy miles in forty-eight hours, including every halt. Our caravan alighted round an old tomb, with a lofty dome, and it was unanimously decided that, so long as the Allamans were abroad, it would not be prudent to prosecute our journey. It was therefore resolved to sleep in Shurukhs, the greatest haunt of the Toorkmun robbers: a paradox truly, since we were to settle among thieves to avoid the thieves abroad.

The Toorkmuns crowded among us during the day, and brought tunics made of camels' hair for sale, which were readily purchased; but there was not an individual of the caravan who trusted himself at a distance from it: and how could it be otherwise, when we hourly saw the Allamans passing and re-passing in front of us, and knew that the chief subsistence of the people was derived from their forays. Shurukhs is the residence of the Salore Toorkmuns, the noblest of the race. Two thousand families are here domiciled, and an equal number of horses, of the finest blood, may be raised in case of need. If unable to cope with their enemies, these people flee to the deserts and await the termination of the storm.

Two days after our arrival at Shurukhs, and when I venture to say we had often congratulated ourselves at the near prospect of success-fully terminating our journey, we experienced an alarm that at least showed our congratulations to be premature. One of the Toorkmun chiefs of the place appeared in our part of the encampment, and summoned the Hajee, one of our people, to attend him, near enough for me to overhear their conversation. He commenced a long list of interrogatories regarding us, and stated that he had heard from persons in the caravan that we possessed great wealth, and had travelled into the remotest parts of Toorkistan. Such being the case, continued he, it was impossible for him to grant us permission to prosecute our journey until the commands of Ullah Koli, Khan of Orgunje, were received concerning us. [This was disquieting news for Burnes, for even if the Turkman chief could perhaps be bought off, it meant there were ill-wishers in the caravan. He decided to take the senior merchants into his confidence, and they were angry and concerned. One suggested that he should produce the firman of the King of Bokhara, given him by his friend and protector the Vizier, but in the end they decided to 'feed the dog of a Turkman', and Abdool undertook to negotiate this. Next morning another blow fell, for Burnes's favourite black pony – which he had brought all the way from Poona – had been stolen in the night. He admitted that he was more upset over this than he would have been over a major disaster, especially when he thought of the treatment it would receive at the hands of its new masters.]

The whole caravan assembled to express their regret at the theft, and assured me I should either have the pony or his value; but they did not understand that in my estimation he stood above all price. I was obliged to turn to other matters, and it was a more solid source of consolation to find that we had satisfied the demands, and silenced the threats, of the Toorkmun chief at a most moderate sacrifice. He became master of our stock of tea, and we should have added the sugar, had it been worth presenting; and this peace-offering, crowned with two gold tillas (each valued at about six and a half rupees), satisfied a chief who had us in his power. We were much indebted in this difficulty to Abdool, who happened to be an acquaintance of the

Toorkmun, and whom we had brought over to us by some acts of civility. We might not have escaped so readily from the talons of any of the other; and it was curious that the fellow who had wished to profit by us was the friend of the merchant with whom we were most intimate.

After the alarm which we had already experienced in Shurukhs, it was not desirable that we should mingle much with the people; but I had great curiosity to see them, and our Toorkmun Ernuzzer said I was invited to a friend's house, and I accompanied him without further consideration. I was very agreeably surprised to find these wandering people living here, at least, in luxury. The tent or *khirgah* was spacious, and had a diameter of about twenty-five feet. The sides were of lattice-work, and the roof was formed of laths, which branched from a circular hoop, about three feet in diameter, through which the light is admitted. The floor was spread with felts and carpets of the richest manufacture, which looked like velvet. Fringed carpets were also hung up round the tent, which gave it a great finish, and their beauty was no doubt enhanced by their being the work of wives and daughters. On one side of the tent was a small press, in which the females of the family kept their clothes, and above it were piled the quilts on which they slept. These are of variegated coloured cloth, both silk and cotton. From the circular aperture in the roof, three large tassels of silk were suspended, differing in colour, and neatly wrought by some fair young hand. Altogether, the apartment and its furniture bespoke any thing but an erratic [i.e. nomadic] people; yet the host explained to me that the whole house could be transported on one camel, and its furniture on another. I was never so much struck with the Tatar features as in this assemblage. The Toorkmun has a skull like a Chinese, his face is flat, his cheek-bones project, and his countenance tapers to the chin, which has a most scanty crop of hair. He is by no means ugly, and his body and features are alike manly. Their women are remarkably fair, and often handsome.

[After a week the Allamans returned triumphantly, with 115 slaves, 200 camels and as many cattle, all snatched from the out-skirts of Meshed. A fifth of the booty had to be reserved for the Khan of Orgunje, the rest they divided among themselves. They were particularly pleased with themselves because there were very few old men among their captives: old people were generally killed at once, for they would command low prices in a slave-market, even if they survived the rigours of the desert crossing. The Allamans had also had a scuffle with a small party of Persian soldiers near Durbund, between Meshed and Sarakhs, killing one of them and capturing fifteen horses.]

At length, on the 11th of September, after a detention of ten long days, we joyfully quitted Shurukhs at sunrise. The Toorkmuns maintained their character to the last. After giving us leave, and agreeing to tax us at the first stage, they waited till we had fairly started and then sent orders to stop the caravan. They demanded a tilla and a half on every camel, which is the customary transit duty for an escort to the Persian frontier. The party came only a few miles and then returned, tired of escorting; nor were we sorry to get so well rid of them. Our caravan had now been increased by the junction of two others, which had come up during our stay, and formed a numerous body; but I fear there were more timid than fighting hearts among us. There were men, women and children, merchants, travellers, pilgrims and emancipated slaves. There were Uzbeks, Arabs, Persians, Afghans, Hindoos, Jews, natives of Budukhshan and Cashmere, Toorks and Toorkmuns, a Nogai Tatar, a wandering Kirghiz from Pameer, and ourselves, natives of Europe. Last, not least, was a young Persian girl, about fifteen years old, whom we had picked up at Shurukhs, and who was said to be of exquisite beauty. [The luckless girl had been captured by Turkman raiders and was at first appropriated by their leader who, however, decided to auction her when wealthy merchants turned up at Shurukhs with Burnes' caravan. She was acquired by a Tehran merchant for twenty-seven gold tillas.]

We halted in the afternoon at a cistern, eighteen miles distant from Shurukhs, the fort of which was yet visible, for we had travelled over a level country, broken in some places by gravelly hillocks. At the third mile we crossed the dry and pebbly bed of the small river of Tejend, which rises in the neighbouring hills and is lost in the sands.

We again set out about eight at night with a full moon, and after an advance of seven or eight miles, entered among defiles and hills, and found ourselves at Moozderan [Mozduran] or Durbund, the frontier post in Persia. [This part of the frontier has since moved slightly further east, and Sarakhs now straddles the border between Iran and the modern state of Turkmenistan.] The whole of the latter part of the route lay in a deep ravine, where there is imminent danger in travelling, from the Allamans of the desert. We pushed on with great celerity and greater fear: every instrument of war was in requisition, every match was lit, and the slightest sound brought the horsemen to a halt; for we expected every moment to encounter the Toorkmuns. After a night of such anxiety, we beheld with pleasure the look-out towers of Durbund, eleven of which crown the crest of the range and command its passage. We here found a few irregular soldiers, the first subjects of the 'Great King' whom we encountered. They were dispirited after the attack of the Toorkmuns, since this was the party which had lost their horses, and one of their fellow-soldiers.

After we had surmounted the pass of Durbund, our caravan alighted in the fields beyond the fort of Moozderan, which stands on an isolated spur of table-land, as you descend the pass. The place was once peopled, but the Khan of Orgunje some years since seized its inhabitants *en masse* and razed their defences. There is a beautiful fountain of tepid water, which makes for itself and some kindred streams a channel down the valley, where the fruit trees and gardens of the exiled inhabitants may still be seen. It appeared a charming spot to us after so long a sojourn among desolation. Our arrival in Persia afforded the greatest source of joy to many of the persons in the caravan who, though natives of Bokhara, were yet Shiahs. I thought that when we quitted that holy city, we should have done with such sanctified spots, but the capital which we were now approaching, Meshid-i-Mookuddus, the sacred Meshed, appeared by every account to be even more holy than Bokhara. When we should behold its gilded dome, I now heard that every one would fall down and pray. [Meshed is much revered by Shia Muslims for the tomb of Imam Reza, who was martyred there in 818. The golden dome was erected in the seventeenth century by Shah Abbas, for the original shrine had been destroyed by Sunni invaders, and it became a place of pilgrimage.]

We could not yet consider ourselves within the protection even of the holy Meshed, which was thirty-eight miles from Moozderan; we therefore moved at nightfall. In the bustle of departure I killed a huge reptile of a tarantula, or an enormous spider, crawling on my carpet. Its claws looked like those of a scorpion, or small lobster, but the body was that of a spider. I was assured of its poisonous nature, and the natives insisted that it squirted its venom instead of stinging.

[The caravan was soon on the march again, for Turkman raiders were no respecters of frontiers, and the danger of being snatched into slavery was still acute. There was general alarm in the night when the braying of a donkey betrayed the presence of other human beings in the vicinity, but fortunately they proved to be a small – and equally terrified – group of nomadic Eimaks who had been gathering herbs for dyeing on the hills. The caravan hurried on, cutting out the usual halts, and only stopped at midday, when it reached the first inhabited village in Persia, about fourteen miles short of Meshed.]

We halted a few hours at Ghoozkan, and had an opportunity of observing the supreme joy of the poor slaves, who had now reached their native land in safety. Many of the merchants gave them clothes and money to assist in their journey homewards, and it was with pleasure that we joined in the charitable feelings of the caravan. Ghoozkan is peopled by Teimurees, a tribe of Eimaks, and has a population of about a thousand souls. They were a miserable-looking set of beings, who used bandages as stockings, and covered their heads with brown sheep-skin caps. The whole of the inhabitants turned out to see us pass, and many of the poor creatures asked, in melancholy strains, of the different passengers, if we did not bring letters from their captive friends in Toorkistan. The Toorkmuns seldom spare Ghoozkan in their forays, and the last party had carried off six of their children and put four of their peasants to death. We loaded the camels after a watch of night, and set out for Meshed, the gates of which we reached long before the sun had risen, not more to our own joy than that of the poor Persian slaves, who had performed every step of the journey with a palpitating breast.

CHAPTER XIV

Meshed and Khorasan

At dawn on the morning of the 14th of September, we found our caravan waiting, in anxious expectation, under the walls of Meshed. At sunrise the keys of the gate were brought, which was at once thrown open to us. A new scene burst upon our view, with a rapidity which one only sees in theatrical representations. We had left a desert and the wandering Toorkmuns, and now advanced in stately order through a crowded city, arresting the notice of all the inhabitants. We had exchanged the broad face and broader turbans of the Toork and Tatar for the slim long-faced Kuzzilbash, with a fur cap on his head, and his ringlets curling up behind, who now stood idly looking at us, with his hands in his pockets. The street which we entered was spacious and handsome; an aqueduct passed through it, and its banks were shaded by trees, while the splendid cupola and gilded minarets of the shrine of Imam Ruza [Reza] terminated the perspective. A hundred and twenty camels passed up this avenue and entered the spacious caravanserai of the Uzbeks. We followed in course, and seated ourselves on the balcony of the building, that we might the better observe the busy scene of the area beneath us.

The Prince Royal of Persia, Abbas Meerza, was now in the neighbourhood of Meshed, and though this country had been visited by few Europeans, we knew that there were British officers in his Royal Highness's service. I lost no time, therefore, in despatching an express to the camp, which was about a hundred miles distant: but we were agreeably surprised to receive a polite message from Mrs Shee, the lady of Captain Shee, who was then in Meshed; and it was equally pleasing to have it conveyed by a messenger who spoke our own language, one of the serjeants of the Prince's army. During our stay in Meshed we found ourselves more comfortable than since we had left India, and experienced many acts of civility and attention. We gladly changed the barbarous custom of eating with our hands, and though our fair hostess was a Georgian, who spoke only Persian, we fancied ourselves once more among the society of our country.

I lost no time in visiting the city of Meshed, but I need not present a diffuse or long account of it, since I find that there is both a minute and correct one in Mr Fraser's admirable work, *Travels in Khorasan.* The holy city of Meshed surrounds the tomb of the Imam Ruza, the fifth in descent from Ali, and three streets branch out in different directions from the shrine. Two of them are wide and spacious, shaded by trees and enlivened by running water. A chain, drawn across the streets, within a hundred yards of the shrine, encloses its bazar and the riches of Meshed, and keeps out cattle and animals from the sanctified spot. The greater portion of the enclosed space is devoted to the use of a cemetery, since it is believed that the dead may rest in peace near an Imam. There are also shady gardens to please the living. About the centre of the city, the sepulchre rests under a gilded dome, which is rivalled by twin minarets of burnished gold, that shed resplendent light in the rays of the sun. A spacious mosque of azure blue rears a loftier dome and minarets close to the tomb, and was built by Gohur Shah, a descendant of the illustrious Timour.

We soon received a reply to our communication from the Prince Royal's camp, and were invited to pay our respects to Abbas Meerza, who had just captured the fortress of Koochan, which was said to be one of the strongest in Persia. The intelligence of its fall was received in Meshed with great enthusiasm, and followed by an illumination of three successive nights, for no monarch since the days of Nadir Shah had ever subdued the chiefs of Khorasan. We dined *a la Perse* with Abdool, our old travelling friend, who is a merchant in Meshed, and then proceeded to view the illumination. Altogether the scene approached much nearer a genuine British illumination than I had ever expected to see in Asia.

We now prepared for our journey to the camp, and took leave of all our Bokhara acquaintances and friends, visiting most of them at the caravanserai, where we had a parting cup of tea. Many of the slaves came to see us, and we now hailed them as freemen. I was sorry to bid adieu to Ernuzzer the Toorkmun, but I gave him a letter to the Vizier of Bokhara; and as it contained all the news of Khorasan he seemed proud to be its bearer, and was anxious to set out on his return. We had now less fear of being thought rich, so we clothed our friend in a dress, and amply rewarded him for his services. I stuck a pistol in his girdle as he was leaving, and though of the coarsest manufacture, it seemed a mighty gift to a Toorkmun. In Meshed, perhaps, our feelings were more pleasing than in any part of the journey, for we had the prospect of soon seeing our countrymen, and the rest of our undertaking was, comparatively speaking, easy.

Since we had entered Khorasan my fellow-traveller, Dr Gerard, had come to the resolution of turning down upon Herat and Candahar, and thus retracing his steps to Cabool, in preference to advancing upon the Caspian. The main object of our journey had been now nearly accomplished, and the route to Herat promised him some gratification. We now, therefore, prepared to separate, after a weary pilgrimage of nine months which we had performed together. Our feelings on such an occasion may be imagined; but we parted with the knowledge that we had almost brought the original design of our undertaking to a close, and that both to the east and west all serious dangers were at an end. At Koochan I also permitted the Hindoo lad to return to India, along with Dr Gerard; and at his own request I discharged my faithful Afghan servant, who had accompanied me from Lodiana. His name was Sooliman, a native of Peshawur. He was quite unlettered, but he had kept both my secrets and my money where there were many inducements to betray. He had proved himself worthy of my confidence, and the feelings with which I parted from him were those of unmingled approbation and regard.

[Dr Gerard also took with him some twenty letters from Burnes, conveying his heartfelt thanks to the many people who had smoothed their way on such a dangerous journey. They ranged from important personages like the Vizier of Bokhara; Dost Mohammed of Kabul and his hospitable brother Nawab Jubbar Khan, with whom they had stayed; the Khan of Peshawar, and Maharaja Ranjit Singh of

Lahore, down to his 'jolly conductor' and guide in Kabul, Naib Mohammed Sharif, who had become a real friend.

This was effectively the end of Burnes's long journey, and his relief is palpable. Although he did travel on to the shores of the Caspian – which he had so longed to see – he now travelled with a large escort, which made the journey safe and comfortable, with no more fears of abduction. But after admiring the 'noble sight' of the ocean-like sea, he dared not linger, for an epidemic of plague was raging and he rode instead to Tehran and reported to the British Minister there. After a formal audience with the Shah of Persia, who was very curious to hear about his experiences, Burnes took ship from Bushire and arrived back in Bombay on 18 January 1833.]

LETTER TO
LIEUTENANT ALEXANDER BURNES FROM
LORD WILLIAM BENTINCK

Political Department
Delhi, December 6, 1831

Sir – I am directed by the Right Honourable the Governor-General to acknowledge the receipt of your several letters, forwarding a memoir on the Indus, and a narrative of your journey to Lahore.

2. The first copy of your map of the Indus has also just reached his Lordship, which completes the information collected during your mission to Lahore, in charge of the presents from the late King of England to Maharaja Runjeet Sing.

3. The Governor-General, having perused and attentively considered all these documents, desires me to convey to you his high approbation of the manner in which you have acquitted yourself of the important duty assigned to you, and his acknowledgments for the full and satisfactory details furnished on all the points in which it was the desire of government to obtain information.

4. Your intercourse with the chiefs of Sinde, and the other Sirdars and persons with whom you were brought into contact in the course of the voyage up the Indus, appears to the Governor-General to have been conducted with extreme prudence and discretion, so as to have left a favourable impression on all classes, and to have advanced every possible object, immediate, as connected with your mission, as well as prospective; for, while your communications with them were calculated to elicit full information as to their hopes and wishes, you most judiciously avoided the assumption of any political character that might lead to the encouragement of false and extravagant expectations, or involve you in any of the passing intrigues. The whole of your conduct and correspondence with the chiefs of the countries you passed through in your journey has the Governor-General's entire and unqualified approbation.

5. In like manner, his Lordship considers you to be entitled to commendation for the extent of geographical and general information collected in the voyage, and for the caution used in procuring it, no less than for the perspicuous and complete form in which the results have been submitted for record and consideration. The map prepared by you forms an addition to the geography of India of the first utility and importance, and cannot fail to procure for your labours a high place in this department of science.

6. The result of your voyage in the different reports, memoirs, and maps above acknowledged, will be brought without delay to the notice of the authorities in England, under whose orders the mission was, as you are aware, undertaken. His Lordship doubts not that they will unite with him in commending the zeal, diligence, and intelligence displayed by you in the execution of this service, and will express their satisfaction at the manner in which their views have been accomplished, and the objects contemplated in the mission to Lahore fully and completely attained.

I have the honour to be, &c.

(Signed) H. T. PRINSEP,
Secretary to the Governor-General.

EPILOGUE

On his return from Bukhara, Burnes published his *Travels into Bokhara*, and found himself an overnight celebrity. He was invited to London to meet both Lord Ellenborough, President of the East India Company's Board of Control, and the King, was lionised by society hostesses, and gave standing-room-only lectures to the Royal Geographical Society, which presented him with its Gold Medal. The French publication of his book, *Voyages Dans Le Bokhara*, was also a bestseller and Burnes went to Paris to receive further awards and more medals. But the success of the book also set in train a series of events that would lead to Burnes's violent death and the unravelling of his reputation.

For it was the French translation of Burnes's work that brought Burnes's journey to the notice of the Russian authorities. Burnes's expedition had been intended to spy out and counter Russian activity in Afghanistan and Bukhara at a time when both areas were off the Russian map. Ironically, it was Burnes's writings that first provoked Russian interest in those regions, not least to head off suspected British intrigues. As so often in international affairs, hawkish paranoia about non-existent threats can create the very monster you fear most.

As the Russian Governor of Orenburg explained it in his memoirs, St Petersburg was becoming as frustrated as London had been with its poor intelligence from Central Asia: 'All the information that Russia procured was meagre and obscure,' he wrote, 'and was supplied by Asiatics, who either through ignorance or timidity were not able to furnish useful accounts. We had reliable information that the agents of the East India Company were continually appearing at Bokhara . . . It was accordingly decided in 1835, in order to watch the English agents and counteract their efforts, to send . . . sub-Lieutenant Vitkevitch in the capacity as an agent . . . '

Ivan Viktorovich Vitkevitch was the Russians' answer to Burnes.

A Polish nobleman who had been exiled to the steppe for anti-Russian activity as a student, like Burnes he rose in the ranks due to his linguistic gifts and twice was sent off to Bukhara. The first time he travelled in disguise with two Kirghiz traders and made the journey in only seventeen days through deep snow and over the frozen Oxus. He stayed a month, but found it much less romantic than the Oriental Wonder House described by Burnes: 'I must note that the tales told by Burnes, in his published account of his journey to Bukhara, presented a curious contrast to all that I chanced to see here,' he wrote back to Orenburg. 'He sees everything in some glamorous light, while all I saw was merely disgusting, ugly, pathetic or ridiculous. Either Mr Burnes deliberately exaggerated and embellished the attractions of Bokhara or he was strongly prejudiced in its favour.'

On his second visit, in January 1836, Vitkevitch went openly as a Russian officer, to request the release of several Russian merchants who had been detained by the Emir of Bukhara. On arrival in the caravan city he recorded that he was immediately asked: ' "Do you know Iskander?" I thought they meant Alexander the Great but they were, in fact, talking of Alexander Burnes.' This early indication of British influence did not stop Vitkevitch immediately trying to reverse it, and it took him only a couple of weeks to uncover the intelligence network that Burnes had established to send news back to India.

It was on this second visit to Bukhara that Vitkevich had an extraordinary break. Completely by chance, his visit coincided with that of an Afghan emissary, Mirza Hussein Ali, who had been sent by Dost Mohammad on a mission to the Tsar. Vitkevitch escorted him to St Petersburg, then led the return mission to Kabul, the first by Russia to Afghanistan. His visit happened to coincide exactly with a second expedition by Burnes.

The two rivals had much in common. They were nearly the same age; both came from the distant provinces of their respective Empires, with few connections to the ruling elite, and having arrived in Asia within a few months of each other, had both worked their way up through their own merit and daring, and especially their skill in languages. Now the rivals came face to face in the court of Kabul, and the outcome of the contest would do much to determine the immediate future not only of Afghanistan, but that of Central Asia.

'We are in a mess here,' wrote Burnes to a friend in India shortly after he heard about Vitkevitch's arrival in Afghanistan. 'The Emperor of Russia has sent an Envoy to Kabul to offer Dost Mohammad Khan money to fight Ranjit Singh!! I could not believe my eyes or ears, but Captain Vitkevitch arrived here with a blazing letter, three feet long, and sent immediately to pay his respects to myself. I of course received him and asked him to dinner.'

The dinner between the two – the first such meeting in the history of the Great Game – took place on Christmas Day 1837. The two agents-turned-ambassadors got on well. Burnes records that the Pole was 'a gentlemanly, agreeable man, about thirty years of age, and spoke French, Persian and Turkish fluently, and wore a uniform of an officer of Cossacks which was a novelty in Kabul. He had been to Bokhara, and we had therefore a common subject to converse upon, without touching on politics. I found him intelligent and well informed on the subject of Northern Asia. He very frankly said it was not the custom of Russia to publish to the world the result of its researches in foreign countries, as was the case in France or England.' Burnes then added: 'I never again saw Mr Vitkevitch, although we exchanged sundry messages of "high consideration", for I regret to say I found it impossible to follow the dictates of my personal feelings of friendship towards him, as the public service required the strictest watch.' This was no understatement: Burnes had already begun to intercept his dining companion's letters back to Teheran and St Petersburg.

Vitkevitch won the first round of the contest, and Burnes, unable to come up with any offer to the Afghans to match that of the Tsar, was forced to retreat to Simla. In response to Vitkevitch's success, in the spring of 1839, the British invaded Afghanistan, in what came to be known as the First Afghan War. Eighteen thousand British and Company troops poured through the passes and re-established on the throne Dost Mohammad's great rival, Shah Shuja ul-Mulk.

At this point Burnes was caught in a dilemma. Not only had he been a guest and a friend of Dost Muhammad but he did not admire Shah Shuja, and strongly suspected that the British invasion of Afghanistan would be the major diplomatic and military mistake that it turned out to be. He made his feelings clear in a series of reports addressed to the new British Governor-General, but Lord Auckland would not listen to this opinionated junior official. Burnes may have been tempted to resign, and may have regretted declining an invitation to join the Foreign Office in Teheran. But in the end, his loyalty to the East India Company, in whose service he had so prospered, won out. It wasn't long before he was promoted to the rank of Lieutenant-Colonel and given a knighthood. In the eyes of his old Afghan friends, these honours looked like a bribe. His perceived duplicity in this matter led to Burnes becoming a hate figure in Afghanistan, and is commemorated as such in the epic poetry of the period.

In the Afghan sources, Burnes is always depicted as a devilishly charming but cunning deceiver, a master of flattery and treachery – an interesting inversion of British stereotypes of the 'devious Oriental'. Mirza 'Ata Muhammad in the *Naway Ma'arek* talks of Burnes's progress up the Indus 'to spy out conditions in Sindh and Khurāsān, which he succeeded in doing thanks to his Plato-like intelligence. Burnes realised that the states of the region were built on very insecure foundations and would need only a gust of wind to blow them down. When the people crowded to stare at him, Burnes emerged from his tent and jokingly remarked to the crowd "Come and see my tail and horns!" Everyone laughed, and someone called out: "Your tail stretches all the way back to England, and your horns will soon be appearing in Khurāsān!" '

This image is developed at greater length by the poet-mullah Maulana Hamidallah Kashmiri, who in 1844 wrote an epic Masnavi in praise of the defeat of the British, the *Akbar Nama*. In this poem, Burnes is again the demonically charismatic incarnation of all the two-faced treachery and deceit of Crusading Christendom:

> One of the Firangi lords of high stature
> By name Burnes, and called Sikandar

Epilogue

Gathered all the necessaries for commerce
And set out with every appearance of a trader

When he arrived, with all haste, in the city of Kabul
He sought intimacy with its illustrious men

With many gifts and open display of favours
He made a place for himself in every heart

With his chicanery, he held everyone spellbound
And insinuated himself into the inner circle of the Amīr

The Amīr, with his kindness and natural grace
Treated him as a most honoured guest

He elevated him above all others
And bestowed every mark of distinction upon him

But he of depraved nature and unholy creed
Had mixed poison into the honey

From London, he had requested much gold and silver
So that this gold may render his own schemes golden

With dark magic and deceit he dug a pit
Many a man was seized by the throat and thrown in

There remained not one amongst the Khāns of power
Whom he did not place thus on the devil's path

When he had bound them in chains of gold
They swore allegiance to him one and all

They said: 'wherever you place your foot we will place
                                            our heads
And we will follow to the end every command you give'

Until finally someone spoke in front of the Amīr
'O Lion-slaying Commander of great fame!

This sedition-sowing Burnes – he is your enemy
On the outside he seems a man, but inside he is the very devil

Beware this evil-spreading foe
Do you not remember the advice of Sādi?

It is better to hold back from strangers
For an enemy is strong when in the guise of a friend

You have been nurturing this enemy day and night
Turn away from him before you find yourself betrayed.'

It was partly because of the hatred the Afghans felt for Burnes
that he was the first to be killed when, in November 1841, the people
of Kabul finally rose against their British occupiers. 'It happened by
God's will,' wrote Mirza 'Ata, 'that a slave-girl of Abdullah Khan
Achakzai ran away from his house to the residence of Alexander
Burnes. When on enquiry it was found out that that was where she
had gone, the Khan, beside himself with fury, sent his attendant to
fetch the silly girl back; the Englishman, swollen with pride, cursing
and swearing, had the Khan's attendant severely beaten and thrown
out of the house.

'The Khan then summoned the other Sardars and said: "Now we
are justified in throwing off this English yoke: they stretch the hand
of tyranny to dishonour private citizens great and small: fucking a
slave-girl isn't worth the ritual bath that follows it: but we have to
put a stop right here and now, otherwise these English will ride the
donkey of their desires in the field of stupidity and have us all. I put
my trust in God and raise the battle standard of our Prophet, and
thus go to fight: if success rewards us, then that is as we wished; and
if we die in battle, that is still better than to live with degradation
and dishonour!" The other Sardars, his childhood friends, tightened
their belts and girt their loins, and prepared for Jihad – holy war.'

Early the following morning, Burnes's house was surrounded and
set on fire; when he ran out into the street, he was hacked to death
by the mob. After a two-month siege, 18,500 cold, hungry and
leaderless East India Company troops and their followers retreated
through the icy passes in the middle of winter. One by one, they
were shot down by Afghan marksmen firing from caves and behind
boulders with their long-barrelled jezails – the sniper rifles of the

nineteenth century – as the sepoys trudged snowblind and frostbitten through the mountain snowdrifts.

After eight days on the death march, the last fifty survivors made their final stand at the village of Gandamak. As late as the 1970s, fragments of Victorian weaponry and military equipment could be found lying in the screes above the village. Even today, the hill is still covered with bleached British bones. Out of the 18,500-strong party that left Kabul, only one man, Dr Brydon, made it through to the British garrison in Jellalabad. A handful of British officers and their wives were taken hostage; the rest were shot. Meanwhile, the Indian sepoys who made up the bulk of the army were either sold en masse into slavery, or disarmed, stripped and left to perish in the snow.

The First Afghan War was arguably the greatest military humiliation ever suffered by the West in the East: an entire army of what was then the most powerful military nation in the world routed and destroyed by poorly equipped tribesmen. In 1843, the army chaplain in Jellalabad, the Rev. G. H. Gleig, wrote a memoir about the expedition. It was, he wrote, 'a war begun for no wise purpose, carried on with a strange mixture of rashness and timidity, brought to a close after suffering and disaster, without much glory attached either to the government which directed, or the great body of troops which waged it. Not one benefit, political or military, has been acquired with this war. Our eventual evacuation of the country resembled the retreat of an army defeated.'

We have allowed ourselves to forget the lessons of Burnes and the First Afghan War – to our cost. But the Afghans have not. Last year, I followed much of the route of Burnes' journey in Afghanistan and the path of the 1841 death march, which leads deep into Taliban territory; the Ghilzai tribe, who massacred the British on their retreat in 1841, now provide the foot soldiers for the modern Taliban resistance. Whatever their tribe, everyone still remembered Burnes's name. At the village of Jigdallick, not far from the site of the last stand at Gandamak, my hosts casually pointed out the various places in the village where many of the British had been massacred.

'It is exactly the same today as 1841,' said my host, Anwar Khan

239

Jigdallick, whose ancestor had led the resistance. 'Both times the foreigners have come for their own interests. They say, "We are your friends, we want to help." But they are lying.'

'Whoever comes to Afghanistan, even now, they will face the fate of Burnes and Macnaghten,' agreed Mohammad Khan, the owner of the orchard where we were sitting. Everyone nodded sagely: the names of the fallen of 1841, long forgotten in their home country, were still common currency here.

'Since the British went we've had the Russians and now the Americans,' said one old man. 'We are the roof of the world. From here you can control and watch everywhere. But we do not have the strength to control our own destiny. Our fate is determined by our neighbours.'

'This is the last days of the Americans,' said the other elder. 'Next it will be China.'

WILLIAM DALRYMPLE

ELAND

61 Exmouth Market, London EC1R 4QL
Email: info@travelbooks.co.uk

Eland was started in 1982 to revive great travel books
that had fallen out of print. Although the list has diversified
into biography and fiction, it is united by a quest to define the
spirit of place. These are books for travellers, and for readers who aspire
to explore the world but who are content to travel in their own
minds. Eland books open out our understanding of other cultures,
interpret the unknown and reveal different environments as well as
celebrating the humour and occasional horrors of travel. We take
immense trouble to select only the most readable books and therefore
many readers collect the entire series.

All our books are printed on fine, pliable, cream-coloured paper.
Most are still gathered in sections by our printer and sewn as well
as glued, almost unheard of for a paperback book these days.
This gives larger margins in the gutter, as well as
making the books stronger.

You will find a very brief description of our books on the
following pages. Extracts from each and every one of them can be
read on our website, at www.travelbooks.co.uk. If you would
like a free copy of our catalogue, please email
or write to us (details above).

ELAND

'One of the very best travel lists' WILLIAM DALRYMPLE

Far Away and Long Ago
W H HUDSON
A childhood in Argentina

Holding On
MERVYN JONES
One family and one street in
London's East End: 1880-1960

Red Moon & High Summer
HERBERT KAUFMANN
A coming-of-age novel following a
young singer in his Tuareg homeland

Three Came Home
AGNES KEITH
A mother's ordeal in a Japanese
prison camp

Peking Story
DAVID KIDD
The ruin of an ancient Mandarin
family under the new communist order

Syria: through writers' eyes
ED. MARIUS KOCIEJOWSKI
Guidebooks for the mind: a selection
of the best travel writing on Syria

Scum of the Earth
ARTHUR KOESTLER
Koestler's personal experience of
France in World War II

A Dragon Apparent
NORMAN LEWIS
Cambodia, Laos and Vietnam
on the eve of war

Golden Earth
NORMAN LEWIS
Travels in Burma

The Honoured Society
NORMAN LEWIS
Sicily, her people and the Mafia within

Naples '44
NORMAN LEWIS
Post-war Naples and an intelligence
officer's love of Italy's gift for life

A View of the World
NORMAN LEWIS
Collected writings by the great
English travel writer

An Indian Attachment
SARAH LLOYD
Life and love in a remote Indian village

A Pike in the Basement
SIMON LOFTUS
Tales of a hungry traveller: from catfish
in Mississippi to fried eggs with chapatis
in Pakistan

Among the Faithful
DAHRIS MARTIN
An American woman living in the holy
city of Kairouan, Tunisia in the 1920s

Lords of the Atlas
GAVIN MAXWELL
The rise and fall of Morocco's infamous
Glaoua family, 1893-1956

A Reed Shaken by the Wind
GAVIN MAXWELL
Travels among the threatened Marsh
Arabs of southern Iraq

A Year in Marrakesh
PETER MAYNE
Back-street life in Morocco in the 1950s

Sultan in Oman
JAN MORRIS
An historic journey through the still-medieval
state of Oman in the 1950s

The Caravan Moves On
IRFAN ORGA
Life with the nomads of central Turkey

Portrait of a Turkish Family
IRFAN ORGA
The decline of a prosperous Ottoman
family in the new Republic